BORDOGNA · MICK TINGELHOFF · PAT FISCHER · LAVERNE TORC
CHICH · KAYE CARSTENS · LARRY KRAMER · LAVERNE ALLERS ·
CH · JOE BLAHAK · LARRY JACOBSON · DA⬚⬚ ⬚⬚ OR MIL
HNNY RODGERS · BRODERICK THOMAS ⬚⬚ TON · S
KE ROZIER · MARC MUNFORD · TOM RATHMAN · STEVE TAYLOR ·
N · AHMAN GREEN · TREV ALBERTS · TOMMIE FRAZIER · AARON TA
FRED MEIER · VIC SCHLEICH · JOHN BORDOGNA · MICK TINGEL
R · LARRY WACHHOLTZ · BOB CHURCHICH · KAYE CARSTENS · L
TAUGH · BOB NEWTON · BILL KOSCH · JOE BLAHAK · LARRY JACO
RAGAMO · JIM ANDERSON · JOHNNY RODGERS · BRODERICK THO
CCORMICK · TONY FELICI · MIKE ROZIER · MARC MUNFORD ·
MIKE MINTER · RUSS HOCHSTEIN · AHMAN GREEN · TREV ALBE
GLENN PRESNELL · FORREST BEHM · FRED MEIER · VIC SCHLE
ZON · DENNIS CLARIDGE · LYLE SITTLER · LARRY WACHHOLTZ ·
N SCHNEISS · JOE ORDUNA · JERRY MURTAUGH · BOB NEWTON ·
R · TOM RUUD · JEFF KINNEY · VINCE FERRAGAMO · JIM ANDERS
DAMKROGER · DERRIE NELSON · JOHN MCCORMICK · TONY FEI
NEIL SMITH · TURNER GILL · WILL SHIELDS · MIKE MINTER ·
RON TAYLOR · AARON GRAHAM · ERIC CROUCH · GLENN PRESN

D1592316

WHAT IT MEANS TO BE A HUSKER

TOM OSBORNE

AND NEBRASKA'S GREATEST PLAYERS

EDITED BY JEFF SNOOK

TRIUMPH
BOOKS
CHICAGO

Library of Congress Cataloging-in-Publication Data

What it means to be a Husker : Tom Osborne and Nebraska's greatest
   players / edited by Jeff Snook
      p. cm.
   ISBN 1-57243-662-X
      1. University of Nebraska—Lincoln—Football—History.   2. Nebraska
Cornhuskers (Football team)—History.   I. Snook, Jeff, 1960–

   GV958.U53W55   2004
   796.332'63'09782293—dc22

                                                          2004051722

This book is available in quantity at special discounts for your group or organization. For further information, contact:

Triumph Books
601 South LaSalle Street
Suite 500
Chicago, Illinois 60605
(312) 939-3330
Fax (312) 663-3557

Printed in U.S.A.
ISBN 1-57243-662-X
Design by Nick Panos; page production by Patricia Frey.
Photos courtesy of the University of Nebraska photo archives unless otherwise indicated.

CONTENTS

FOREWORD

Growing up in Hastings, Nebraska, I remember attending a few University of Nebraska football games in Lincoln in the late 1940s. My uncle A. H. Jones had tickets and would invite my dad and me at least once each year. You can say that I was immediately awestruck by Memorial Stadium, Nebraska fans, and Cornhusker football.

I just never knew that it would be the beginning of an enduring relationship that would become a very large part of my life for the next six decades.

Occasionally, we would pay 50 cents and sit in the knothole section to watch games, and I remember seeing Tom Novak and Bobby Reynolds play. Back in those days, the stadium had only two sides and the end zones were open with bleachers. The capacity was around thirty-five thousand, and there were empty seats at many games.

But Nebraska Cornhusker football would change and grow as the years passed.

In January of 1962, when I was about to turn 25 years old, I enrolled in graduate school at Nebraska and arrived on campus at about the same time as a man named Bob Devaney. He had been hired as the new football coach, and I had written him a letter while he was still at Wyoming, indicating that I would like to explore the possibility of working for him as a graduate assistant coach.

When he got to Lincoln, I went to see him, and he told me that he had all the coaches he needed, but he asked if I could help out in the dormitory.

There were several players living in one wing of Selleck Quadrangle—most were from Chicago—and they intimidated the dorm counselors.

Devaney was concerned that nobody could handle them, so he said that if I lived there and got the situation under control, he would help me out. He said that I could eat my meals at the training table, but he made no promises about a coaching job.

I did show up for spring ball in 1962, and I began coaching as a graduate assistant with the freshman team that next fall. I finished my master's degree in 1963 and then my Ph.D. in 1965. For the next couple of years, I rode the fence teaching classes in educational psychology and coaching at the same time. Coaching or teaching? I did not know which way to go, so I went in to see Devaney. I told him I wanted to become a full-time coach, but I needed to make $10,000 because I would make that much as a professor. He said he could do that for me.

So I became a full-time assistant coach in 1967, and my recruiting area was western Nebraska, Kansas, California, and Arizona. Signing day back then was in May, so I spent much of my time on the road.

In 1967 and 1968, things did not go well—Nebraska finished 6–4 both years. Now those records would have looked pretty good in 1960 or 1961, but Devaney had come in and put up records of 9–2, 10–1, 9–2, 10–1, and 9–2 in his first five seasons. People got used to winning big (and it seems they never do get used to losing). After losing to Oklahoma 47–0 in 1968, there was a petition going around Omaha to fire him, and all the coaches were catching a lot of flak.

This entire period was very instructional to me later in my career. The thing that most impressed me about Bob Devaney was this: he was getting pressure to make some changes, and most people wanted him to make changes on his staff, but he said no.

"There will be no sacrificial lambs," he said. "If one of us goes, we all go."

That taught me something about loyalty, and I carried that with me during my coaching career.

To his credit, Devaney was always looking for something a little different and a little new on offense. He had come from Michigan State, which had used an unbalanced line, and an offense that was the precursor to the wishbone. He took it to Wyoming and then brought it to Nebraska, but it seemed like we were not moving the ball as well in 1967 and 1968. He asked me to redesign the offense and put more emphasis on the passing game. I took a look at what Oklahoma had been doing, and then decided to go to the I formation as our basic set and also used a four-receiver set as a changeup.

One day after Nebraska's 62–24 win over Florida in the 1996 Fiesta Bowl, Tom Osborne stands tall between the Cornhuskers' consecutive national championship trophies at a homecoming rally in the Devaney Sports Center. Two years later, Osborne's Cornhuskers would add a third national title in four seasons—and the school's fifth overall—by beating Tennessee in the Orange Bowl in the Hastings, Nebraska, native's final game. Osborne finished his 25-year head coaching career with an amazing 255–49–3 record. *Photo courtesy of AP/Wide World Photos.*

Fortunately, we rebounded the next season. After a 2–2 start, we won the next seven games, including a win over Georgia in the Sun Bowl, to finish 9–2. I really think one of the keys to the improvement was that we had better players and, specifically, better offensive linemen. Alabama had beaten us in a couple of Orange Bowls with smaller, quicker offensive linemen, and we had made the mistake of thinking that was the way to go. However, with smaller, quicker linemen, we just were not getting the job done. Then we got bigger, stronger, quicker offensive linemen and started moving the ball again.

We would have been in real trouble as a coaching staff if we had had another bad season in 1969.

Late in that season, after we had played at Kansas State and won a close game, 10–7, we were riding back to Lincoln on the bus when Devaney called me up to the front where he was sitting.

"I am not going to do this a lot longer," he told me, "and I want you to take this thing over as head coach."

Now I had wanted to become a head coach; I almost got the Texas Tech job and I also had looked at South Dakota and Augustana. I could have had the Augustana job if I wanted it, but I decided to stay at Nebraska. Devaney had six or seven assistants with him that he had brought from Wyoming, and they were older than me, and here I was—just an upstart young guy who had been a graduate assistant just two years earlier.

I really liked Nebraska, and I really liked Devaney. But I knew what the history book said about those who followed the Bob Devaneys of the world. It is well known that it is tough to follow a legend. But I also knew that if you passed up a head-coaching job, another might never come again.

Then something happened that made Devaney stay a year or two longer than originally intended: Nebraska won national championships in 1970 and 1971 and it was hard for him to quit then. So he stayed on through the 1972 season.

Bob Devaney and I got along well, and yet, we were so different. He was an Irishman with a really good sense of humor and a quick temper, but he was very quick to forgive and he never held a grudge. I was more reserved and I know that some people saw me as aloof. We were an odd pair, but we did get along well, and football-wise we pretty much agreed on philosophy.

After beating Alabama in the 1972 Orange Bowl to complete a second unbeaten season, Devaney announced that the next season would be his last and that I would become the new head coach in 1973. That gave everybody a year to get used to the idea.

That season, we beat Notre Dame badly in the Orange Bowl to finish the season 9–2–1, and I realized this would be a very difficult job for me. Devaney had done it all, including winning back-to-back national championships. He left me with a good coaching staff, and as athletic director he was always supportive.

In my first five years as head coach, we had some rocky times because we did not beat Oklahoma. I realized winning 9 or 10 games each year wouldn't be enough if we could not beat Oklahoma, and I would not be able to last a lot longer without beating them. In 1978, Oklahoma came to Lincoln ranked

No. 1 and, fortunately, they fumbled—or we caused the fumble—late in the game as we beat them 17–14.

The problem was that we had to play them again in the Orange Bowl six weeks later, and even though we outgained them in that game, they beat us. So our victory celebration was short-lived.

As the years went on, we played Oklahoma pretty evenly, and then we finished with seven consecutive wins over them, from 1991 to 1997.

People have asked me over the years about recruiting and what type of person we aimed to bring to Nebraska. We always looked hard at character, but that does not mean we did not get fooled once in a while. But 90 to 95 percent of our players were really solid people. We always believed in strong academic performance, and when they began to publish graduation rates, we had some objective evidence that we were doing well in that area. We always had one of the better graduation rates in the country, and we had 44 Academic All-Americans from 1962 to 1997. We figured if a player did not have a degree when his eligibility was up, then we had failed him; therefore, if a player did not go to class, he did not play for us in the upcoming game.

There has always been a strong sense of community within our football program. We had an unbroken tenure from 1962 until 2003 when it came to the coaching staff. There are not many places that have that type of continuity. A player from any one of those teams always could come back to Lincoln and find coaches he knew or somebody he had played with.

We had the Husker Nation reunion in August 2003, and it was estimated that there were 1,200 living football lettermen at that time and more than 800 of them showed up. That is an amazing figure. Being around them, I sensed a strong camaraderie and a strong feeling for the program.

I have to say that my fondest memories of Nebraska football are the relationships I developed over the years—more than the trophies and the championships. The greatest personal satisfaction I get to this day is when a player calls and wants to have lunch or writes me for a recommendation. When I hear from them, I realize that the experiences players shared at Nebraska mean a great deal to them. The emotional bond is very strong.

Our players, for the most part, always had a really good work ethic. Many of them grew up in small towns or on farms, and they knew what hard work meant. They had a good level of integrity and the majority of them left Nebraska with degrees. I really believe that the groundwork for their success was laid for most of them before they came to Nebraska. Their parents had done their jobs before they arrived. All of this led to the success that most of them enjoyed in whatever career they chose once they left Nebraska.

What can I say about Nebraska fans?

Generally, they are some of the more knowledgeable fans in the country. They really do follow football. They can recite statistics, scores, and facts all the way back to Nebraska's games against Notre Dame in the twenties. They also are knowledgeable of strategy and the nuances of the game. There are those who just want to win, but by and large, they understand almost everything that goes into winning and losing. And by and large, they are very courteous fans. Opponents generally were treated well when they came to Lincoln over the years. When we went some places to play around the country, it was not always that way for us, but I was always pleased that our opponents were treated well. Nebraska fans appreciate the effort and the skill that goes into playing the game of football.

You can say that Nebraskans are generally fair and friendly and have good values, and that leads to them being good football fans.

What do I think it means to be a Cornhusker?

To me, it symbolizes a quest for excellence. We tried to be excellent on the field, and we tried to excel in other areas, such as community service and academics. We tried to cultivate an attitude of unselfishness, to realize that if the team won on the field, then we all won. We tried to move players from a self-centeredness to a team-oriented concept. We tried to teach that if you sacrificed personal goals for team goals, it would benefit everybody in the end. And we consciously promoted spiritual values. I believe that all of this went into making those who have played Nebraska football, generally speaking, individuals of whom all Nebraskans can be proud.

I would like to take this opportunity to thank all the coaches, players, and fans whose loyalty and efforts helped make Nebraska football a great experience for me and for all of those involved.

I have never regretted a day of my 36 years as a coach at the University of Nebraska . . . and I will always value those countless experiences and enduring relationships.

—Tom Osborne

EDITOR'S ACKNOWLEDGMENTS

FIRST OF ALL, I WANT TO THANK U.S. Representative Tom Osborne for his efforts, and also those of his staff in Washington, D.C., especially Erin Hegge. Tom Osborne personified great character, unmatched class, and pure excellence on the football sidelines for more than 25 years, and I am sure he has made Capitol Hill a much better place.

Many Cornhuskers have demonstrated a sincere concern for their communities over the years by creating or contributing to public-service organizations. This is no coincidence, given the fact that coach Osborne constantly stressed to his players the need to give back to their community. To borrow a page from coach Osborne's playbook of life, please consider giving to these organizations:

- Tom Osborne is personally involved with the TeamMates Mentoring Program, a one-on-one mentoring program that "builds positive relationships to help young people reach their full potential." Contact teammates.org.
- Jerry Murtaugh's GoalOmaha, which places fitness coaches in Nebraska's high schools to promote physical fitness and to fight obesity among youth. Contact GoalOmaha.com.
- Will Shield's Will to Succeed Foundation, which aids abused and neglected women and children in the greater Kansas City area. Contact

willtosucceed.org or write: Will to Succeed Foundation, 11730 W. 135th Street, PMB 43, Overland Park, Kansas 66221.

- Dave Humm, the Huskers' quarterback from 1972 to 1974, was diagnosed with multiple sclerosis in 1988. To help fight MS, contact MultipleSclerosis.com.
- Bob Hohn, cocaptain of the 1964 team, died in 2003 from complications of ALS, commonly known as Lou Gehrig's Disease (read more about Hohn in Lyle Sittler's chapter). To help fight ALS, contact ALSFoundation.com or write ALS Foundation for Life, PO Box 504, Franklin, Massachusetts 02038-0504.

Also, I would like to thank Jerry Murtaugh and Broderick "the Sandman" Thomas. From two different eras, they were linebackers with real heart. I appreciate their special contributions in believing this was a worthwhile project.

Most of all, I want to thank all of those who wore the Nebraska uniform and took the time to do the work necessary to make this book a reality.

—Jeff Snook

INTRODUCTION

What It Means to Be a Husker

O NE DAY DURING THE MID-1920S on the southeast side of Lincoln, Nebraska, five-year-old Forrest Behm and his buddy accidentally started a brush fire that immediately spread like a juicy rumor. While flames shot into the air and the other boy ran for safety, Forrest stomped and stomped, using all he had as makeshift extinguishers—his feet.

By the time he was overcome by the intense heat and smoke, his little body was covered with third-degree burns. It was only a brush fire, harmless flames that threatened no homes, but Forrest was now on death's doorstep for literally trying to stomp out a childhood mistake.

A doctor immediately told the family that he must amputate his right leg to avoid infection and, thus, save the boy's life.

"That's what they did back then when you were burned," Behm said. "Amputation was the only way."

But his father, Forrest Sr., had dreams and goals for his namesake, and no doctor was about to cut them all away. "You are not amputating my son's leg," he said. "He's going to walk again, he's going to run again, and he's going to play sports some day."

For hours each day, Forrest Behm Sr. tended to his son's scarred and mangled leg, rubbing it with ointment while the boy screamed so hard the entire family made it a daily routine to leave the house. Finally, his father resorted to putting a piece of pine in young Forrest's mouth to prevent the screaming.

With a strip of wood in his mouth and tears in his eyes, young Forrest would dream his way through the intense pain while his father worked his miracle. With each raw nerve exposed, his desire grew day by day, treatment by treatment.

He would play sports like his father said, and he would become a success in life. He would make something of himself. Nothing would stop him.

Determination would lead him there.

In 1936, a boy named Fred Meier befriended an All-American football player. It was a typical case of hero worship, as the boy followed the star full-back everywhere he went. The boy even had access to the team's locker room, where he would fetch his hero's helmet and pads.

The hero, Sam Francis, had a night job answering the telephone at the old *Lincoln Star* newspaper. It was a good time for Sam to study because the phone rarely rang after hours. Young Fred would sit with him, watching his idol study, with hardly a word spoken between the two.

"Once in a while he would say something to me," Fred remembers. "It was the highlight of the day for me. I went about anywhere Sam went, just following him around. And I think, after a while, he kind of liked me.

"He certainly knew what I wanted to be when I grew up—I wanted to be just like him."

In the early sixties in McCook, Nebraska, a boy named Jeff Kinney couldn't wait for the weekends. It wasn't that he detested school, but Saturday afternoons meant Nebraska Cornhusker football, and Sunday mornings meant reading about it.

"I would go pheasant hunting on Saturday mornings and listen to the football game on the radio in the afternoon," he recalls. "I couldn't wait to hear it . . . I would just visualize the plays as they were happening through that radio.

"But the real highlight was getting up the next day and seeing the pictures in the newspaper. They would show a sequence of a certain play and how it developed. I loved that. I devoured that sports section from cover to cover, reading every word and staring at every picture of Nebraska football."

On New Year's Day, 1964, on a farm outside of Monroe, Nebraska, nine-year-old Clete Pillen fell off a horse while rounding up cattle and sustained a badly broken leg.

"Actually, the horse fell on me," Clete said. "I think a rabbit ran out in front of him and spooked him."

When the doctor finished casting the young lad's leg, Clete asked two simple questions:

"Will I be able to play football again?" and "Did we win the Orange Bowl today?"

On hearing the affirmative to both queries, young Clete smiled and realized this little mishap would not ruin his boyhood dreams. He would play football again. His beloved Huskers won a bowl game. Broken leg or not, all was right in his world.

On November 27, 1890, Dr. Langdon Frothingham, a faculty member who had recently arrived at the University of Nebraska from Harvard, took a bunch of young boys to Omaha to play a relatively new game. The Nebraska boys scored 10 points that day. The Omaha YMCA team scored none.

The next year, the Nebraska boys played four games, three of which were against Doane College.

By 1893, the university paid Yale graduate Frank Crawford to become the school's first official coach. They paid him $500, and he led the team to a 3–2–1 record.

For the next few years, coaches blew through the state capital like the whipping winter wind, with even the legendary Fielding Yost passing through Lincoln for one season. But by 1900, Princeton grad William C. "Bummy" Booth arrived and remained for six years, compiling a 24-game winning streak and an excellent 46–8–1 record.

After the university's team had been called various nicknames such as the Rattlesnake Boys, Antelopes, and Bugeaters, Booth's first team was officially given a new name: the Cornhuskers.

And the state of Nebraska's greatest tradition was born.

For the next century and beyond, the Cornhuskers would become entrenched as the state's obsession, passion, delight, pride and joy, agony, and ecstasy all rolled into one.

Hundreds of young men have grown up with a goal and a dream of playing football for the University of Nebraska. Among them were Forrest Behm, Fred Meier, Jeff Kinney, and Clete Pillen, who all became star football players for their beloved Cornhuskers.

Through dedication and desire to overcome his crippling burns, Behm became an All-American tackle on the school's first Rose Bowl team of 1940. He is now in the College Football Hall of Fame. Meier was a teammate.

Jeff Kinney became the workhorse running back and an All-American on perhaps the finest team to ever play college football, the 1971 Cornhuskers, which swept through the season like a Kansas tornado on its way to a second consecutive national championship.

And Pillen became an All–Big Eight linebacker and one of Nebraska's all-time leading tacklers.

Following their college football careers, they each became successful businessmen. Behm even worked his way to the top of the corporate ladder, becoming CEO and president of Corning International.

The great state of Nebraska is full of stories like theirs. Little boys playing in the yard, imitating their heroes who wear the scarlet and cream. "Someday when I grow up . . ." they say. "Someday . . ."

It has become a cycle of adoration that has sustained the Nebraska football program for more than a century. Glenn Presnell, a star running back in the twenties, was a hero of Sam Francis', who was a hero of Fred Meier's. Dennis Claridge was a hero of Jeff Kinney's, who was a hero of Marc Munford's.

The Cornhuskers have not been exclusive only to the natives, however. Nebraska's program has been a powerful magnet to those outside its borders, perhaps more so than any other college football program, with the exception of Notre Dame.

Of All-Americans, consider that LaVerne Allers and Trev Alberts hailed from Iowa; Dennis Claridge from Minnesota; Jim Anderson from Wisconsin; Dave Humm from Nevada; Vince Ferragamo and Steve Taylor from California; Tommie Frazier from Florida; Larry Jacobson from South Dakota; Turner Gill, Broderick Thomas, Junior Miller, Aaron Graham, and Aaron Taylor from Texas; Neil Smith from Louisiana; Marc Munford from Colorado; Mike Rozier from New Jersey; and Will Shields and Mike Minter from, of all states, Oklahoma.

"When you look at the Nebraska program," Aaron Graham said, "it really has been just one big melting pot. There were kids from all over the United States and kids from Nebraska, and the coaches always made it work."

On September 7, 1985, I stood near the end zone in the northwest corner of Memorial Stadium as the visiting team that day, the Florida State Seminoles, pranced happily to their locker room, celebrating along the way. They had just defeated the favored Cornhuskers 17–13 to leave the sunburned fans clad in red and white sullen, shocked, and extremely disappointed.

Suddenly, a slow clapping sound busted the silence that had gripped Memorial Stadium. It spread and grew into consistent applause, as if a Broadway play had just lowered its final curtain.

Why are these Nebraska fans applauding? I wondered. And why are they standing? Didn't their team just lose this game?

Oh Lord, I realized, they are applauding *the opposing team*!

I stood in pure amazement and gazed into the crowd, as if I was seeing with my own eyes a solar eclipse, or the Grand Canyon for the first time, or a spaceship landing in the middle of a cornfield. Could this really be happening?

In this win-at-all-costs, boo-at-will, throw-objects-at-the-visiting-team era of big-time college athletics, I was told this sight was a frequent occurrence at Memorial Stadium, where all gates read: "Through these gates pass the greatest fans in college football. . . ."

Now I understood why.

Of all of the school's unique football traditions—defensive starters called "Blackshirts," Herbie Husker, the consecutive bowl streak, and consecutive sold-out games at Memorial Stadium—the fans are Nebraska's greatest asset.

The famed Sea of Red can and will travel anywhere and turn another university's stadium into the site of a Nebraska road party.

"That's what I will always remember from walking out of that tunnel at Notre Dame," Eric Crouch said of the 2000 game in South Bend, Indiana. "I expected to see all blue and gold, and all I saw was red. You can't imagine how good that feels for a Nebraska football player."

A few hours later on the day of Florida State's upset, as I walked to my car outside of Memorial Stadium, Bob Devaney walked next to me.

Then serving his 19th year as the university's athletic director and 13 years following his retirement from the sidelines, he was disappointed at the game's outcome. Still, we conversed as if we were sitting on neighboring bar stools at the nearby American Legion, which Bob liked to frequent.

He asked where I attended college, where I lived in Florida, and what I thought of my first trip to Memorial Stadium. It is safe to say I liked him right away. I only wished that two-block walk could have lasted five miles.

Bob Devaney the football coach was a living legend. Bob Devaney the athletic director was a catalyst of ideas that established a solid foundation for the university's athletic future. Bob Devaney was a man of character. And Bob Devaney the character was a composite of Bob Hope and Jimmy Stewart. He was as funny and entertaining as he was devoted and thoughtful.

He coached the Huskers for only 11 seasons, a relatively short period to parallel his legendary status, but he accomplished as much for Nebraska as Bear Bryant did for Alabama or Darrell Royal for Texas or Bud Wilkinson for Oklahoma.

The fact is, Nebraska had been a perennial loser before Devaney was hired away from Wyoming in 1962, recording only three winning seasons in those 22 years since the 1940 Rose Bowl team. After Devaney arrived in Lincoln, the Huskers never had a losing season, beginning a four-decade run of consistency that hasn't been matched in major college football.

Furthermore, Devaney hired Tom Osborne.

By writing about Florida State's and later Miami's football programs, I came to meet Osborne several times during the eighties and nineties when Nebraska matched up with either the Seminoles or Hurricanes in bowl games. From that first introduction on a Scottsdale, Arizona, practice field before the 1988 Fiesta Bowl, I realized immediately that I was meeting greatness.

In dealing with college football coaches for the past 25 years, I can tell you that the Pat Dyes, Danny Fords, Jimmy Johnsons, and Jackie Sherrills come and go because, by and large, they put themselves first.

But the Tom Osbornes make a lasting difference and leave legacies because they put their *players* first.

I think of a quote I once heard: "Great people talk about ideas; average people talk about events; petty people talk about people."

As a coach, nobody had more original ideas than Tom Osborne. His players who sustained long NFL careers will tell you a simple fact: nobody who coached in the pro game—nobody—could match Xs and Os with Dr. Tom.

His impeccable 25-year record—255 wins, only 49 losses, an NCAA fifth-best .836 winning percentage, and three national championships—is a testimonial, but those are mere statistics that illustrate Osborne's success.

What distinguishes it is the long list of future doctors, lawyers, businessmen, clergymen, CEOs, and corporate presidents and vice presidents whom he recruited, nurtured, motivated, taught, and inspired through the University of Nebraska.

When he recruited them, he didn't tell them they would become All-Americans and Heisman Trophy winners. He didn't even tell them they would become great football players or even starting football players. And he surely didn't promise them material goods.

He told them they would receive a college education if they applied themselves.

Not coincidentally, Nebraska has had more Academic All-American football players than any other NCAA university.

To me, he was college football's Abraham Lincoln. He was honest until it hurt, caring to a fault, as dignified as any of our nation's finest leaders, and as humble as an everyday follower.

When I hear of the scandals surrounding NCAA head coaches in recent years—involving gambling, cavorting with strippers, and drinking with coeds—I can't help but wonder what coach Osborne must have been thinking about the game he left behind.

Here is a man whose character was exemplary. Even in the heat of battle, when his anger simmered, the worst phrases he could possibly mutter would be a "dadgummit" here or a "gosh-darnit" there.

Frankly, he is what we should all aspire to be: A person of excellent morals, extreme loyalty, and unselfishness, and one who has a deep sense of community and is committed to public service.

While coach Osborne was a great, great football coach, U.S. Representative Tom Osborne is a great, great man.

If only Capitol Hill had more like him . . .

★　　★　　★

As I talked to Lyle Sittler, the All–Big Eight center from the 1964 team, while researching this book, he told me the story of his friendship with Bob Hohn. It began when he tackled Hohn on one play in a high school game and became stronger when the two became cocaptains together at Nebraska.

Hohn affectionately called Sittler "the fat SOB that caught me from behind."

The two, along with several former Husker teammates, would meet at Brewsky's and share a few laughs over a beer on Mondays as the years passed since their playing days. They met there with Hohn for the final time on a Monday, November 24, 2003.

Three days later, Bob Hohn died of Lou Gehrig's disease. The next day, his beloved Cornhuskers whipped Colorado in Frank Solich's final game as head coach.

"Losing Bob was tough," Lyle said, sobbing. "I always enjoyed it when he called me 'that fat SOB that caught me from behind.' I'll sure miss him."

Now that the Devaney-Osborne-Solich era is gone, some wonder, what will happen to the solid Nebraska foundation?

The truth is, the rich Nebraska tradition will always remain alive in the memories and in the names from its storied past. It is alive and thriving in men like Forrest Behm, Fred Meier, Lyle Sittler, Jeff Kinney, and Tom Osborne. It is alive in those who remember Bob Devaney, Jake Young, Brook Berringer, Tom Novak, and Bob Hohn.

For it is the people—players, coaches, and fans—who have made Nebraska football what it is.

And for those who know what it means to be a Husker, it will always remain very much alive.

Here are their stories . . .

—Jeff Snook

The
TWENTIES

GLENN PRESNELL

HALFBACK

1925–1927

MY STORY WITH NEBRASKA FOOTBALL BEGAN WHEN we moved from Kansas to DeWitt, Nebraska—just a little place about 40 miles southeast of Lincoln—when I was a freshman in high school. I loved sports. I played basketball, football, and ran track, but my favorite sport was always football. A lot of my high school friends went on to Nebraska and joined the fraternity Alpha Gamma Rho, so when I got out of high school, they all got me to come up there to go to school and join the fraternity.

When I arrived in Lincoln in 1924, I thought, "Wow, now this is a big, big place." We had about 100 kids in our whole high school, so you could say I was impressed by Lincoln's size. I was just a real country boy who had worked hard growing up. I shocked wheat, baled hay, and worked on a farm.

I decided I would try out for football, but I didn't know how good you had to be to play at Nebraska. I was about 5'10" and 185 pounds then. I had no idea then if I would be a good player or a bad one. I just went out and had pretty good luck, I guess. I had played high school football, but nobody out there knew my name. They just called me "DeWitt." There were about 40 players out there my first day as a freshman. In one of our first scrimmages, I scored five touchdowns, and that got me noticed right away. I figured then I would love college and love playing college football.

Coach [Ernest] Bearg came in as head coach of Nebraska after my freshman year, replacing Fred Dawson. Bearg had been an assistant at Illinois and

2

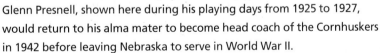

Glenn Presnell, shown here during his playing days from 1925 to 1927, would return to his alma mater to become head coach of the Cornhuskers in 1942 before leaving Nebraska to serve in World War II.

had coached the great Red Grange. He was a great big man, about 6'4", and a stern man. But I think he was a really good football coach. I know that he worked us hard.

I remember we opened my sophomore season at Illinois, and I got to make the traveling squad, so that was quite a thrill for me. I had never been east of

Omaha, but I remember the porter on the train waking us up as we crossed into Illinois so that we could see the Mississippi River. I expect that night was the first time I ever stayed in a hotel, too. I got in the Illinois game for the final five minutes [of a 14–0 win], but didn't do anything.

The thing I remember most about my sophomore year was finishing it up by beating Notre Dame [17–0] in Lincoln. They were coached by [Knute] Rockne, and it was quite a feat for Nebraska to beat Notre Dame in those days. There was a big party in Lincoln that night, I sure do remember that.

My junior year, I started playing more and we had a pretty good season [6–2], and the same for my senior year. I guess I ran the ball quite a bit, and scored some touchdowns, but one thing I really remember is that we never beat Missouri in my three years. We lost to them 9–6, 14–7, and 7–6. That stuck with me a while. Never beat 'em. I was picked to play in the East-West Shrine Game in San Francisco after my senior year, but I got hurt early in the game and didn't get to play much. We were on the East team back then, and I remember we lost. I guess that was the first time I ever saw the ocean, too. It was a great big city, and we had a few parties and banquets before the game. [Nebraska tackle] Ray Randels made the trip with me. We sure had a lot of fun on that trip.

4

I live in Ironton, Ohio, now, but I love Nebraska very much. It was always home to me. That was why I coached as an assistant and then became head coach [in 1942], but then with the war on, I went into the service. I still watch the Cornhuskers, and being from Nebraska meant a lot to a small-town country boy like me. I can tell you this: watching all those national championship teams through the years meant an awful lot to us old-timers. I was always proud to say I was a Cornhusker.

Glenn Presnell led the nation in rushing in 1927. Notre Dame coach Knute Rockne said of Presnell: "Unless you stop him behind the line of scrimmage, he'll average seven yards a try on you." He was all–Missouri Valley Conference in 1926 and 1927. Born July 28, 1905, he was the oldest-living Nebraska football player and oldest-living former NFL player as of April 2004. He played four seasons with the Portsmouth (Ohio) Spartans, which then became the Detroit Lions, with whom he played another three seasons (1935–1937). The 1942 Cornhuskers finished 3–7 in his only season as head coach. Presnell was inducted into the Nebraska Football Hall of Fame in 1973.

The THIRTIES

FORREST "FORRY" BEHM

TACKLE

1938–1940

I was one of seven children, living out on the edge of town, the south-east part of Lincoln. A lot of vacant fields out there were the original prairie. There were five girls and two boys in our family, and it was a much different age back then. The amazing thing about our household was that we had three bedrooms and only one bathroom, and at one time I had four sisters that were either in school at the University of Nebraska or had jobs. How they got through the morning with one bathroom, I'll never know. Those were tough times. The drought was so bad—one year leaves were off trees by the Fourth of July. We used to talk about the seven years of drought . . . that plus the Depression was when I grew up. I had one pair of shoes, and if your shoes had a hole in them, you didn't get them repaired right away—you put paper in them to cover the hole. But nobody thought you were poor. It was a common thing to have hoboes come to the door to work for food then. We would just save apple peels and potato peels to give them. We never turned them away without something. I think there was about 35 percent unemployment in those days.

When I was five years old, I did something that changed my life forever. I was with a friend from the neighborhood and we had found some candles. Against all common sense, we were out in this huge field playing with these candles, and we set the field on fire. My friend was smart—he ran away. I tried to put out the fire, but it was too late and too big. I got badly burned over most of my body, but my right leg was really bad. I had third-degree burns from my heel, where I was stomping on the fire, all the way up to my hip, and I still have some bad scars to this day. Back then, the way they treated a burned limb was to amputate it, because they were scared of infection setting in. Nine times out of ten you got an infection, and when you got an infection, you died. But my dad, who was Forrest Senior, said, "No way. You are not amputating my son's leg. He's going to walk again, he's going to run again, and he's going to play sports some day."

From that day on, Dad put me on my belly and worked that leg. He bought Ungentine; I can still see the can with the yellow decoration. He would plaster my whole leg with it, then wrap the leg in cotton padding. When he worked on me, I would scream so hard that the rest of the family had to leave the house. This went on for a year. At times, he would give me a piece of pine to bite on to keep me from screaming. So I bit on pine, and my dad worked my leg. Day after day after day. At one point, Dad had me starting to do deep knee bends to exercise it. At first they weren't very deep, and when I would bend, the scars would rip open and bleed. I had a brace on my leg at this point. By the time I was 10, at his insistence, I started playing some sports. I would come home crying because guys beat me up all the time. So he taught me how to fight with a brace on my leg. My dad loved sports. He would race all the kids, and we would have baseball throws and play any kind of sports, especially on the Fourth of July. He was a lineman for the telephone company and a hard worker.

7

By the time I was a sophomore at Lincoln High, I loved basketball. I really wanted to be a basketball player, but I guess I was pretty clumsy. I got put on the sophomore team. And as a junior, I got put on the sophomore team. So before my senior year, I went to the coach and asked, "Is there any chance I can make varsity this year?" He said, "None whatsoever!" So then I went to the football coach and asked, "Can I play football?" He stuttered around, looked me up and down, and finally said, "OK, you can come out."

So I became a football player. That coach recently told me before he died that I was the only player he ever let come out for the first time right before his senior season. I played a few games, but mostly sat on the bench.

Later on, the principal called me into the office and said, "You are going to graduate next week. Your grades are good enough, you are graduating." I said, "I am?" What he was doing was watching out for the budget. I guess they had too many kids in school and they were graduating some of them early. So I got a diploma and went to work for the telephone company that January. I was digging holes and climbing poles. Now that really built up my legs. It was wonderful training for me. I put on more weight and got stronger by the day.

Then I went to Nebraska, and that was a tremendous change. That campus looked monstrous to me. I didn't think I was going to make it. But I found out I could make it academically if I worked hard, and I worked at making new friends, too. I wanted to major in mathematics and become an actuary. Then I found out what an actuary earned and decided to major in economics.

One time, one of my friends, Leroy Farmer, said, "Let's go sign up for football. We'll have a lot of laughs." So I went to the freshman coach and he said, "You can try out. Go down there and get a uniform." I went down and they asked me, "What size shoes do you wear?" I said, "Fifteen." They said, "We can't afford to buy those." So I ended up buying my own shoes—they were beautiful kangaroo hide, nice and soft. When they came, they came in two boxes. Do you think I heard about that from my teammates? I was 6'4" and about 185 pounds, not bad for a tackle back then. I remember walking down the street one day and seeing the president of my high school class, who was black. I asked him, "Why don't you come out for football?" He told me he was too busy with his studies and so forth. We had no racial problems in Nebraska then, but what I realized much later was that he hadn't come out for the team because Oklahoma and Kansas and other teams wouldn't play us if we had black players.

It was such an upgrade from high school on the football field. Those guys were so much bigger and faster. I remember the first day, I had those nice new shoes on, and I was on the punt coverage team. I ran down as fast as I could. I sort of galloped, and as I was trotting back, I heard this big, deep voice: "Kid, you run like a cow stuck in the mud. I am going to teach you how to run!"

I walked over to this voice, and it was some shriveled-up old man in a wheelchair. It was coach Henry Schulte, who was one of the great track coaches of all time. [Schulte was the football head coach from 1919 to 1920 and track head coach from 1919 to 1938 at Nebraska.] So he did—he taught me how to run. I ran very upright and my right foot tended to turn out. He

Forrest Behm overcame a childhood tragedy to become an All-American. He is one of 12 Nebraska players to be inducted into the College Football Hall of Fame.

put me through a series of exercises to get the weight over my body and correct my posture, and he got my right foot turned in. It worked. I got faster.

Our head coach, Biff Jones, was an absolute gentleman. He was tough, but in a kind way. He was a real leader of men. I would have done anything for Biff Jones. He once told me a story about when he coached down at Louisiana State, when Huey Long was the big boss down there. At one of the games, Huey Long came to the door of the dressing room at halftime. He wanted to talk to the team, but the guys wouldn't let him in the door. Biff told him, "Nobody talks to my team but me." Huey told him, "I got five big guys out here who say I talk to the team right now." Biff replied, "I got 40 in here who say you don't." That's the kind of guy he was.

I remember my first game at Nebraska like it was yesterday. We played at Minnesota, and Minnesota just beat the hell out of me. I had a twisted knee and a broken nose, and I thought, "This is what I got myself into?" We got beat 16–7 on the scoreboard, but it was about 50–0 from a physical standpoint. But I never got beat up like that again.

I do remember a bad game I had against Indiana that year. We came into the Monday afternoon review and Biff said, "I have never had a football team play as poorly as you did. And of the defense, the line played the worst. And of the line, the tackles played the worst. And of the tackles, Behm, you were the worst." We filed out of there, and nobody said a word to me.

We always had fun traveling by train. We were headed to Indiana to begin my junior season, and [fullback] Vike Francis had false teeth. Well, Vike fell asleep in a lower berth and he had his mouth wide open. Harry Hopp went by and very carefully pulled Vike's teeth out and put them in his pocket. So Vike wakes up later and starts gumming his words to find out who had his teeth. Biff Jones comes in, surveys the situation, and asks, "OK, where's Harry Hopp?" Biff knew his players.

By the time I was a senior, I realized I was a pretty good football player. It was a really bad year with the Depression and everything. Nobody could get jobs. That summer, I found out they were building a highway, which is now the Cornhusker Highway. I went out there and they put me to work shoveling concrete. We had to shovel concrete in front of the concrete spreader to keep the blade wet. You shoveled nonstop for a six-hour shift. No breaks. Then I found a job stacking sugar in a warehouse. I stacked bags of sugar for another six hours, so now I was working 12 hours each day. I got Sundays off on the road and Saturdays and Sundays off in the warehouse. But I was in good shape. I was strong after all that working, and I really had an unfair advantage my senior year. We didn't lift weights back then, but all that shoveling concrete and stacking sugar served as my weight lifting. I weighed about 230 by then.

We lost the first game my senior season at Minnesota, 13–7, and never lost again. I remember going to play in Pittsburgh, standing on the field, and not being able to see the top of the stadium because of the smog. We were used to the clean air. Nebraska had never been to a bowl before and a lot of people took pride in that because we considered ourselves an academic school. But after the season, the athletic board of control had to meet to discuss accepting an invitation to the Rose Bowl—they were leaning toward not going. I was a student representative on the board, and I just asked, "What are you going to tell the hometown folks when you tell them you turned down the Rose Bowl?" There was a silence, and then they decided to go.

Before we got to California, I had what I considered a real personal tragedy that bothers me to this very minute. We went to Phoenix to practice, and during one workout, some of the scout-team players were on the sidelines horseplaying. I was running down near the sideline when one of those big lineman from the scout team stepped on my foot, and I hurt my hip joint. This was one week before the Rose Bowl! It was a freak thing, but I had never been hurt before, other than the normal bumps and bruises.

I didn't start the game, but I played about half of it on my press clippings only. I was in quite a bit of pain in that game and I didn't enjoy it one bloody bit. I feel I let the team down. We lost to Stanford [21–13] in what was my final game. That always has and always will bother me.

But a great thing came from that game. My dad, who had saved my leg when I was a boy, got to see me play in the Rose Bowl. I just would have given anything for him to live long enough to see me inducted into the College Football Hall of Fame.

You know, I have lived in New York State since 1944, but my heart is still back in Lincoln. When people ask me where I am from, I just say, "Nebraska." I was so proud of coach Devaney and coach Osborne for how they turned the game around for Nebraska, and I always considered myself part of the Nebraska family.

Forrest "Forry" Behm was an All-American in 1940. He was inducted into the Nebraska Football Hall of Fame in 1980 and the College Football Hall of Fame in 1988. He later worked his way up from the production line at Corning Glass Company to serve as president and CEO of Corning International in Corning, New York.

11

FRED MEIER
CENTER
1939–1941

WHEN I WAS IN JUNIOR HIGH SCHOOL, my brother Frank was on the football team at Nebraska and I couldn't wait to go down to watch them practice every day. Then on gamedays, there was one special gate where the players entered, and I would go stand there to watch the players go in. One time, a player I knew put his arm around me and took me in. I sat on the bench that day, and that continued all the way through my high school days.

Sam Francis was an All-American fullback in 1936 and probably the most famous Cornhusker. He also later became a shot-putter in the Olympics. Well, he was my hero. The players had metal tubs in those days for their clothes and football uniforms. They would come to practice, take out their uniforms, and put their street clothes in the tub. I would go over and get Sam Francis' tub and bring it to him every day. He also had a job at the old *Lincoln Star*, now the *Journal Star*, answering the phone after hours. He would sit there and study, waiting for the phone to ring, and I would sit there with him. Once in a while, he would say something to me.

You could say that I always wanted to follow in my brother's and Sam's footsteps and become a Cornhusker football player.

They were tough times. Frank, who became a third-team All-American, and I slept in the same bed until he left home. In the summertime, my dad farmed me out to a cousin for work. I went to work at the age of 13 on my cousin's farm, taking care of the horses. We would hook them up to a cultivator and cultivate the corn and pitch hay on the rack by hand. When I was 16, my cousin took his family on a vacation and I ran the whole farm for two weeks. There were nine cows to milk twice a day. There were horses, hogs, and chickens to take care of. We had a walking plow. I made a dollar a day, plus I got room and board. Now that taught me about hard work and how to withstand suffering. Later on, that would come to help me, because when you are getting the hell beat out of you on the football field, some guys fold and some guys don't.

But I was unathletic as a sophomore in high school. I couldn't run worth a damn and I couldn't get on the football team. As a junior, I got better and got on the team. I played center—like my brother—and linebacker, and Lincoln High won the state championship that year. That was quite a thrill for us. We lost a lot of good players before my senior season and didn't have a very good year. After that, there was hardly any question what I was going to do. My parents had graduated from the University of Nebraska. I had three brothers and a sister and all but one brother graduated from the University of Nebraska. My father's family had 14 children and most of them went to the University of Nebraska.

So my dream was to play football for the Cornhuskers. There were no scholarships then, of course. You just went out for the team. So I was lucky to be on the team because I wasn't really talented, but I worked like hell to earn my place. I remember one of the first practices. They had two posts about four or five feet apart for the linemen. One lineman would be on one side and one on the other, and you blocked while the other guy tried to get through, but you had to stay between those posts. It was murder. The upperclassmen beat the hell out of me. We learned how to hit hard and how to take a hard hit. The thing was to be tough. Anyway, I had a badly sprained ankle that took me out of about half of my freshman season.

I wasn't a great athlete. I had a hard time snapping the ball back to the player in the backfield. But we had a discus net in the stadium, and I decided to put it to good use. It was about 10 feet high and wide, made of a mesh of rope. I practiced centering the ball into this net for hours on hours until I could do it damn hard. From that point on, I don't think I ever made a bad snap on punts or kicks.

I started to get to play quite a bit during my junior year in 1940. I remember that very first game at Minnesota. They had a great back named Sonny Frank, and he could run to one end and then cut back to the other. Well, I remember it because when he would cut back, somebody was blindsiding me the whole game. I remember we were really tackling Sonny hard, too. He

Cornhuskers football became a lifelong affair for Fred Meier and his family.

was really getting hit. But after the game [a 16–7 Minnesota win], we were in the locker room, and I'll be damned, here comes Sonny, who wanted to meet us and talk to us. That meant a lot to us. Minnesota went on to win the national championship that year.

We beat Missouri 20–7 a few games later because we had been so mad at them for beating us the year before. We were so fired up that Missouri finished the game with minus three yards rushing.

In the next game, we beat Oklahoma [13–0] at their place. Now there are two remarkable things I remember about that game: one was when Allen Zikmund went down to catch a pass and the pass hit the defender in the back and bounced up into the air. Allen caught it and ran for a long gain that set up a touchdown. The other was when we had the ball at Oklahoma's 20-yard line with a fourth-and-10. We had this trick play from the single-wing formation where I centered the ball back to our fullback, Vike Francis, who charged into the line next to me. He handed the ball to me, and I was supposed to lateral it back to Bob Kahler, who was coming around from the end on a reverse. But I looked up and Bob was nowhere to be found because somebody had already tackled him even though he didn't have the ball. So I just turned around and started running, and I made it to the 2-yard line. Now that was every linemen's dream!

When we had one of our team reunions about 25 years later, our coach, Biff Jones, asked me, "Freddie, what the hell happened on that play anyway?" I really don't know what happened to Bob, but I almost got it into the end zone.

After the season, they announced Nebraska would play in the Rose Bowl, and we were all excited about that. I remember being in one building on campus, milling around with other kids on the first floor, when this old-time army guy who taught military science on the second floor came down the steps. Everybody was talking about Rose Bowl this and Rose Bowl that, and we thought he would be one of the people who would be all upset about it because nobody would be coming to class. All of a sudden he blurted out, "Let's go west!" All the kids whooped it up.

Then came the Rose Bowl. It was just a marvelous experience to play in that big stadium with all those people [ninety-two thousand]. That was the first time I truly saw wide receivers and the T formation. Stanford lined receivers up way out there, and their quarterback, Frankie Albert, would get them the ball. They were very good. So we came out to Los Angeles early for that game and our eyes were so big, seeing that big town and Hollywood and everything. We were given $10 per person. That didn't go far in old Los Angeles. We went to watch the Chicago Bears play out there. The idea was to learn this new defense we would be playing with three down linemen and four linebackers. A few of the linebackers would rush the quarterback and some would stay back, but on each play, we would change which players rushed and which didn't to try to confuse Stanford.

15

A man named Chuck Taylor made my Rose Bowl experience a tough one. He was a defensive guard and the guy was so quick. I would snap the ball and turn one way to block him and he would be by me. I could never get him because he was so quick. I got so damn mad at him, but they had designed their defense to stop our strong off-tackle running plays of Harry Hopp (who was the toughest guy I ever knew) and to stop our reverse play with Bob Kahler. They did a great job at that, but we had noticed their interior defensive linemen were spread apart farther than normal. So I remember our coaches did a great job of changing our plan, and we just started trapping their defensive guards. We let them go up the field and we didn't even have to block them. So I would let Chuck go by, and we would run it on them up the middle. That's how we got all of our yards that day.

Later in the game, I was on defense and I was rushing the passer. I had a head of steam built up and I saw this blocker setting up to block me. Then I saw who it was. It was Chuck Taylor. I hit him harder than I hit anybody in my life. I got underneath him and flipped him over backward and accidentally kicked him in the head on the way through him. He got up, but he didn't get up right away. I just wanted to hit this guy because he was making me miserable on the other side of the ball. [Taylor later played for the 49ers.]

Anyway, we were in a very close game [with Stanford leading 14–13], and Stanford got the ball down to our 4-yard line near the end of the game. We stopped them, got it back, and—we were very conservative back then—we punted on first down! We were just playing for field position. It was about a 60-yard punt, and this guy [Pete Kmetovic] takes it back all the way for the game-breaker. That was the most memorable play in my mind, and we got beat 21–13, but Nebraska put a team into the Rose Bowl.

It seemed that Rose Bowl changed the way every team in college football played offense. Most all of them changed to the T formation like Stanford after that.

In my senior season, my weight was up to about 193 and I got stronger, but we had lost so many good players the year before that we didn't do nearly as well [4–5 record]. But we did beat Oklahoma [7–6] in the final game. They had a noseguard who would hit me with the palm of his hand right on my headgear to begin every play, and my head got so damn sore by the end of that game. But we got the last laugh on the scoreboard. What happened the following week? Pearl Harbor was bombed.

I've lived in California now most of my life since leaving college, but let me tell you that I have corn in my blood. I just love the University of Nebraska. So does all of my family. Our house is full of Cornhusker stuff. You can say that I am very proud to be a Cornhusker.

A Meier brother held down Nebraska's center position from 1932 to 1934 (Frank) and from 1939 to 1941 (Fred). Frank Meier was All–Big Six in 1933 and 1934. Fred was president of the "N Club" from 1941 to 1942. The Meier family was presented the Family Tree Award from the University of Nebraska Alumni Association in 1999 for having 67 members from five generations attend—and 53 graduate—from the university. Since then, several more descendants from the Meiers have attended and graduated from the university.

The
FORTIES

VIC SCHLEICH

TACKLE

1940–1942

Y PARENTS WERE RUSSIAN IMMIGRANTS, who moved to Lincoln, Nebraska, in 1907 along with one son. Once there, they had eight more children, and I was the youngest. I had five brothers and three sisters. Anyway, I grew up to love sports. I learned how to throw the shot put and I learned to play football. I had a good friend who was ahead of me in school, Bill Pfeiff, who helped me with each sport. We got to be good friends, and Bill was just like a player-coach, even in high school. He went on to play at the University of Nebraska for a season [1937] before he got injured and couldn't play anymore.

I was always a lineman because of my size—I was about 6'2" and 220 pounds by my senior year at Lincoln High. And I was a big Nebraska fan. We would sneak into games or sit in the old knothole section, where if you didn't have a lot of money, they would let you in for something like a dime. My hero then was George Sauer, the All-American fullback. I loved to watch him run.

Anyway, I had some great high school teammates like Forry Behm, Eddie Schwartzkopf and Freddie Meier, and they all ended up at Nebraska. I wasn't that good in high school, but the biggest thing I had going for me was that they said I was "coachable," whatever that means. But I guess I was, because I always worked hard at the game. I wanted to become better.

I had an offer from Alabama, but I had no intention of going there. I couldn't wait for Nebraska coach Biff Jones to call me. Finally, one day, he did. I went down to talk to him, and he said, "We'd like to have you. You have a chance to be on one of the best teams in Nebraska football history." Those were magical words to me. What he didn't know was I would have scraped up the money to pay him to play football at Nebraska.

I remember seeing our freshman squad at Nebraska, and we had about 125 guys out there. And we ran a lot of wind sprints! We were tough, too. We had that "between the posts" drill where you had to see who was the toughest. And we had a simple drill where they would throw the runner the ball and you had to tackle him, one-on-one. The hardest I ever got hit in my life was by Forry Behm in high school in that drill. He creamed me.

You can say I liked our coaches right away. Biff Jones was very fair. He knew everybody by name from the time he met you. He never forgot your name. Our line coach, "Link" [Roy] Lyman, was a former Chicago Bear, and he was a great coach. Then there was Glenn Presnell, who coached the backfield. I remember that Link, Glenn Presnell, Bill Pfeiff, and I used to play handball for hours, and we would just beat the hell out of each other. Boy, that was fun. It kept us in great shape, and it was good ol' competition.

I had a rude awakening in my freshman year. It was during practice the week before the season opener against Indiana when somebody fell on me from behind and broke my lower right leg. It sidelined me for the whole year. But that's how I learned how to kick—I spent much of the time over there with the kickers.

In the first game of my sophomore year, we played at Minnesota and I can remember my first entrance onto the field. We were supposed to report into the game in those days, and I was so excited I forgot who to report to and who I was coming in for. I didn't play much, but it was the beginning of my Nebraska career. We always had fun on those road games. I remember coming back from Kansas [a 53–2 win in 1940], and we were eating our meal on the train. All of a sudden, somebody pulled the brake and we heard a boom and stopped on a dime. We were all covered with food!

That season also ended up as one of the most memorable seasons in Nebraska football history, as Biff had promised. Near the end of the season, we had won all of our games but that Minnesota game, and we heard that if Texas A&M beat Texas on Thanksgiving Day, we would be going to the Rose Bowl. Sure enough, A&M came through for us. Now that was something I never thought would happen in all my life. Me, a kid from a huge family growing up in the Russian Flats of Lincoln, playing in the Rose Bowl?

You dream about things like that, but I never thought it would happen. The day we got the invitation, they canceled classes. We had a big tackle, Royal Kahler, and he showed up for class that day, not realizing what they had done. I guess we all were very excited about the thought of playing in the biggest football game there was.

We went to Phoenix to practice and then went on to Los Angeles and saw Hollywood, and it was such a thrill. I still have the Rose Bowl itinerary to this day. They treated us like kings out there.

In those days, Biff Jones liked to use a two-team system. He would play one team for a quarter, and the second team for the second quarter, and so on. I remember we went ahead because Vike Francis was gaining big yards on that trap play. He scored and kicked the point and we were ahead 7–0. But Stanford was a great team and they came right back. The play I remember most was when Allen Zikmund caught that long [33 yards] pass from Hermie Rohrig to score a touchdown and got hit right after he crossed the goal line. He broke his leg badly. As everyone knows, we didn't win the game, but the experience was special. And today, so is the memory.

But we lost a lot of good players after that season, and we weren't nearly as good the next season [4–5 record]. I remember we trailed Oklahoma 6–0, and Wayne Blue ran an interception back for a touchdown. Biff was screaming from the sideline, "Let Vic kick it! Let Vic kick it!"—meaning the extra point. Jack Hazen heard it and made the call in the huddle, "Quick kick! Quick kick!" But Hermie figured it out. There was no way we would quick kick after scoring a touchdown. So I kicked the extra point and we beat Oklahoma 7–6. That would have been Biff Jones' final game at Nebraska. I know I heard he wanted to come back for another season, but apparently certain people in Lincoln didn't want him back. That was a big mistake, in my opinion, because I knew him as a great coach, but Biff was an army guy and went on to become athletic director at West Point.

In my senior year, Glenn Presnell became head coach and he was very well liked by everybody, but we didn't have too many good players left. We had linemen playing in the backfield on that team, and I know we didn't score many points. [The 1942 team was shut out in five games and scored only 55 points in 10 games.] Against Oklahoma that year, I blocked a punt that set up a touchdown. In those days, you couldn't substitute a lot, and they had some small back in there who was trying to block me. I think I weighed about 230 and was up to about 6'3" as a senior, so I got through him pretty

Vic Schleich, a tackle and kicker from 1940 to 1942, scored all of Nebraska's points in the 1942 victory over Oklahoma—the Cornhuskers' last victory over the Sooners until 1959.

easily. After we scored, I kicked the extra point and beat them again [7–0]. It would be the last time we beat Oklahoma for 17 years. Then we lost our final four games. Whatever our record was [3–7], it wasn't the coach's fault, I know that.

The one thing I know about playing football at Nebraska is this: I was fortunate. I think there must have been one thousand kids just like me who wanted to play football at Nebraska, and I got to live my dream. For me, it was always quite an honor. I remember this secretary from the alumni association who used to travel with us to all of our games. I heard him make speeches a number of times, and he always ended them with this: "Once to be a Nebraskan is always to be a Nebraskan . . . in the deep down constitution of your soul!"

I think that says it all.

Vic Schleich, a three-year letterman, was named All–Big Six as a tackle in 1942. He later played one season (1947) with the New York Yankees of the All-American Football League.

The FIFTIES

JOHN BORDOGNA

QUARTERBACK

1951–1953

I'LL NEVER FORGET MY FIRST NIGHT IN LINCOLN in the fall of 1950, when I arrived from my home in Turtle Creek, Pennsylvania, which is about 15 miles east of Pittsburgh. It was kind of lonely, to be honest. I had arrived late at night, probably 11:00 P.M. or so. As we—I was with two other recruits from my area—came up from the train station to what we called O Street, nobody was around. It was dark, it was unknown to us, and we spent some time searching for a hotel.

In all honesty, there were times I questioned myself, "Why did I come here? What am I doing here?" And that was the first time.

I am often asked how I wound up in Nebraska—both to play college football and to live the rest of my life. The answer is simple: my high school head coach at Turtle Creek, Ralph Fife, had accepted a job to become the line coach at Nebraska. I had gone to Notre Dame to visit, and I had also considered the University of Georgia, Clemson, and North Carolina. Notre Dame's Leon Hart was from my hometown and I may have ended up there, but Frank Leahy believed I was not tall enough at 5'10" to play quarterback. But I trusted Ralph Fife, even though I had never met Nebraska head coach Bill Glassford.

When we arrived, it was kind of tough on us because we were not Nebraska people. Most of the players on Nebraska's team were from Nebraska, but my goal from the start was not to be just another player. I just believed that I had to work doubly hard to become a starter. As a freshman, my immediate goal was to become the starting quarterback of the freshman team. I did that and played reasonably well in our three freshman games. I was up against Ray Novak, who was from Omaha, for the quarterback's job. But Ray went on to play fullback, and I played quarterback.

I have to say that it took some time to like Lincoln, and as I said, I had questioned my decision to follow Ralph Fife here. I had left all my friends back home, but as time passed I made new friends, and then the team became more than friends to me. It became an extended family. My teammates became my brothers. And that is a camaraderie we still have to this day.

For my sophomore year, the entire team reported to Curtis, Nebraska, for fall camp. We called it "Camp Curtis," and it was way out west in Nebraska. We were there for 18 days in August, and it was rough, very rough. It was very hot, too, with most days over 100 degrees. This camp became somewhat like a boot camp, and we had similar camps in high school before the football season, so I was used to it. Some of the local boys, the farm boys, weren't used to it. I saw many people who were upset about being there and having to go there in the first place. We practiced twice a day and sometimes three times each day.

As far as the quarterback job goes, Fran Nagle had been the starter in 1950 and he graduated, so I knew the job was open. My goal was to win the job as a sophomore, and I think I did that in Camp Curtis.

Nineteen-fifty-one was an unhappy season for us for the most part because we didn't win many games [2–8 record]. We had Bobby Reynolds, but he was hurt most of the time. We were counting on him because he had been an All-American in the previous season. But he was hurting so bad—he had broken his femur and then broken his collarbone—that we had no choice but to use him as a decoy.

In 1952, we won our first four games and the highlight had to be beating Oregon 28–13 at their place. It must have been 100 degrees on the field that day, and I scored on an 80-yard touchdown run that must have looked like an option. I went down the line of scrimmage and our running back was out too far, so I just made a fake to him, and the defensive end went for it, and I went the rest of the way.

In the fourth game, we went to Penn State. It was a homecoming of sorts for me, and my entire family was there for the game. My mother didn't really like me playing football, and she even refused to sign the letter of permission

John Bordogna was one of the toughest quarterbacks in Nebraska history.

for me to play in high school. My dad supported me more, but even he had been to only one game in my high school career.

Anyway, our offense just sputtered for most of the day at Penn State. Early in the game, I was rolling to my right and Roosevelt Grier hit me from the blind side with a forearm to the face, and remember, we had no face masks. I was spitting up blood so bad, and two of my front teeth went through my jaw and two more were smashed downward. I lost four of my bottom front teeth. My eyes were dilated and I couldn't see, and it took me a little while to regain consciousness, too.

I am not bragging by saying this, but I came back in and played the rest of the game, but we lost 10–0. It was the first time, and only time, that my mother ever saw me play football, and after the game I tried to sneak by my family onto the bus so she wouldn't see me. When I got back to Lincoln, I went to the dental college, and they went to work on me. It wasn't very pleasant, and I wear a bridge there today.

That Monday, we got a letter from [Penn State coach] Rip Engle saying something like "We're very sorry this had to happen." But Roosevelt Grier [who later became an NFL great and acted in movies] never apologized. Yes, it was a really cheap shot. And no, I never saw him again.

As a senior, I got to throw it more, and we were changing the offense a little bit because of our personnel. We went to Illinois and played very well in a 21–21 tie. But my biggest regret is that we never beat Oklahoma. They just had too many horses—about four-deep. Oklahoma was always powerful, and those were Bud Wilkinson's best teams.

I remain very close to Bill Glassford to this day. He was only about 5'6", and I remember him getting in the faces of guys who were about 6'4". Now he could do that to the Eastern boys who didn't have a problem with it, but the farm boys didn't take it too well. Glassford and I had a bond from the beginning. I understood him, and I think he understood me. That's why we have always stayed friends.

Before 1955, a few people in the downtown area wanted to oust him, and some players had signed a petition to do so, but I would never sign it. He was my coach and always will be my coach. I was helping out with the quarterbacks after my playing days, and that's how I stayed in Nebraska. Coach Glassford stayed one more year and then left after the 1955 season, but I never felt right about the way he was treated.

I now have a lifetime pass to Nebraska games, but that is not why I attend. I attend the games because I like them. I knew Bob Devaney and Tom Osborne and Frank Solich very well, and they all put Nebraska on the map. I stayed here because I liked Lincoln. I married a Nebraska girl, and I feel very strongly that this part of the country has a lot of things going for it, especially in the game of football.

Some people don't realize that at Nebraska, we don't get money from the state. It is through donations, and that makes me very proud. I like to think that I have become a strong supporter as an alumnus of the University of Nebraska. And I have very strong feelings for my school. For the University of Nebraska, whatever I can do, I will do.

John Bordogna was named All–Big Seven in 1953. In this three years as starting quarterback, he completed 113 of 271 passes for 1,608 yards and six touchdowns. He also led Nebraska in rushing in 1952 with 576 yards and eight touchdowns. His 89-yard interception return against Colorado in 1953 is the third-longest in school history. He was inducted into the Nebraska Football Hall of Fame in 1988.

MICK TINGELHOFF
CENTER
1959–1961

I GREW UP WAY OUT IN LEXINGTON, NEBRASKA, a small town of about five thousand people in the middle part of the state. I was the youngest of six kids, and we lived on a farm about eight miles outside of Lexington. We raised beef and corn, and that taught us a lot about hard work at a very young age. I went to school in a one-room schoolhouse, which is hard to imagine these days, but that's what it was.

I didn't play any sports whatsoever until my freshman year in high school, but we always listened to Nebraska football games on the radio. I dreamed of playing football for the Big Red when I was younger, but I never thought I would get a scholarship to play anywhere, much less at the University of Nebraska. Bobby Reynolds and Tom Novak were heroes of mine when I was growing up, but I never got to go to Lincoln to see a game.

Our football coach in high school was named Merle Applebee, and he was a great, great coach. We won the Class A state championship during my senior year, which was quite an accomplishment for such a small-town school. Seven of us off of that team would get scholarships, and the big catch was a guy named Monte Kiffin. Everybody now knows Monte as the defensive coordinator at Tampa Bay, but he was the big star back then. He was about 6'3" and 205 pounds, and everybody wanted him. I was about 6'1" and 180, played center on offense and linebacker on defense, and my only offers were from South Dakota, Iowa State, and Nebraska.

You realize that I did not have a tough decision.

If I could get a scholarship to the University of Nebraska, I was gone. And I got it. I don't really remember much about my freshman year—I think that I took so many hits to the head for all those years in the NFL that it's tough to remember that far back, but I know I respected coach [Bill] Jennings. I played some as a sophomore in 1957, some at center, but more at linebacker in our 6–2 defense. I was the linebacker on the right side, and we didn't have a very good team that year [3–7 record].

Something very special in Nebraska history happened when we played Oklahoma in Lincoln. The Cornhuskers had not beaten the Sooners in 17 years, and nobody gave us a chance to do it that time, either. We weren't that good of a team [2–4 at the time], and Oklahoma [ranked No. 19] was very good. But we held on to beat them 25–21, and oh, man, the celebration was wild. They tore the goalposts down and right now, as I write this, I am looking at a piece of that goalpost. They filled it in, painted it red with the score of the game and gave each of us a piece of it.

The next year, we weren't any better [4–6], but we beat Oklahoma again [17–14] after about four losses in a row. We had some good players, but it just didn't work out for us. As a senior in 1961, we went 3–6–1, and there was talk that coach Jennings would be fired. He was, and it was a very tough situation. Everybody seemed to know it was coming.

30

Then, in a few days, I met the man who would turn Nebraska around for good. They chose me and a couple of other players to show him around campus. I can tell you that I was very impressed with Bob Devaney from the beginning. Why they chose us to show him around, I don't know, but I am glad they did. I don't think he had taken the job yet, but he was a very impressive guy. He was very polite. We had no idea he would do what he did at Nebraska, but he turned it around right away. We started winning and became the powerhouse that we are today, but I never looked back. I was in pro football when Nebraska started winning and I have no regrets about my college days. It worked out for me very well.

I thought I was going to be drafted [by the NFL], but I wasn't. So right after the draft, coach [Norm] Van Brocklin was in Minnesota, and he called me. He said he needed a center. I think his exact words were: "I saw you enough on film that I am going to fire that son of a bitch of a center I have right now!" But I almost signed with the St. Louis Cardinals first. They

Mick Tingelhoff was a solid center on Nebraska's last teams with losing records from 1959 to 1961, and then he became a fixture with the Minnesota Vikings.

wanted me, and I was ready to sign until Van Brocklin rented a plane and flew into Lincoln. He signed me for $10,000. I had just got married to Phyllis, whom I met at Nebraska, so we needed the money. It isn't much compared to today's signing bonuses, but it was a lot to us back then.

I remember that after two weeks of camp as a rookie, coach Van Brocklin was walking off the field and he came over and put his arm around my neck and said, "I told you I was going to fire him!" He had just cut the Vikings' center, and now I was the man.

We have been in Minnesota ever since, some 40 years.

But Nebraska was a great start for me, even though we didn't have winning records back then. It was a dream of mine to play for the Big Red, and I got to live my dream. For that, I will always be very thankful.

Mick Tingelhoff played the second-most games (240) on offense in NFL history. He started at center for the Minnesota Vikings from 1962 to 1978, and he was named All-Pro six times. He also played in four Super Bowls and seven Pro Bowls. He was inducted into the Nebraska Football Hall of Fame in 1980.

PAT FISCHER

HALFBACK, QUARTERBACK, DEFENSIVE BACK

1958–1960

What can I tell you about my days at Nebraska? Well, first of all, let me say that I played so many years in the NFL that I heard the "Star Spangled Banner" played a lot in between my final game with the Cornhuskers until the end of my days playing professional football.

In other words, my memory may not be perfect.

To begin with, there were six Fischer boys, and Nebraska football was in our blood. My brothers, Cletus, Kenny, and Rex, all played there when I was growing up. So when it was time for me to decide where I wanted to play football, it was a done deal. Joseph, our father, was a carpenter and he loved all sports, too. It was just the natural thing for us to do. We ran, we tackled, and we blocked as we grew up.

I used to go watch games at Nebraska when my brother Rex played. I remember being so excited just to carry his helmet. He would introduce me to other players, and I would be awed by that. Growing up, yes, I had heroes like the other boys—and they were all my brothers. I was coached by my brothers, too.

Our family, which included three older girls, started out in St. Edward, Nebraska, which is about 20 miles outside of Columbus. Then we moved to Oakland, Nebraska, and by the time I was in high school, we were in Omaha.

I played at Omaha Westside High as a halfback and a linebacker. By the time I was a senior, I had one thing on my mind—I would follow my brothers to Nebraska. I never wanted to go anywhere else. I could have gone to a couple of the military schools, probably, but I never took a visit anywhere. I just did it. I just went to Lincoln, and that was that. In fact, I don't think Nebraska had to recruit me at all. There was nothing to talk about . . . coach [Bill] Jennings just knew I was coming.

We were in the single-wing when I got there, and in one of the first practices, I got in serious trouble because I was supposed to hand the ball off, but I saw an opening and took off with it.

I remember when I got there that Monte Kiffin and Gene Ward roomed together right across the hall from me. We formed a close group and we would run around together. Our big thing was to try to get a booth at the student union and watch the girls go by and just hope one of them would sit down with us. It was fun to be in college and make new friends. My brother Rex had been in the Phi Gamma Delta fraternity, and I went up there some, but I never joined.

Was I a great student at first? No. But I became a better student. I knew then that if you become a better student, you become a better person. And I later came back to school, needing only nine hours to get my degree in business administration. In fact, four of us six Fischer boys graduated from Nebraska.

The play I remember most from my whole career is the opening kickoff of 1958 against Penn State in Lincoln. I took it back [92 yards] for a touchdown and we won [14–7] that day.

Heading into my senior year, they moved me to quarterback, but I couldn't throw the ball very well. I could run it though. I know that we beat Oklahoma 17–14 to end the season and had quite a time that night. We all went to a big dance, and I even had a date that night.

We never won big then, because that was the pre-Devaney era, but we had a lot of fun, made great friends, and all made contributions. Just because we didn't win championships doesn't mean we loved Nebraska any less than the players from those teams that did win championships.

When Devaney came in [1962], Cletus stayed as an assistant with him and they went around the state setting up quarterback clubs in every little community. That told all of those people in the state that they were significant, and that turned out to be the strength of Nebraska football over the years.

Pat Fischer played several positions for the Cornhuskers, including quarterback in 1960, before a long and storied NFL career.

Devaney sent his coaches out to keep in touch with the people, and it seemed that every community has contributed something to that program.

And with Devaney, they won and won and won.

What can I say about Nebraska people? Nebraska people will say hello to you or share a smile every day. It is a place you get to know your neighbors. I have lived here in northern Virginia for a long time, and I hardly know my neighbors. In Nebraska, there isn't anything people won't do for you.

All in all, Nebraska is very close to me and my family. We played there, and my brother Cletus coached there for so long [1959–1985]. Football at Nebraska means everything to our family. It is our identity. It is who we are and who we were. I look at it this way: all my brothers and I made contributions to the program, which in turn makes a contribution back to the state of Nebraska. That will always mean a lot to me.

Pat Fischer was one of the most versatile players in Nebraska history. He led the Cornhuskers in kickoff-return yardage, punt-return yardage, and all-purpose yardage for three straight seasons, 1958–1960; receptions in 1958; and passing and total offense and scoring in 1960. His 92-yard kickoff return against Penn State in 1958 is the eighth-longest in school history, and his 84-yard punt return against Oklahoma State in 1960 is the fifth-longest. He was a team tri-captain in 1960. Fischer played seven seasons with the St. Louis Cardinals and 10 seasons with the Washington Redskins. He was inducted into the Nebraska Football Hall of Fame in 1974. Brothers Cletus and Rex were inducted into the Nebraska Football Hall of Fame in 1979 and 1987, respectively.

LaVERNE TORCZON

TACKLE

1954–1956

I GREW UP ON A FARM TWO AND A HALF MILES NORTH of Platte Center, Nebraska, a town about 13 miles northwest of Columbus. Platte Center had about five hundred people in it while I was growing up, and it's not any bigger today. There was a lot of work—baling hay and picking corn. We picked corn by hand in the 1940s, but we always had plenty to eat.

We played six-man football back then, and I had been a lineman before switching to running back. I was about 6'3", and I was pretty fast. I also ran track—the 440 in 50.5 seconds on a cinder track—and played basketball, averaging 26 points per game. We were the Platte Center Explorers. Now Platte Center doesn't even have a high school anymore.

Anyway, I was never recruited to play football. Nebraska told me if I came to school for basketball, they would pay for my books. My dad drove me to Lincoln, and on the way we crossed the Loup River Bridge in Columbus. Right there, we saw this guy hitchhiking his way to Lincoln. We picked him up and gave him a ride. His name was Jim Murphy. So I got down to Lincoln and went to the spring football game because back then all the kids went to the spring football game.

As we watched the spring game, I just decided: I am going to try out for football in the fall. I walked on. That fall, when we crossed the Loup River Bridge on the way back to Lincoln before classes started, guess who was standing there? Jim Murphy.

I went out for football, and as the freshmen stood in line, the coaches didn't know who was who. As we introduced ourselves, they asked me what position I played. I told them. "Running back?" one of the coaches asked. "Look down the line here. You are one of the biggest guys here—you are not going to play running back!"

At those freshman practices, we started out with about 110 players, and after a week we were down to about 30. I played center on the freshman team, and I was a middle guard on defense. They still wanted me to go out for basketball, too, but I told them I couldn't play two sports and graduate on time. And one of my goals was to graduate on time.

Becoming a lineman was not that big of an adjustment for me. Nobody was huge at that time, and I basically was lining up against people my own size.

It would have been tough to hang in there as a walk-on, as tough as they worked us, but right after our last freshman game, the freshman coach came to me and said, "LaVerne, you have earned yourself a scholarship." Dad had always told me, "What do you want to play football for when you get nothing out of it?" That changed, although the cost of a scholarship was nowhere close to what it is today. I think we had to pay $80 each semester no matter how many hours we took. Getting a scholarship was a big boost in my incentive to play football.

Nineteen fifty-four—my sophomore year—was also the year they built the football dormitory and the training room, and we got to eat at the training table three times each day, except for Sundays. That year, I didn't make first team, but I got playing time. If you substituted then, you couldn't go back into the game in that quarter, and you played both ways.

In the second game of the season, we played Iowa State, and I rushed the passer, tipped the ball up into the air, caught it, and ran it in for a touchdown—into the south end zone. It was the only touchdown I ever scored in college.

At the end of that season, we went to Hawaii for 10 days and had a great game [beating the University of Hawaii 50–0]. It was an absolutely fantastic 10 days, and the weather was fantastic for most of the time. We stayed in this resort that had these little grass shacks. On the Sunday before we left, it rained 10 inches, and there was water standing all over the place. Then we went to Miami for the Orange Bowl, but Duke had a great team and beat us [34–7]. Those were two great trips for a bunch of small-town Nebraska boys.

That same Hawaii team that we had beaten so badly came to Lincoln and beat us [6–0] to start the 1955 season. I remember it was about 100 degrees that day, and that was the worst day. I don't know how we could have lost to Hawaii.

Back then all you heard about was how great the Big 10 was. For the next game, we went to Ohio State, and they had the great "Hopalong" [Howard] Cassady, who won the Heisman Trophy. They also had a guy named Jim Parker, an All-American lineman who was really big. Well, Jim Murphy—yeah, the same Jim Murphy we always had picked up by the bridge—just really handled him. And Jim Murphy weighed about 190 pounds. We were leading Ohio State 20–14 and driving in the fourth quarter when they intercepted a pass and ran it in for a touchdown. If we had scored on that drive, we would have beaten them [Ohio State won 28–20]. The highlight of the season was when Colorado came to town and they were supposed to beat the pants off of us. We beat them 37–20 and that was the biggest win I can remember. We finished 5–5 in 1955.

I had moved to tackle as a junior and then to guard as a senior. There were a lot of people in Nebraska who knew it was time for Glassford to go. Everybody felt the same way. I mean, how do you recruit when your current players don't like you? I think kids went home and told their parents how tough it was and about the conditions we were under, and the parents told a lot of people. I think, finally, Glassford more or less just quit.

The next year Pete Elliott came in as head coach, and he appeared to be a very nice person. He tried to inspire the players, but by the time we got to my senior year, the talent level was decimated, and freshmen weren't eligible. He had a decent coaching staff, we just had no talent.

We could never beat Oklahoma. We would hang tough for a little while, but they would wear us out and overcome us. [Oklahoma beat Nebraska 55–7, 41–0, and 54–6 from 1954 to 1956.] In my senior year at Oklahoma, I took the hardest hit of my whole football career. Their quarterback, Jimmy Harris, rolled out, and it looked like he was going to pass, but then he started running. I was trying to catch up to him, and their fullback, Billy Pricer, came up from the side and just leveled me. He hit me neck-high and I made a complete flip. I heard the crowd go, "Woooo!" It was the hardest hit! But they whipped us that day, and we finished my senior season 4–6.

Well, I graduated in four years as I had planned, getting my B.S. in education. Jim Murphy graduated, too. He married Monte Kiffin's sister and now

LaVerne Torczon went from walk-on to two-time All–Big Seven, chosen in 1955 as a tackle and in 1956 as a guard.

lives in Lexington, Nebraska. We became good friends and I have stayed in contact with him all these years.

I made a lot of great friends at Nebraska. I have to say that any time you play football for a major school, it is a real honor. I made some achievements, but you can ask, "How can a boy who played six-man football from a small rural area go to a big city and do all those things?"

The answer is that it reflects on what you are able to do at a school like Nebraska.

LaVerne Torczon, who was named All–Big Seven in 1955 and 1956, was awarded the Novak Trophy in 1956 as the player who "best exemplifies courage and determination despite all odds in the manner of Nebraska All-American center Tom Novak." Torczon played seven seasons of pro football and was inducted into the Nebraska Football Hall of Fame in 1987.

The
SIXTIES

DENNIS CLARIDGE
QUARTERBACK
1961–1963

I WAS BORN IN PHOENIX AND GREW UP IN ARIZONA as an only child. My parents had divorced when I was one year old, and my mom and I moved to Minneapolis when I was in junior high. She remarried and we settled in Robbinsdale, a suburb in the northwest corner of the city. I loved sports and played football, basketball, and ran track at Robbinsdale High. I guess I was average in basketball and track. But I was all-conference in football as a quarterback and safety. We hardly threw it at all, maybe four or five times per game, but I learned how to run the offense. We had a great audible system, and I was responsible for it. I remember I was in a Minnesota all-star game, and I was selected as the MVP of the game. At that time, I thought I was about to get a call from Colorado to go play for the Buffaloes. I had visited there and loved the campus. But the call never came. Then I focused on playing at Minnesota. Wisconsin also had recruited me. And Nebraska had contacted me, too, but I actually registered at the University of Minnesota. I had my dorm room and all my books for my freshman year, and I had gotten to know some of the kids who had played in that all-star game. They had gone to Nebraska, and they really enjoyed it. They told me, "Geez, you really need to come down here. This is a great place."

At that time, Minnesota had Sandy Stevens as a sophomore quarterback, and he was highly touted. Nebraska had two seniors and a sophomore at quarterback, but what really sold me was that Nebraska was a small campus at that time, with about seven thousand students. Minnesota had about thirty thousand students. Ironically, Nebraska played in Minneapolis against the Gophers that year [a 32–12 Cornhuskers win], and after the game, my dad went into the locker room to see [Nebraska coach Bill] Jennings. They still wanted me, so the very next day, I left Minnesota. Because classes had started, Minnesota made a big deal out of me leaving because it was a transfer. But in the end, the NCAA ruled that I would have to sit out of one of two games in my second year, which was no big deal anyway (since I ended up redshirting my sophomore season).

So in late September of 1959, I arrived in Lincoln.

I didn't know if I was good enough as a quarterback to make it, but I was going to work to get there. I remember my first practice. We had two quarterbacks ahead of me, and they were both good throwers, and I was not. We did not have a punter on the freshman team and I had punted in high school, so I got that job. I had a way to go as a quarterback, I knew that. Our offense was somewhat basic. We didn't have a split end—just two tight ends and the standard T formation. It was basically all power, with some option. And all the passes, when we threw them, were play-action. That freshman season . . . you were basically just fodder for the varsity, getting beat up in scrimmages and learning the game. Under coach Jennings, we scrimmaged often during the season. I redshirted the next year as a sophomore. After they moved Pat Fischer from halfback to quarterback, I saw the writing on the wall that he would be the guy. And I knew I needed the time to develop. I had strained some knee ligaments, and I guess I felt like a lost soul. I was about 6'2" and 205 pounds, and I realized that if I ran the stadium steps, I got stronger legs and I got faster. And that's what I did. I gained a lot of speed over those first two years.

43

In the spring of 1961, the job was thrown wide open. Ron Meade and two freshmen were thrown into the mix, and in that third week, I had a particularly good scrimmage throwing the ball and it just sort of picked up from there. I guess I actually won the job in fall camp, though.

I remember our first game, against North Dakota, and I was on the kickoff return team. Sure enough, they kicked it to me. How far did I return it? I really don't know, but evidently not very far, because it was the last time I was on a kickoff return. It really was a tough season. I remember, though, in the fourth game, against Syracuse, they had Ernie Davis [who later died of leukemia], and Bill Thornton out-rushed him that day [in a 28–6 Nebraska loss]. Like I said, that season was very difficult and I learned a lot, but we lost a lot [3–6–1 record]. I give coach Jennings credit for having patience with me, because I know I made a lot of mistakes and I had an awful lot to learn. I guess all the talk was going around about him maybe getting fired, but I really was ignorant of all that. I just assumed he would be the coach, and at that stage, most kids don't like change. Most people like the known, and we knew what to expect from him.

Then he got fired.

I didn't hear the name of our new coach until he was hired and we were summoned to the basement of the dorm to meet him. You can say I was very impressed with this man Bob Devaney right away. He did a number of things that got everybody's attention. He came in and right away he said, "Now, I don't know any of you, but we are all starting from scratch. You will have an equal opportunity with everybody else."

And he meant it—it was wide open in the spring. He was humorous, too, where the previous staff was very serious all the time. There wasn't much joking around with coach Jennings. The other thing was, coach Devaney brought in a different offense. We had an unbalanced line but the same full-house backfield. It was fun to be excited about something new like that. From then until spring practice, we never had a one-on-one meeting, and I was the returning quarterback. But in quarterback meetings, he was very involved. He would say, "Now here are your keys. On this play, this is what you are looking for . . ."

As we got near the season, I think we all thought we would be better, but not as good as we turned out to be. But Devaney was the biggest reason for it. In the previous season, we had scrimmaged a lot. Bob knew we didn't like that. Why leave your game on the practice field, right? He made an announcement that there would be no contact during the fall once the season started, and everybody loved that idea. Plus, we used to practice three hours. He said, "An hour and a half or an hour and 45 minutes if you practice well . . . if you goof off, we'll go more." That won over everybody.

To open 1962, we beat South Dakota pretty easily [53–0] and then prepared to go to Michigan. It was an unspoken thing among all of the team that "Bob was going home." He was from there, and some of the assistant coaches made it known to us that he really wanted to win this game. Plus the Big 10 was the premiere conference then. In the first or second series, I rolled out

Dennis Claridge was Bob Devaney's first Nebraska quarterback and, as the legendary coach frequently said, his finest.

and got hit. When I got up, I looked at the guy who tackled me, and he just didn't have that look of confidence in his eyes. It wasn't exactly fear, but it certainly wasn't confidence. I knew right then that the game was over—and we were going to win it. Bill Thornton had been hurt, but he scored our last touchdown and we beat Michigan [25–13].

Two games later, we were trailing North Carolina State near the end of the game in Lincoln, and we were driving. I was calling the plays, and with a minute or two left, my mind just went blank. We were down near the end zone, and I got in the huddle and faced everybody, and I couldn't think of what to call. I looked at [halfback] Dennis Stuewe, who was also from Minnesota and was my roommate. He just winked at me and I knew what he meant. I called a pitch to him around left end. He scored and we won the game [19–14]. We beat Kansas State and Colorado, and all of a sudden we were 6–0.

The loss to Missouri [16–7] was a real tough game, and I know it wasn't as close as the score indicated. That was a disappointment, and then Oklahoma was really good. They beat us badly [34–6]. We got invited to the Gotham Bowl in New York. The funny thing about that game was we were sitting in the airplane in Lincoln waiting to leave for something like three hours. We kept asking each other, "What's taking so long? Why aren't we leaving?" The reason was they were waiting for the check [$35,000] for the game to clear. The school wanted to be paid first.

When we got to Yankee Stadium for the game [against Miami]—and I swear to this day, no matter what they announced as the attendance [6,166], there was nobody there. You could actually count the fans in the stands. It was a frozen field. It was snowing. And it was a great game. We scored. They scored. We scored. They scored. I remember throwing for one touchdown [Claridge finished 9-of-14 for 146 yards] and batting down a [George] Mira pass. After the game [a 36–34 Nebraska win], one of the New York sportswriters asked coach Devaney to "give Claridge a kiss so they could take his picture." It was typical Bob Devaney. He told the sportswriters, "I don't know about you guys in New York, but back in Nebraska, we kiss girls."

And that was Nebraska's first-ever bowl win.

Heading into my senior year, we expected to have a great year, because we had some really great athletes returning. And we did have a great year. I had called plays in high school and in college so far, and then Tom Osborne joined the staff in my senior year and things changed with my decision making. Coach Osborne wanted to see things from the press box so he could see what area of the field to attack. So from the sideline, they would signal in areas to attack. For example, a right hand on the right calf might mean "attack right end." So I spent most of my senior season looking to the sideline to think of an area in which to call a play. Coach Osborne brought that in, and that's why he was the genius he was. He was very impressive with his knowledge and the way he created new things.

A big thrill for me was going back home to play at Minnesota [a 14–7 Nebraska win]. I had a good game and it was very satisfying. But the disappointment of all disappointments was that Air Force game [a 17–13 loss]. No matter what we tried, it didn't work. Nothing worked that day. We got down to the end of the season to play Oklahoma and we were 8–1. [Nebraska was ranked No. 10; Oklahoma No. 6.] I remember in a quarterback meeting we were going over plays to run and it seemed we were running right at Ralph Neeley, their big defensive lineman who later became a star with the Dallas Cowboys. I said, "Coach Devaney, shouldn't we be running away from Ralph Neeley?" He looked at me, and said, "Don't you worry about Ralph Neeley— [offensive tackle] Lloyd Voss will take care of Ralph Neeley!" He knew his players, and he knew what they could do.

47

On the day before the game, President Kennedy was killed in Dallas. What I remember about it is this (put it in the context of an immature 21-year-old who loves football): I wanted to play the game. When we played Oklahoma, it was the season. You would trade three wins over somebody else and make them losses if you could beat Oklahoma. That game meant everything to us. It was a terrible tragedy for the country, but the ramifications don't register with you when you are so young.

But we played the game and won 29–20. And coach Devaney was right— Lloyd Voss took care of Ralph Neeley.

Then we had a lot of fun down at the Orange Bowl against Auburn. I remember the start of the game very well. I had wanted to call this quarterback trap early, and I did. But I didn't expect it to result in a long run like that. I scored [on a 68-yard run on the game's second play], and I remember Frank Solich returning two long punts, but one of them was called back when he stepped out of bounds. We were on the verge of blowing the game open in the first half, and then we had to hold on to win it 13–7.

That team ended 10–1, and I really don't think we get the credit we deserve as being one of the all-time great Nebraska teams.

You can talk about great teams at Nebraska . . . we had eight guys from that team who played three or more years of pro football. We lost only one game and that was by four points. But what I really think is important to say is that we had fun. It's still just a game, and I think that gets lost these days in college football. Kids work harder now with all the meetings and lifting weights, and I don't think kids in college football today have as much fun as we did back then. Everybody now thinks about making it to the next level. We didn't think about that at all. We never thought about pro football. We practiced hard, played hard, and had a blast doing it. The thing is, we lived in the moment, not in the future.

I really have to say that I have been blessed to have the opportunity to have some success in college athletics—and to play at Nebraska. I have stayed here. I married a Nebraska girl. I have my business here, and I raised my family here. This state always loved football and football's always a topic of conversation. Sometimes it gets out of control and people lose sight of what it is. But it is still a very special tradition—one that I will always be proud to have been a part of.

Dennis Claridge, a cocaptain his senior season, was a player whom Bob Devaney often called his finest quarterback. Claridge was named All–Big Eight in 1962 and 1963 and an Academic All-American in 1963. He played two seasons with the Green Bay Packers and one with the Atlanta Falcons. He is an orthodontist living in Lincoln.

LYLE SITTLER

CENTER

1962–1964

WHAT DOES IT MEAN TO BE A CORNHUSKER? By the end of my chapter, I may be crying as I tell you in my words, especially when I tell you about my dearest friend and teammate. The university, the football program, the memories, and the people all have meant so much to my life. I hope I can properly express it.

I grew up in Crete, Nebraska, on a ranch farm. I was a Crete Cardinal, a small Class B school, which had not been a football factory by any means. I was not recruited heavily, as injuries forced me to miss several games, but I did well as a shot-putter in track. During the Doane Relays here in Crete, Nebraska, coaches Bill Jennings and Dick Monroe came to look at two brothers— Roger and Gale Sayers.

They walked in and saw me uncork the shot put and coach Jennings later told the press he was impressed with my physique and strength. We had films of only two high school games, and fortunately, I had played pretty well in each. I guess the coaches had watched those later on.

In one game—this became a lasting, enduring memory as you will discover later—we were playing Beatrice High which had the great Bob Hohn. Bob was all-everything, the prep athlete of the year in track and football. In the final game of my senior season, Bob was running a sweep and I was playing middle linebacker. As the play developed, Bob thought he was going to score easily, but I happened to have a great angle to tackle him. I dove at him and tripped him up to save the touchdown.

As I got up, I offered my hand to Bob, who rolled over and looked me in the eye. I can still see his face to this day as he said, "Why you fat SOB! How could you have caught me from behind?"

From that moment, Bob Hohn became one of the most important people in my life.

So coach Jennings offered me a scholarship. I thought I'd died and gone to heaven. I would be playing football at the University of Nebraska. So, too, would Bob Hohn.

I was about 6', 230 pounds when I played on the freshman team at Nebraska, moving from fullback to center. In the spring of 1961, I had worked my way up to number one on the depth chart at center, and on the last day of practice, I faced a great disappointment. We were not wearing pads in a punt-coverage drill. I snapped the ball and ran down the field as the receiver muffed the punt. As I dove, someone landed on me, and I dislocated my left knee. It was sticking out at a 45-degree angle and I knew surgery and rehab were to follow. Rehab was slow, so I redshirted in the fall and learned everything I could about playing center. At first, my center snaps were so bad that [assistant coach] Carl Selmer later accused me of trying to prepare Ron Kirkland, our punter, into trying out for shortstop of the New York Yankees. But I worked and worked at it until I got it down. I stayed out nights practicing it over and over.

50

When you come into a program in college, you always look at your coach as sort of a father figure. Coach Jennings was kind to me, and he had recruited me. He gave support, but worked us hard, very hard. I guess when he was fired that year it was like losing a member of the family.

Then we met Bob Devaney. He was fairly short and fairly round, and he had a very unique voice. I thought, "If this guy knows anything about football, I will eat my hat."

Those were my first impressions, but we knew he had been an apprentice to the great Duffy Daugherty and that made us listen to him. We knew he did well at Wyoming, too. Coach Devaney would say, "Now my name rhymes with 'fanny' folks, so that's how you pronounce it." He hated when people pronounced it "De-VAIN-ee."

I remember he would actually send Western Union telegrams to certain players who didn't play well the week before. They went something like this: "Thank you very much for making me Player of the Week," and he would

Lyle Sittler, an All–Big Eight center, cocaptained coach Devaney's 1964 squad.

sign the name of a player from the team we had just played. He sure knew how to needle guys! But this caused that player to give a much better effort the following week, so it worked.

He had a great sense of humor, too. One time I was out eating breakfast—eggs and hash browns at Don and Millie's at three in the morning. All of a sudden, a policeman recognizes me and says, "We got a burglary going on next door and we could use your help." They tossed me a shotgun, and in the end, I helped nab the guy.

Fortunately, he wasn't armed, but they thought he was. Coach Devaney found out about it and read me the riot act: "What in the world were you doing out at 3:00 A.M.?"

I told him, "Coach, I just had to get up early and get at it!"

Devaney said that was the first time anybody had come up with that line, so it kept me from extra running.

The day Bob Devaney arrived at Nebraska was a great omen of things to come. He was a great man and a great coach.

I remember that in my early years at Nebraska, a young guy by the name of Tom Osborne was coaching the scout squad. Little did I realize that this gentleman would become so big in football history. He was organized, knowledgeable, and thoughtful. And he became a legend, as we all know now, much like Bob Devaney.

The game in 1962 that sticks out in my memory is the Gotham Bowl in New York City. Like coach Selmer predicted, we did get to play in Yankee Stadium! There was a 40 mph wind and the wind chill was below zero as we played Miami and the great George Mira. In the first half our footing had been so bad that we had to change from cleats to tennis shoes at halftime. The coaches had sent our trainers to a store and they bought enough shoes for the first two teams. And we won a thrilling game, 36–34.

During the next season, I'll never forget our game against Kansas in October. On fourth down, I snapped for a punt, raced down into coverage, and downed the football inside the 1-yard line. The fans were in a frenzy at that point, as we had kept them in a hole. I had to stay in at middle linebacker because of the substitution pattern, and on the next play, the great Gale Sayers, who was at that track meet with me years earlier, swept around the left side. I had a great angle to tackle him, but he just made me look like I ran into a strong wind at about the 45-yard line.

As Sayers scored, my momentum took me off the field and into the Kansas bench. Coach Jennings, who had recruited me at Nebraska, was now a Kansas assistant. He offered me his hand and just said, "Nice try, Lyle."

Our family still has a videotape of Gale's run, and my three daughters have always humbled me by playing that tape. It has become a ritual of ours every year at halftime of the Super Bowl. We stop the game on television and put the tape in and watch it. My daughters all scream, "Dive, Dad! Dive!" as Sayers races by me.

I am telling you, one of these years, I am going to alter that tape so I make the tackle!

A few weeks after that game came one of the most terrible days in American history—November 22, 1963. It was the day before we were to play Oklahoma in Lincoln, and their team had already arrived in town when we got the terrible news about JFK being assassinated in Dallas. We went into the fieldhouse to have a meeting, and both teams were there. Oklahoma coach Bud Wilkinson was going to speak. As we sat there, I met Newt Burton, who was Oklahoma's center, and he said, "Whatever coach Wilkinson says will be the truth because he's a great man." Other than that, we didn't really talk much to the Oklahoma players.

Coach Wilkinson was the chairman of President Kennedy's Fitness Council at the time, and he got up to speak. "I knew President Kennedy very well, and he would have wanted this athletic contest to be played tomorrow," he announced. So we prayed and then played the game the next day. (I remember going against Newt Burton the entire day, and the following summer, I drove down to Norman and visited with him.) We beat Oklahoma 29–20 that day, but we didn't celebrate much.

We beat Auburn in the Orange Bowl, and what I remember from that is the fishing trip the day after the game. Willie Ross grew up in the South, but he had never fished in the ocean. So we got out to sea, and Willie hooked this gigantic sailfish. Right away, we could tell it was a trophy fish. All the guys were telling Willie, "Get this thing on ice, get it mounted, and take it home to put it on your wall."

Willie thought that was a great idea, and we told him to check with the skipper to see what it cost to have it mounted. "Oh, for that size, I would say at least $500," the skipper told him.

Willie looked at his beautiful fish with a sad look on his face and just said, "Cut the line, boys."

53

The 1964 season was supposed to be a rebuilding year for the Cornhuskers. But you don't shortchange Nebraska farm boys and you don't forget that our coach was Bob Devaney. Bob Hohn, the friend who always called me "that fat SOB who caught me from behind," and I were named cocaptains.

By this time, when I was a senior, I weighed about 228. Coach Devaney believed in quickness over being terribly big. We won our first nine games before losing to Oklahoma 17–7. Then we went to the Cotton Bowl. Arkansas, with players such as Jimmy Johnson and Jerry Jones and coached by the great Frank Broyles, beat us 10–7 and won the national championship.

I figured my playing days were over with that game, but coach Broyles was scheduled to coach the Coaches' All-American Bowl in Buffalo that summer and I was chosen to play in the game with Larry Kramer, our great tackle. I graduated from the University of Nebraska on June 12, got married to Alice on June 13, and then left for Chicago with Larry Kramer and our wives on June 14. We continued on to Buffalo for the game. It was an all-expense-paid honeymoon for us.

Some 33 years later, in 1998, we had a reunion at Nebraska, and Bob Hohn and his wife Sandy walked in, and right away, he looked at me and said, "There's that fat SOB that caught me from behind."

We had a great friendship. Bob was a great hurdler—his state record in the low hurdles was just recently broken. He was a very dedicated athlete. But at about the time of the reunion, Bob had been diagnosed with Lou Gehrig's disease. He had trouble controlling his legs and he limped some at that time.

For the next five years, we would meet on Mondays at 4:00 at Brewsky's in Lincoln and other teammates would join us. Denny Claridge and others would come by to see Bob and we would relive the good ol' days.

On Thanksgiving Day, 2003, Bob died. The last time I saw Bob was on the Monday before he died. He had written his own memorial service, and this is the closing: "By the way, several friends contributed to my success. I will mention them here . . . one is that fat SOB who caught me from behind. . . ."

They also read this for his service, which I find very touching and I have kept it: "I wish you all the following":

I wish you enough sun to keep your attitude bright,

I wish you enough rain to appreciate the sun more,

I wish you enough happiness to keep your spirit alive,

I wish you enough pain so that the smallest joys in life appear much bigger,

I wish you enough gain to satisfy your wanting,

I wish you enough loss to appreciate all that you possess,

I wish you enough "Hellos" to get you through the final "Good-bye."

Don't be sad because it is over, smile because it happened!

And I smile because I knew a man named Bob Hohn, but yes, I do have tears in my eyes.

Through my experiences with all the great people—teammates, coaches, and fans—I continued to be reassured through their support, and through what I believe about Christ in my life, as well. I will continue to examine myself as to the real purpose of my life. Through all this, I am sure that I have found that my faith is greater having been a part of the family of Husker football.

In the end, I must say it was an unbelievable experience to play football at Nebraska. Coach Devaney turned it around and he did it right away, and it is hard to believe to this day how it worked out so well. We had every personality you could imagine, and the coaches were great—with one thing in mind: to help their kids become better players and better people.

Our family has remained loyal Husker fans through the years. Look at the consecutive sellouts we have had since 1962. And while it is a tough place for a visiting team to play, win or lose, they receive a standing ovation as they leave the field from the fans in the Northwest corner. That is our tradition. We have had great players. We have great fans. We have great people. To me, that's what it means to be a Cornhusker.

Lyle Sittler was a cocaptain with Bob Hohn in 1964. He also was named All–Big Eight and presented the Tom Novak Award, given to the Cornhusker senior "who best exemplifies courage and determination despite all odds in the manner of Nebraska All-American center Tom Novak." Sittler was inducted into the Nebraska Football Hall of Fame in 1999.

LARRY WACHHOLTZ
DEFENSIVE BACK
1964–1966

I HAVE TO THANK A HIGH SCHOOL TEAMMATE, Pete Tatman; a local booster, York Hinman; and my high school coach, George "Crump" Redding, for leading me down the path that led to the Nebraska Cornhuskers.

Prior to 1961, North Platte High School had not enjoyed much success on the football field, but that changed overnight when coach Redding arrived. He was the toughest guy I ever played for. We won immediately. We were unbeaten and won the state championship in my senior season. I was a running back as a junior and a quarterback as a senior, and we had Pete, who was a heck of a football player. Pete was a very good fullback, and Nebraska was recruiting him, but I don't think that they wanted me. Coach Redding just kept trying to sell me to them. Finally, they said, "Oh, all right, we'll give him a scholarship, too."

However, for a while it looked like Pete wanted to go to Colorado. I really wanted to go to Nebraska, but Pete and I wanted to play together. I had followed Nebraska football from an early age because John Edwards was a local boy and he had played there. His brother Jack had been a classmate of mine, and I had followed the Big Red very closely after coach Devaney turned it around and made Nebraska a winner.

Finally, we all had a meeting at North Platte High School, and Pete and I weren't sure what we were going to do. At that point, Pete really thought he might go to Colorado. But coach Redding said we really owed it to the state of Nebraska to stay home and play for the Cornhuskers. Then York Hinman, who just loved the Cornhuskers, suddenly slammed his fist on the table and said, "Let's get this over with once and for all—you both sign those letters of intent right now!"

I signed that day with Nebraska and so did Pete.

I really knew the University of Nebraska was the place for me in the beginning. The coaches were very friendly and Bob Devaney was an excellent salesman. He was a great recruiter, and he sold the program to me.

As a freshman, I was in awe of the size of the campus and of the number of students there. In some classes there were 125 kids, and I felt it was easy to get lost in the shuffle. Plus, where we lived there were about 40 scholarship football players in the same dorm, and it was easy to get distracted. Let me put it this way—it wasn't very conducive to an academic environment.

On the football field, I was amazed at everybody else. I weighed about 160 as a freshman and I wasn't too fast, either. I was timed at 4.8 in the 40, and I know the coaches weren't too impressed with that. I didn't get off on the right foot, and I didn't impress anybody.

57

I remember when I was on the scout team—there was Tony Jeter, who was an All-American end. Now Tony was about 6'3", 230 pounds, and I was about 5'8", so I was giving up about seven inches and 70 pounds when we went head-to-head. One week I was running the offensive plays for Iowa State on the scout team, and I was scared to death. I was playing at wingback, and on the first play, Tony came by and just brushed me. It wasn't supposed to be live, but on the next play, we were in another formation, and I was a little relaxed. Well, Tony came by and gave me a forearm to my chest and head and knocked me six ways to hell. My helmet was on sideways with my nose sticking out of the ear hole, and he had knocked the wind out of me. It was embarrassing. After that, the war was on. It didn't matter if the play was over or not: I was looking for Tony and he was looking for me. And I got even with him eventually.

Prior to 1963, players played both ways, until the NCAA made the rule change that allowed 11 on offense and 11 other players on defense. The change gave me an opportunity to get on the field as a defensive back, where I might not have otherwise. I also did some kicking.

In 1964 it was my first year with the varsity, and I really had no great expectations of seeing playing time. We had a lot of good players, and I didn't know of many sophomores who got to play. In the second game of the season, we went to Minnesota and I learned I would be on the traveling squad. I started that game and learned it was quite an experience to play in front of a large crowd. The thing that gave me confidence was our upperclassmen were very encouraging and they were always giving me confidence.

Then came the Kansas game, in which I made a few tackles of Gale Sayers and started to return punts. I do remember one time that Gale got behind me and would have scored on a reception, but he had such high knee action, fortunately for me, that he knocked the ball right out of his own hands with his knee.

In 1965, we went undefeated through the regular season. In the Missouri game, we had fallen behind 14–0 and came back to win 16–14. The reason I remember that game so well is that Pete Tatman and I scored all the points. I had missed an extra point and we were trailing 14–13 late in the game, but we drove down the field and I kicked the winning field goal from about 27 or 28 yards with a few minutes left.

But Alabama beat us in the Orange Bowl 39–28 in a game for the national championship. They had recovered a few onside kicks in that game, or we would have won it. Of the five losses in my college career, that one hurt the most—by far. Alabama was not big, but they had a lot of speed, and I felt we were a better team.

58

We lost only two regular season games in three years and both were to Oklahoma and both were in Norman [1964 and 1966].

In 1966, I was a cocaptain with Bob Churchich, and we had won 9 out of our 10 games, but after the loss to Oklahoma, coach Devaney called me and Bob into his office. We were going over our bowl options, and Bob and I both decided we wanted another shot at Alabama. So we went to the Sugar Bowl to play them, and that was a big mistake. They just beat the hell out of us [34–7]. We had started my three seasons 9–0, 10–0, and 9–0, but lost our last games in each of those seasons. It was very frustrating that we couldn't close it out to win a national championship.

I really liked coach Devaney, but he could blow up at times. I remember we had a defensive back, Maynard Smidt, who now is a good fishing buddy of mine. We were playing South Carolina [in 1964] and they had Dan Reeves at quarterback. In the first half, he threw a couple of passes over Maynard's head. At halftime, coach Devaney told Maynard in no uncertain terms: "If that happens again in the second half, you will never player another down."

Larry Wachholtz was a ball-hawking safety who also recorded 153 tackles.

On the first series of the second half, it happened again, and Maynard didn't play a hell of a lot after that.

There also was a guy who was built like Charles Atlas, a guy named Bill Brown. Well, Bill came to camp two days late one year, and while he was suiting up, coach Devaney heard he had arrived. Bill had on about half of his equipment when coach Devaney went into the locker room. He told him: "Get the hell out of here—go back to Detroit." We never saw Bill Brown again.

You have heard the old adage: "There's No Place Like Nebraska." That is the truth, especially when it comes to Nebraska football. Nebraska fans revere their heroes. I have actually been to funerals where the Nebraska fight song is played. I consider myself very lucky to have played there because as small as I was, I never knew if I would have the opportunity. And then to have the success I had. . . . I am very proud of it, and I was always proud to be a Cornhusker.

Larry Wachholtz was All–Big Eight in 1965 and 1966 and an All-American and team cocaptain in 1966. He also was awarded the Novak Trophy which "best exemplifies courage and determination despite all odds in the manner of Nebraska All-American center Tom Novak." He finished his career with 11 interceptions—tied for third on Nebraska's all-time list. He was inducted into the Nebraska Football Hall of Fame in 1982.

BOB CHURCHICH
QUARTERBACK
1964–1966

My Dad loved sports and took me to all the great sporting events in Nebraska, such as the College Baseball World Series. When I was 14 years old, Dad took me to a Nebraska football game for the first time. My brother Ely was a great baseball player for Nebraska, and he got us tickets. Nebraska lost to Kansas that day, but it didn't matter because I got to see the Huskers play in person. Dad took me down on the field, and as we stood on the 50-yard line, he said, "Would you like to play football at Nebraska?"

Looking back on it now, I've always felt that it was his wish as much as my desire that led me to be a Husker football player.

In high school, I played three sports, but baseball is where I felt I had a future, even though I had a good senior year as quarterback for Omaha North High School. Following high school, I had professional baseball offers as well as scholarship offers to some of the top baseball and football schools in the country. Coach Devaney offered me a football scholarship and said if football didn't work out that I could always fall back on baseball. Nebraska's baseball coach, Tony Sharpe, could not offer me a baseball scholarship. Coach Devaney also told me that if I became his starting quarterback, I could forgo spring football and play baseball.

I arrived on the Nebraska campus in the fall of 1963 and went through freshman orientation. Our campus guide and host pointed out two very big guys sporting very large biceps who were breaking up concrete in front of the girl's dorm. He said they were incoming freshman football players. One was a fullback from Detroit who weighed 255 pounds, and the other was a defensive end from Washington, D.C., who was 6'5" and 230 pounds. At the time, I was a skinny 168 pounds. What was I thinking? Could I possibly play big-time college football?

I knew I was about to find out. The first time I put on a football uniform as a freshman, I found myself listed on the depth chart as the fifth-team quarterback. The quarterbacks ahead of me were bigger and threw the ball farther and with more velocity. I spent a lot of time running the scout team as the opposition quarterback against the varsity. The other quarterbacks were with the other freshmen learning the offensive system. Maybe running the scout team was a good thing for me, because the varsity coaches saw me play against the big boys and perhaps thought I had some ability. President Kennedy was assassinated the week of the Oklahoma game and the game was almost canceled, but the decision was made to play.

The varsity was 8–1, and practices were intense because the Orange Bowl was on the line. Bob Brown, the great collegiate and pro football Hall of Famer and all-everything almost ended my career before it started. I saw Brown break the face masks of two linemen in a blocking drill a few weeks earlier. He was big, fast, and mean. We were in a live scrimmage when I rolled out and Brown came off a block and was chasing me on this play. He swung those big arms that had broken face masks, but fortunately he missed mine. After that, I always paid attention to where Bob Brown lined up.

In the fall of 1964, with attrition in the quarterback ranks, I found myself competing with starter Fred Duda, fellow sophomore Wayne Weber, and senior Doug Tucker. Fred was a great competitor, runner, and leader. Wayne was a great athlete, but was plagued with injuries most of his career, and Doug was a fifth-year player and a very good passer.

During the third game of the season against Iowa State, Fred broke his leg right in front of our bench—just a few feet from me. It was an ugly break with the bone penetrating the flesh. Doug Tucker immediately ran right up to coach Devaney's side, assuming that he would be the logical replacement—which I too thought would be the right choice under the circumstances. Coach Devaney looked at Doug, looked at Wayne, and then looked at me. He hesitated a moment and then motioned to me. Coach gave me the play to call and pushed me on to the field. There was nobody in the stadium more surprised about it than me.

Here I was, with the score tied 7–7, a 19-year-old sophomore looking in the eyes of 10 upperclassmen who were as surprised as I was to be standing before them. A few seconds passed in the huddle, and team cocaptain Bob Hohn, his hands on his knees, looked up and said these words that I will never forget: "OK, it's all yours now kid. Now call the &% #?★ play!"

I don't think I called the play that coach Devaney had sent in with me, but I did call a nice safe play. Devaney never told me if the play was right or not. We won the game 14–7, and Tommy Vaughn, Iowa State's captain, came up to me after the game and said, "You played a great game kid. You're going to be all right!" Coming from a great player like Tommy Vaughn, that gave me a lot of confidence.

The next game we were at home against South Carolina, and it was my first start for the Huskers. Their quarterback was the legendary Dan Reeves, whom I met years later when he was coaching the Denver Broncos. (We were paired together in a golf tournament, and I walked up to him on the first tee and said, "We crossed paths years ago." He said, "Don't tell me it was in a bar someplace!" I told him that we played against each other in college, and that I was the other quarterback for Nebraska. He remembered that game like it was yesterday, and so do I. He said that his coaches thought they had a great chance to beat Nebraska because I was starting my first game).

63

Reeves set a South Carolina passing record that day, but we won 28–6. Over the years, a lot of quarterbacks have had great passing games against Nebraska. Reeves said he took the hardest hit in college in that game from our defensive end, Langston Coleman. Langston was the player from Washington, D.C., mentioned at the beginning of this chapter. Reeves explained to me that South Carolina had installed a new play for that game, and on that play he took that vicious hit from Langston. He was helped to the sideline by the trainers and he then told his coach, "If you call that play again, you go in and run it!"

I missed most of spring ball in 1965 because I played for the baseball team. Like I said, coach Devaney told me during recruiting that I could play baseball if I earned the starting quarterback position. We had a good baseball team. I led the Big Eight in batting average, and I made All–Big Eight and the All-America baseball team. But as I look back, I could have used the spring football practices.

We were favored not only to win the Big Eight again, but some preseason publications picked us to compete for the national championship. We were a

Quarterback Bob Churchich was named All–Big Eight in baseball and football for the Cornhuskers.

perfect 10–0 in the regular season and played Alabama in the Orange Bowl. Coach Devaney started Fred Duda, who came back after his broken leg, in the Orange Bowl. Fred had never lost a game he started from the beginning of his high school career, and I believed that coach Devaney was superstitious. I was very disappointed that I did not start this game, and it got away from us in the first quarter before Devaney sent me in for the second quarter. We played catch-up all night. After the game, coach Carl Selmer said,

"We started the wrong guy!" I would agree: I threw three touchdown passes (tying an Orange Bowl record that lasted for 30 years), scored on a sneak, and threw for a two-point conversion. But we lost the game and, thus, lost our chance at Nebraska's first national championship.

The game that most fans recall was the 1966 comeback thriller against Colorado in Boulder. We were undefeated and playing the team that I thought was the best in the conference. In the first half, Colorado knocked us all over the field and took a 19–7 lead. In most halftime speeches, coach Devaney usually talked strategy, adjustments, etc. But at the half of this game, he ripped into every one of us. I mean he didn't miss one guy, and he told us we were an embarrassment to our fans, our parents, and our coaches. We were crammed into this small metal field-maintenance building, and the students were pounding on the walls. It was loud, and after Coach's fiery speech, we made our own noise in the second half. The defense came up with big stops and the offense came up with big plays. We got one final possession from our 30-yard line with 2:30 left. We all knew this was our last possession, so we used the run and short passes to set up a long pass play. Colorado's defense was playing us for deep passing routes, so we used runs and passes under their coverage for the first few plays. Then, for whatever reason, their defensive backs came up to within a few yards of the line of scrimmage. We thought it was going to be an all-out blitz. Luckily for us, we had the right play called, and I found Tom Penney behind their coverage for a 30-yard gain. From the 9-yard line there was only one guy who was going to carry the ball, and that was Pete Tatman, our fullback. Three isolation plays later, with great blocking from the right side of the line, Tatman scored with less than a minute left. I had passed for more yards, attempts, and completions than in any game of my career, and I had seven completions in that last drive. But I can honestly say that this game was a great team effort on both sides of the ball. It was one of those games you never forget.

We won a lot of great games, including three Big Eight championships, but we also had some huge near misses. I will always cherish the fact that I was a part of the teams that started the great Nebraska football tradition as a player for the legendary Bob Devaney. Tom Osborne was an assistant in those years, and Frank Solich was a teammate of mine. As everyone knows, those three combined to coach Nebraska for more than four decades.

Our teams were a combined 28–5 from 1964 to 1966. That included trips to the Cotton, Orange, and Sugar Bowls, respectively. We lost to Arkansas

10–7 in the Cotton Bowl. The 1965 team finished the regular season 10–0, but we lost 39–28 to Alabama in the Orange Bowl. We would have given Nebraska its first national championship if we had won that game.

In 1966 we were 9–0, had already clinched the Big Eight championship, and accepted an invitation to play in the Sugar Bowl against Alabama again. We lost a disappointing 10–9 game to Oklahoma in the last regular season game and then were humiliated 34–7 in the Sugar Bowl. After that game, coach Devaney got on the bus and told us, "I don't care if I see you seniors again, and you juniors and sophomores better get ready for spring ball."

I believed then that Nebraska needed to recruit more speed and quickness to play with the teams in the South like Alabama. In fact, our longest run from scrimmage in 1966 was a play for 28 yards in which I scored. I've always thought I was the fastest 5.0 40-yard dash quarterback in Nebraska history.

Years after my career ended, I attended banquets where coach Devaney, then the Nebraska athletic director, spoke to the Husker faithful. He was a great speaker with great stories and a charming wit and he always recognized his former players at these events. He always would introduce me as the only Nebraska quarterback to lose three bowl games. I guess he never got over that—and neither have I.

On the bus ride into Boulder for the game in 1966, we approached a high hill that overlooked the city of Boulder and you could see the snow-capped peaks of the Continental Divide. I remember saying to Pete Tatman, who I always sat next to on the bus, "Wouldn't this be a great place to live someday?"

I moved to Boulder in 1974, and it has been home to me, my wife, three children, and three grandchildren. We have many friends here and we attend Colorado football games.

However, we will be Husker fans forever.

Bob Churchich was named All–Big Eight in 1966. He completed 179 of 342 passes for 2,434 yards in his career—ninth best on Nebraska's career passing yardage list. He was inducted into the Nebraska Football Hall of Fame in 1989.

KAYE CARSTENS
DEFENSIVE BACK
1964–1966

GROWING UP ABOUT 13 MILES from the Kansas border, in Fairbury, Nebraska, I could get both the Nebraska football games and the Kansas football games on the radio on Saturdays. So I listened to both. Kansas had John Hadl at quarterback then and won quite a few games, while Nebraska struggled to have winning seasons under Bill Jennings.

Still, I was always a fan of the Nebraska Cornhuskers. I just always wished they would have a winning season. In high school, I followed them when [Bill] "Thunder" Thornton and Willie Ross played, and I always looked forward to Saturdays so I could listen to the games on the radio.

I played football, basketball, and some track in school, but I was noted more for football than anything else. I was good enough to be honored as all-state in football as a running back and safety during my junior and senior years at Fairbury Senior High.

Kansas State and Iowa State were interested in me, but my loyalty was always to Nebraska. When my high school team played in Lincoln against Lincoln Southeast, coach Devaney and coach [John] Melton were there, but we lost the game and played terribly. I figured they wouldn't want me after that. But they talked to my coach, and after that [assistant coach] Cletus Fischer came down to Fairbury, and I decided to sign with Nebraska with him present.

My first memories of getting to Lincoln as a freshman are of feeling quite intimidated. Unlike Fairbury, which was a small town of about six thousand people back then, now I was in a larger place with a large number of bigger, better athletes. I was about 6'1" and 190 pounds, and these people were pretty big, and faster, and they could jump higher. That's quite intimidating for a freshman.

I'll never forget coach Melton during one of our freshman games at Kansas State. We were leading 8–0 at the half, and we came into the locker room feeling pretty good about ourselves. We were all sitting there on these little old wooden chairs in this dirty, dusty locker room, waiting for him to come in. Suddenly, coach Melton came in, picked up one of those wooden chairs, and threw it across the locker room against the wall, smashing it into a million little pieces. He was mad that we weren't ahead 60–0! Well, we then went out and beat Kansas State something like 69–7.

The next year, the coaches gave me the option—offense or defense? I was used to carrying the ball, and when I did play defense, I played safety. But they wanted me to play cornerback, and it did not come naturally to me. I probably was fast enough, but I don't know what my 40 time was.

I played a few minutes as a sophomore, enough to letter, but nothing to speak of. I was on the kickoff team, and I remember in the first game, I went down on the kickoff and made the tackle. In the second game we played, I did the same thing. In the third game, they must have watched film pretty well because I went tearing down the field and I absolutely never saw anybody coming at me. I was hit so hard that it seemed like I was in the air for about five minutes. I'll never forget this—I still had not made contact with the ground, and I could hear coach [Mike] Corgan yelling at me, "Get up! Get up and make the tackle!"

The NCAA then changed the rule about substitutions, which meant they would now allow platooning, so players did not have to play both ways. I started at right cornerback on defense, and that rule change was probably a good thing for me. That was the beginning of when college football became more specialized.

In 1965, we had a really good year, starting the season by winning our first 10 games. That was the best team during my tenure at Nebraska.

I remember in the Missouri game I intercepted a pass and took it back 20 or 30 yards, but I didn't get it into the end zone. That was our closest game, because Missouri was driving at the end of the game and all they needed was a field goal to beat us. They had a crucial play in which, to get the first down and then kick the field goal, they ran a sweep around the corner. The running

After the NCAA rule concerning substitutions changed, Kaye Carstens became one of Nebraska's first true cornerbacks who did not play both ways.

back's name was Charlie Brown, and I came up and got him in the backfield for a loss, but he knocked out my tooth on the play. The good thing was that we held them out of field-goal position and won the game 16–14.

The next season we started 9–0 and then went to Norman to play Oklahoma. We were in for a very tough, close game. We had a chance to win it at the end, but lost 10–9. That has to be the most disappointing loss I think we had in my three seasons.

Then we went to the Sugar Bowl to play Alabama, and they had [Ken] "Snake" Stabler and Ray Perkins. I matched up with Ray a lot that day, but they just killed us [34–7]. They ran wild. They threw. They beat us badly. Alabama was a very good team, but the discouraging thing is that we were a lot better team than we had showed. Sometimes, it is just a mental thing causing you to not play your best, and that was probably the case with that Sugar Bowl.

Playing football for the University of Nebraska was a tremendous opportunity for me. I was just elated that they would recruit me in the first place. Then to play, to travel, and to represent the state was a great experience. Interacting with the fans and feeling their support during every game was always special as well.

Football taught me a lot of discipline and hard work and what it takes to succeed. That is the special thing about sports, especially with the right coaching staff. We had a great coaching staff. Coach Devaney would get upset and irritated, and rightfully so at times, when he sensed people were not giving 100 percent. It takes more than talent. You have to put the effort in, and that carries over into your business life as you get older. You have to make things happen. It just doesn't happen if you sit out on the doorstep and watch.

I have always considered it a real privilege to play at Nebraska, and I have remained a big fan of the Cornhuskers.

Kaye Carstens was named All–Big Eight in 1966. He was inducted into the Nebraska Football Hall of Fame in 2000. Dr. Carstens, a Nebraska medical school graduate, currently practices family medicine in Omaha.

LARRY KRAMER

TACKLE

1962–1964

I ORIGINALLY WANTED TO ATTEND THE UNIVERSITY OF MINNESOTA to play football, but it didn't work out that way for me. Growing up in Austin, Minnesota, which is about 15 miles from the Iowa border, I was a Minnesota guy. A lot of my high school friends went there, and the Minnesota coaches wanted me, but I failed to meet the criteria then. First—and I was told that this was a Big 10 rule back then—you had to be in the top 25 percent of your graduating class, or you could also qualify if your parents didn't make enough money [to pay for college].

Well, I was in the 67th percentile of my graduating class, and both of my parents worked at a meat-packing plant. I had lettered in football, baseball, and wrestling. I was an all-state baseball player as a catcher, so I could have gone on to play baseball. And in football, we were state champs during my senior year.

Initially, not being able to go to Minnesota was a disappointment for me, but it would turn out to be the best thing that ever happened to me. At that time, Nebraska was not doing very well in football, but they showed a lot of interest in recruiting me. I took a visit to Lincoln, and right away, I was impressed with the players and the community. I could tell that Lincoln was a great town, so I chose Nebraska.

I couldn't believe it when I got to freshman practice and there were about 100 freshmen out there. There were no restrictions on numbers back then, and it was a crowded practice field. We were all scout-team fodder as freshmen, but the toughest thing was practicing the long hours we practiced. We were on the field from about 3:30 to 7:30 every day, preparing different units of the varsity . . . and in the end, that is one of the things that hurt coach [Bill] Jennings. He was a good guy, but as far as practices, they were so long that there were times I thought this wasn't where I needed to be.

Fortunately, we had a good group of guys to hang around with and we all got through it together.

Standing on the sideline of the 1961 opener against North Dakota, I was hoping to see my first playing action. All of a sudden, coach Jennings turned around, looked at me, and said, "We're redshirting you, Kramer." Now, that is one thing I thought he could have done in an office. Here I am, hoping to get into the game, and I am suddenly told this would be my redshirt season.

Like I said, coach Jennings was a pretty good guy, but his mentality was to work 'em, work 'em, work 'em. And we would hear what went on in other programs. Nobody practiced as long or as hard as we did. I think that really was his downfall—and not winning enough games, of course. We all just felt, "Let's have normal practices, not four or five hours."

When coach Devaney was hired in 1962, I'll never forget our first meeting with him. The first thing he said to us was, "We're going to have shorter practices." We all liked him from the start after that. Plus, he knew my name. For the first two years, the coaches called me "Jerry" Kramer. Coach Devaney called me Larry from the beginning.

As the season started, I was a third-team tackle, but coach Devaney prepared three units on both offense and defense, and he would get the second-teamers about four or five minutes of playing time in each quarter. That was a pretty good deal. I remember my first road trip, and I was just excited to make the traveling squad. I was playing behind Tyrone Robertson, who was from Toledo. In the second game that season, we went to Ann Arbor to play Michigan. Tyrone had a death in the family, and he left to go back to Toledo before the game. As a result, I ended up playing quite a bit that day [a 25–13 Nebraska win]. Midway through the season, I got elevated to second team. We played an unbalanced line then, so two tackles lined up next to each other. Coach Devaney got that from Duffy Daugherty at Michigan State. So I lined up next to Lloyd Voss, who became a really good friend of mine.

At the end of the season, we were 8–2 and headed to the Gotham Bowl to play Miami. I'll never forget that we sat at the Lincoln airport for about four hours waiting for the money from that bowl game. We got to New York and there was a newspaper strike, so nobody knew about the game. Yankee Stadium was empty except for the five thousand boy scouts who attended, but it still was a thrill to play in Yankee Stadium. It was so cold. It must have been in the teens, and we were wearing tennis shoes so we didn't slip.

The next season, I was a full-time starter, and the only slip-up we had all season was at home to Air Force. Now coach Devaney was very, very upset about that game. We were probably much better than Air Force but still lost [17–13].

That was our only loss for the whole season.

On the Friday before we were to play Oklahoma, JFK was shot in Dallas, and we didn't think we would play the game. At a team meeting later that day, coach Devaney said we probably wouldn't play. But later on, [Oklahoma coach] Bud Wilkinson talked to one of the family, I think it was Bobby Kennedy, and he said, "Go ahead and play the game." Let me tell you that it was an eerie feeling that day. A lot of guys didn't want to be there, and a lot of fans didn't want to be there. You could just sense it, and it was very, very strange. [Nebraska won 29–20.]

We had earned a trip to the Orange Bowl to play Auburn, and it was the first bowl game that we went to that was a first-class bowl. We stayed at the Ivanhoe on Miami Beach, and the weather was great. . . . It was just a great experience for a bunch of guys from the North. Dennis Claridge made a long run early in the game, and then Frank Solich's punt return clinched it for us [Nebraska won 13–7].

Things were good in 1964, my senior year. We won our first nine games, and we were on a roll until playing at Oklahoma. It was really cold that day, and we just weren't mentally prepared like we should have been. It wasn't the coaches' fault; it was our fault. I just remember how quick Oklahoma was that day compared to my junior year. They just seemed so much quicker.

After that game [a 17–7 loss], we really felt we let coach Devaney down, because we had had a shot at the national championship at that point. He was very unhappy, very upset after that game. When he took us down to Brownsville, Texas, for 10 days to prepare for the Cotton Bowl, he made us pay for it. Let's just say we left a lot of sweat and blood on those practice fields for 10 days in 90-degree weather. Then we flew into Dallas for the Cotton Bowl, and it was about 30 degrees. It was really cold on New Year's Day, too, and Arkansas beat us 10–7 to win the national championship.

A native of Minnesota, Larry Kramer became one of the nation's best tackles while playing for Bob Devaney's first Nebraska teams.

I still have to say that coach Devaney was the fairest man I ever met. He treated the first-stringers like the fifth-stringers, and I always appreciated that. I remember one time that Bob Brown missed a Friday meeting, and Devaney sat him down for a game the next day because of it. Now Bob Brown was probably the most heralded lineman in the nation, but coach Devaney treated him like he would have treated anybody else.

In between my sophomore and junior years, I got married to Sandy, who was a Nebraska girl, and I remember going into coach Devaney's office to talk about it. I thought he would say, "What the heck are you doing?" But he didn't. He was supportive. And we have been married for more than 40 years and have four kids.

I just thank God I was able to play for three years under coach Devaney. He treated me right. He treated me like a man, and he never demeaned me. I really got to know him better than some other guys because I worked at the Legion Club during my junior and senior years after I got married, and coach Devaney would stop in after the game on Saturday.

When you talk about Nebraska football tradition, you can't say anything else but it started with coach Devaney. That should be the introduction to Nebraska football: his arrival from Wyoming in 1962. That's it. That is the beginning of a great tradition, and it was because of that man. I am just so sorry he is gone.

75

At Nebraska, not only did I meet my wife, but I formed several lasting friendships. We sort of formed our little fraternity because nobody else would have us, I guess. We call ourselves "the Uglies," and believe it or not, we still get together once a year on the East Coast. We have T-shirts and hats printed up with our names on it. We are all out-of-state guys who played at Nebraska, guys like Lloyd Voss from Minnesota and Walt Barnes from Chicago.

Considering my friends, my family, my playing career, and all the coaches, I can honestly say that attending Nebraska was the best decision I ever made.

Larry Kramer was named an All-American in 1964. He was a college football coach for 32 years, with head coaching jobs at Emporia (Kansas) State, Austin (Texas) College, and McCook Junior College. He also was an assistant under Bill Snyder at Kansas State from 1995 to 1997. He was inducted into the Nebraska Football Hall of Fame in 1987.

LaVERNE ALLERS
Guard
1964–1966

Y THE TIME I ARRIVED IN LINCOLN in the summer of 1962, Nebraska had already started its football practices. It was the first time I had ever been there—I never even took a recruiting visit to see the city or the campus. I took the train from my home in Davenport, Iowa, arrived in Lincoln at about 11:00 that night, and an assistant coach picked me up to take me to the dorm. My roommate was already sleeping, so I just dropped my bag and jumped into bed. The next day, I woke up, met my roommate, and went to meet all the other coaches and players.

It certainly was unusual: I never had a formal visit, had never been to Lincoln, and really knew nothing about the school.

But there I was, a Nebraska Cornhusker.

Growing up in Davenport, I was always interested in sports, but Dad was from the old school, and he was kind of against me playing sports. He had gone through the Depression and believed you should work to help out your family. I know he wanted me to get a job, but my mother, brother, and sister sort of softened him up some so he finally gave in and allowed me to play sports.

I was able to go out for football in junior high, and by the time I was a sophomore, I was one of only two sophomores playing varsity at Davenport High. Then, because the city was growing so much, the schools split, and I went to Davenport West for my remaining two years. I took up wrestling and track, too. In football, I played fullback and linebacker and was second-team all-conference. I had some inquiries from Iowa, Iowa State, and New Mexico, and had planned to go to New Mexico to study wildlife conservation.

Doug Tucker, who was from my hometown and was a quarterback at Nebraska, changed all that. Doug talked to the Nebraska coaching staff about me, and they looked at some film of me, but they still declined to offer me a scholarship.

Then I won the state wrestling tournament at 175 pounds, and I was offered a few wrestling scholarships. Still, I really wanted to play football, and following my wrestling championship, Doug persisted with the Nebraska coaches. Finally, assistant coach Carl Selmer came to see me, and Nebraska finally offered me a scholarship. Nebraska appealed to me because it had two campuses in the same city—one for liberal arts and one for agriculture. The University of Nebraska is unique that way, because most universities are split up and spread out. And my main goal at the time was to get a college education and play college football.

The first time I ever met coach Devaney, who had just arrived himself, was the next morning after I woke up in my dorm and met my roommate. Anytime you meet the head coach, you are impressed, and I had heard some great stories about him, but meeting him was very special. And Doug had told me so many good things about him.

As a freshman, I started out as the third-string fullback and second-string linebacker, but I was the first-string punter. We played a few freshman games, but it really was like a year of orientation for me. The great thing was that the coaching staff wanted me back, but not on a full-ride scholarship. They said they would pay half of my tuition, the wrestling program would pay half if I wrestled, and I would pay for my room and board. Some of the freshmen had not been invited back, so I felt fine about it. I had practiced with the wrestling team in 1962, but remember, freshmen weren't eligible then.

In football, I knew something great was happening with the program with coach Devaney there. They had finished his first season 9–2, but over that summer I started to reconsider. "Maybe I won't go back," I thought. My mother said, "No, you're outta here! You're going back to school!" I probably could have stayed home and got into the family construction business, but I headed back to Lincoln.

At that time, coach Selmer talked to me about converting to guard. I weighed about 205 pounds and faced a year of trying to learn a new position.

77

He said, "You've got good speed and quickness and the strength." He just thought it would be a natural position for me. The position really is the same as being at fullback except you are in a three-point stance. None of us lifted weights in those days. They said if you lifted weights, you got big, bulky, and slow. Times have changed, right?

In 1963 when I was punting, I didn't stretch properly and tore my back up. That sidelined me for the season. They said, "Allers, you will be redshirted," and during the second semester, they put me back on full scholarship.

The game I remember watching that season was when we beat Oklahoma 29–20 and the crowd pelted both teams with oranges all day long. The team then went to the Orange Bowl and beat Auburn.

The next year was when everybody started to platoon, playing either offense or defense, but I was on the third team that backed up people both ways. We had a great season, losing only to Oklahoma, but the tragedy of it was when [quarterback] Fred Duda broke his leg at Iowa State. We then lost to Arkansas in the Cotton Bowl.

I remember my first action on the field because it was overwhelming for me to play in front of all those spectators. I have to say that Nebraska has the greatest group of supporters in college football. The entire state supports the program, and that makes it special. There is no division in the state like Iowa and Iowa State or Kansas and Kansas State.

At about this time, the coaches became like second fathers to us. I remember Mike Corgan used to have me out to his house, and we would do some landscaping or construction work, and then he would make a big bowl of spaghetti and some homemade wine. We had a lot of fun with our coaches. They were always very honest, very friendly, and very caring.

I learned never to be late to practice that year. We always had a light Sunday morning practice at 9:00. It wasn't very physical—you would get treatment and do a little jogging just to get the blood flowing. We had a policy around the dorm that all the guys would get everybody up on Sunday mornings so nobody overslept and missed practice. At midseason on one Sunday, my roommate and I overslept because nobody woke us up. As we were trotting onto the field, coach Devaney was walking off. He said, "Go see coach Corgan." For sleeping in, we ran 10 100-yard sprints and 10 alpines—that's 10 times up the steps of the stadium to the top and 10 times down. Now I was in good shape, but my legs felt like rubber after that. I was never late after that. In fact, nobody was late after that!

LaVerne Allers was a powerful guard who gained All-American honors after converting from the backfield.

I placed second in the Big Eight wrestling tournament in 1964 in the 191-pound class, losing only to the eventual national champion. I didn't get much wrestling practice, and wrestling conditioning is much different than football conditioning, so I felt pretty good about what I had accomplished. I had had a wrestle-off with Lynn Senkbeil, a cornerback on the football team. That reminds me of a running joke among Lynn, me, and Carel Stith, a defensive tackle. We were all good friends and we always kidded each other, saying, "With girls' names like ours, we had to be tough." (Since my college days, I have gone by "Verne," but most people at Nebraska would know me by "LaVerne.")

In 1965, I became a starter at guard. In preseason one day, I remember being in the training room and grabbing some ankle tape when some of the guys wanted Frank Solich, our fullback, to weigh more at a weigh-in. So we stuck about 10 pounds of tape to his butt, and he weighed in. I don't remember what Frank weighed, but suddenly he was about 10 pounds heavier. He went along with it, but it wasn't Frank's idea. To most Nebraska fans, he probably seemed so serious as the head coach later, but he had a good sense of humor.

We had the school's first perfect [regular] season in a half-century that year, but then we played Alabama in the Orange Bowl. I really believe if we played Alabama 99 more times, we would have beaten them 99 times, but everything worked for them that day [Alabama won 39–28]. We had a great, great team, but like they say, "On any given day . . ."

That was very disappointing, and that's all I can say about it.

I started loving football at that point. I had been named All–Big Eight and worked hard in the off-season because my ultimate goal was to be named All-American as a senior. In the spring of 1965, they flew me to Chicago for the *Playboy* All-America team, and I sat down with Bear Bryant there and we talked football. He talked about how they converted fullbacks to guards at Alabama, which is what happened to me.

We won our first nine games in 1966, and the game I remember the most was against Colorado. We were trailing 19–7 and scored two touchdowns in the fourth quarter to pull it out. When we flew back to Lincoln, there were so many fans at the airport that we couldn't get to our bus. Kelly Peterson, our center, and I had to get a police escort just to get back.

The low point, however, was the 10–9 loss to Oklahoma that ended our chances at another undefeated season. I remember that we were threatening in the closing moments, but Bob Churchich threw a pass up for grabs in the end zone, and it was incomplete. Oklahoma had put a hellish rush on us all day.

After the game, we had a choice of a few different bowl games, and we wanted to go down to the Sugar Bowl, mainly because we wanted another chance to play Alabama. But Alabama played a great game and we just fell apart [Alabama won 34–7].

I was scheduled to play in the Hula Bowl but arrived late because we got fogged in after the Sugar Bowl at New Orleans. When I arrived, I had breakfast with the coaches for the North team and they talked me into playing both ways in the game. One of their linebackers had been hurt in a bowl game, so I played guard and linebacker for three quarters of that game. We beat the South 28–27. The quarterbacks that day were names you would know: Bob Griese of Purdue was the North quarterback, and Steve Spurrier of Florida was the South quarterback.

Also, I made All-American like I set out to do, along with [middle guard] Wayne Meylan. [Meylan later died in an airplane crash.]

I would like to close this chapter by thanking the late Bob Devaney and his assistant coaches, especially Carl Selmer. The trainers, George Sullivan and Paul Snyder, kept me together when I was injured so much. A special thanks to our SID [sports information director], Don Bryant, who always did a great job getting exposure for our program. Last but not least, my teammates were very special to me.

We now know that we were all part of something really great, which is Nebraska Cornhusker football.

LaVerne Allers was named All–Big Eight in 1965–66 and an All-American in 1966. He was inducted into the Nebraska Football Hall of Fame in 1995.

DAN SCHNEISS

FULLBACK

1968–1970

I CAME FROM A SCHOOL IN WEST BEND, WISCONSIN, which had a pretty good football tradition—fortunately for me. Several of the kids in front of me there had gone on to play college football. One, Ron Kirkland, had played at Nebraska. Another I knew had gone on to Purdue. I was a quarterback and safety in high school, but I was recruited as a defensive back by most of the Big 10 and Big Eight schools. I was about 6'2" and 210 pounds, and I also played basketball, but it really was just something to do in the winter. I was a sprinter and threw the shot put in track, and I also had good success in baseball. Ron always told me how great Nebraska was, while the other guy always told me how great Purdue was. So my decision came down to those two schools.

It was a tough decision because I loved both schools, but I suppose the difference was Bob Devaney.

When coach Devaney recruited me, he spent time selling my mom more than he did selling me. He was always a very positive guy, and the other coaches from Nebraska that I had met were very down to earth. The head coach at Purdue ran down the other schools. He said, "Don't go to Wisconsin because they were 0–10 the last three years." He said, "Don't go to Nebraska because the Big Eight does not have the quality of football that the Big 10 does." That turned me off some. And at Nebraska, everybody was very friendly and they were not into the negative recruiting.

In the end, I knew I made the right choice when I became a Cornhusker.

We played five games in our freshman season and won all five. Monte Kiffin was our coach, and he was just full of piss and vinegar, but we loved him. He would always praise us when we did well, and he would talk to us, teaching us the game. We loved to play for him. The week before our first freshman game, one of our running backs, Al Montgomery, went down. So they asked if I wanted to switch to the backfield, and I said, "I'll do it."

We were still in the full-house backfield then, and I became the left half-back. We had a really nice freshman team with good talent, and we all got along pretty well. After my freshman year, we switched to the I formation, and I was up to about 220 pounds, so coach Devaney said, "You are not fast enough to be an I-back, we're moving you to fullback." We didn't have many weights around then, but I lifted some on my own and put on that weight.

Coach [Tom] Osborne had brought about the switch on offense. He had spent time visiting some other schools, like Tennessee, and the staff had reevaluated what we had been doing on offense. At that time, it was just smashmouth football. We would line up and say "We're coming at you. Can you stop us?" And they had been stopping us, so it was time for something new.

As the 1968 season unfolded, I got to see some playing time at fullback, and I became the punter. We went to Iowa State, and our starting fullback, Dick Davis, hadn't been producing the way coach Devaney wanted, so he started me. I had about 50 yards in the first quarter, but after that, I never got back into the game. Dick came in and got about 150 yards after that. I guess that motivated him, which is what they were looking for. We ended the season with that humiliating loss [47–0] to Oklahoma on national television, and things changed after that. Workouts got intense. Winter conditioning was very run-oriented and skill-oriented, and we started to lift weights. It was no more checking in and playing racquetball. We punched in and went to work and there was no kidding around.

In 1969, we had a sense of unity, too, that maybe wasn't there in 1967 and 1968 [back-to-back 6–4 seasons]. Guys then had gone their own way, but we seemed to do things more as a team by the time we were juniors. It wasn't really intentional, but we just got along better. On the practice field, we would knock 'em down and help 'em up. We all had the same goal in mind, which was to win games.

We got beat by a very good USC team [31–21] in that opening game, and lost to Missouri a few games later (Missouri wasn't that bad, either). After that, we got on a roll. We went down to Oklahoma again to end the season, and I remember at the Friday walk-through practice, coach Devaney went over to talk to [Oklahoma coach] Chuck Fairbanks. Coach Devaney came back to us and said, "He's worried about us this year. He knows we're better this year."

Early in that game, I remember the wind was blowing so hard across the field that on my first punt, the ball went straight up in the air and came right back at me. We were on our own 25-yard line, and everybody ran down-field—so I had to down my own punt. I knew the big boy would be hot, so I tried to sneak over to the sidelines, but he caught me. Man, coach Devaney was mad. On the next play, [Jack] Mildren scored on an option and we were down 6–0 just like that. Fortunately, we came back and dominated them [44–14], and that took me off the hook.

We went down to the Sun Bowl to play Georgia, and they came in and didn't have any black players. We had quite a few and couldn't figure that out why they had none. Well, leading up to the game, the Georgia players were saying things . . . now you would call them racial slurs. So by the time the game came around, we were chomping at the bit to get at them. They couldn't move the ball on us, and we just ran up and down the field on them all day [in a 45–6 win]. After the game, coach [Vince] Dooley said, "Either we didn't belong in this bowl game, or they belonged in another."

Heading into 1970, our confidence was very high. We had a 9–2 season behind us, and we now knew we could play with the big boys. The coaches were more confident, too. You could just tell. They knew this could be special that season. Jerry [Murtaugh] was never one to make brash predictions, but he came out and predicted we would win the national championship. He really believed it. In fact, we all did, so we stood behind him.

We thought we had a team that nobody could beat. USC was ranked No. 3 when we went out to play them. They had this fast defense, and they were pretty powerful on offense. We had practiced a play in a single-back formation where we spread the I-back out and kept the fullback in the backfield. We gave the defense an option look and pitched to the fullback, who passed it. We practiced it, but I never thought we would actually call it in a game. Well, what did we do? We called it early in the USC game, and it went for a touchdown—I threw it to [Guy] Ingles, who was wide open. USC thought it was a run all the way. That put us up 7–0 and we eventually ended in a 21–21 tie. But we were better than them that day. Poor Joe Orduna had a

Dan Schneiss, here blocking during a field-goal attempt against Oklahoma, was one of Nebraska's finest blocking fullbacks.

problem hanging onto the football that night. He was a great runner, but he dropped one now and then.

At the end of that game, we had a chance to kick a short field goal and a bad snap ended it. We were near tears after that. We thought we were superior to those guys all night long, but never has a tie felt more like a loss.

I remember that game well because my dad was trying to get it on the radio back in Wisconsin. He couldn't quite get the reception, so he went up on the roof of our house and got it. It was like midnight or 1:00 A.M. in Wisconsin, and Dad was sitting up on the roof listening to the game. It was a good thing it was in September and not November.

We just felt like we wouldn't lose after that, and we would take it out on the next team. We did, and kept doing it all the way through until we got to Oklahoma. We were loaded, and they felt they were just as good talent-wise. I always felt Oklahoma had a little more talent than us, but maybe they weren't as disciplined. Late in that game, we had a third-and-17 and [Jerry] Tagge went back to throw. I slipped out of the backfield and went down the middle and was wide open. I could see out of the corner of my eye that I was going to get hit from both sides. I did, and the tacklers sort of bounced off of each other, and I fell down at the 3-yard line. I should have scored, but we punched it in to win 28–21, and we just knew the following year that everybody would be back on both teams. (That's why it became the Game of the Century.)

On New Year's Day, we sat around watching the other games and we knew Stanford beat Ohio State and Notre Dame beat Texas, so all we had to do was win our game against LSU to win the national championship. That night, we both had very good defenses and nobody moved it much, but they went ahead 12–10, before Tagge went over on that sneak to win it. In the locker room, we were all chanting, "We're number one! We're number one!"

86

We get back to the hotel, and Devaney says, "I want to see you and Murtaugh." We were the cocaptains, and I thought, "Oh no, what have we done now?" But Jerry told me, "Don't worry. We're finished—what can he do to us now?"

He called us in and said, "Now this group of guys has given me a lot of trouble over the years . . . but it's the best team I've ever had!" And he thanked us. That meant a lot to me. Bob Devaney was a great, great man. I learned later that he often had written letters to my parents.

In January, President Nixon came to Lincoln, and Jerry and I got to be up on the podium with him. We had to be there before the event started, and they told us, "Now, don't you dare shake his hand. Don't make any sudden movements toward him. If he wants to shake your hand, he'll come over to you." I think Jerry broke that rule. Anyway, we got to meet him, and it was a big thrill for us, even though Nixon didn't finish as one of our fantastic presidents. And we got our rings that proved we were the best in college football.

How much do those rings mean to us? I remember Dave Morock, one of our defensive backs, got robbed once later, and he said, "I didn't care that they took my television and I didn't care that they took my VCR, but the SOB took my national championship ring! How could he take something so personal?" When you look at that ring, you knew that all the aches and pains, and bloody, stressful times in practice were worth it.

You know I never left Lincoln. Even in the summers, my parents would call and say, "Why don't you come back to Wisconsin?" But I loved it here. My girlfriend from high school—now my wife of 34 years—transferred to Nebraska. We never left and we couldn't be happier. Nebraska was definitely the best choice I could have ever made.

> Dan Schneiss was cocaptain of the Cornhuskers' first national championship team in 1970. He teaches elementary education in Boys Town, Nebraska, and coaches youth football and track.

JOE ORDUNA
RUNNING BACK
1967–1968, 1970

THE ORDUNA STORY IN AMERICA BEGAN WITH my father's father, who immigrated from Mexico. He said he came to the country to kill the man who had killed one of his sisters. He never did do that, but he married a black woman and settled in Omaha, Nebraska. They then had six kids.

My mother's family came from the South with an Irish background and settled in Omaha, too.

My parents had four boys and two girls, and I was the second oldest. My dad had built our house, and we always figured we had the best house in Omaha, which was still racially segregated at that time. Dad worked as a chef at a restaurant, and one day I asked him, "Dad, when are we going to go eat at that restaurant where you work?"

Then he told me we couldn't eat there because we were black. That was when the Civil Rights movement was starting, and certain things scared me to death when I was a youngster. There were certain places that we could not go, and establishments that we were not allowed to visit.

Along came the 1960 Olympics, and as I sat and watched Wilma Rudolph and Rafer Johnson run, I suddenly developed this fantasy about becoming an Olympic hero. That's what I wanted to be. I started training at this huge park, and if it sounded hard, I did it. I ran this huge hill, ran sprints, and trained on my own just to be like the Olympic stars.

I had a sister who was taking ballet at the time and she was very limber. She taught me some stretching exercises, and I used to lie on this old mattress in the basement and stretch.

When I got to be a sophomore, I was one of the best hurdlers in the state of Nebraska—I was even undefeated until the state meet. In the Junior Olympics, I set a national record in the triple jump—45'7"—as a 15-year-old, breaking the national record by 1'1". That remains a Nebraska state record. When I was 17 years old, I ran a 13.9 in the 120-yard high hurdles, and then I sustained a hamstring injury. Me and two other guys on the track team somewhat single-handedly won the state track meet for us two years in a row.

I went to the same high school—Omaha Central—as Gale Sayers and I wore his No. 48. We didn't have a very good football team; I think we lost almost every game, but our school was known for its academic prowess. We just got whipped on the football field. Our boys were not physically tough, and it got to be a running joke at times. I remember going to Sunday school and one of the teachers asked, "How was the track meet?" He was making fun of our football team because the other team always made the game a track meet.

I had a few long runs and played both ways, but I fumbled a lot. It was not a spectacular football career by any means.

I really don't know why Nebraska recruited me. Bob Devaney just showed up at my house one day and met my parents. I asked, "Why is he here?" I don't really remember what he said that day, but he had a twinkle in his eye and one of the warmest smiles you ever wanted to see. I think I am a pretty good judge of character, and he was a genuine person, not a phony. I know he impressed my parents.

89

When I came to Lincoln for recruiting day, I sat on the sideline and watched the Nebraska football team jog out onto the field. It was like watching a pack of Clydesdales. They all had these big muscles, and I marveled at the size of these people. Everyone looked so good in those uniforms—that image always stuck with me.

I guess I was recruited because of my accomplishments in track, rather than football, but I know I was smart enough to sign with Nebraska when they offered it to me.

When I got to Lincoln, I was bug-eyed in the big city. I was 50 miles from home and could do anything I really wanted to do for the first time. The running backs there were bigger than any linemen I had played with. I remember some of the other recruits walked around like peacocks with their chests stuck out. Some of them were drinking and smoking and carousing. I had never been around that type of behavior before.

On the other hand, I went to bed early, ate right, and didn't smoke, drink, or chase girls. I was known as a "Goody Two-Shoes," and I think it became a joke at times. Somebody in the locker room would say a bad word, and then follow it up with, "Oh, excuse me, Joe." They weren't always kind to me.

One time I went to a Fellowship of Christian Athletes [FCA]event at Estes Park, Colorado, and it really changed me. I started reading my Bible every day, and that would make me the object of comments from my teammates. But our coaches always supported me that way. At that time, I was being asked to go out and speak at local high schools and in small towns, and I did that almost every weekend.

One time I visited with this family of a friend from church. They lived on a farm in Mead, Nebraska, and it was right out of the 19th century. They had this .30–06 gun out there shooting at targets, and I had never shot a gun that big before. I put my eye right up on the scope, and when I fired it, it came back and hit me in the head. It opened a big slit, which took six stitches to close. As I was bleeding all over the place, they were laughing and howling, and I thought, "These people play hard out here."

That freshman year was a stressful time for me. I started at tailback on the freshman team, and all I know is when they called my number, they gave me the ball and I ran it. Against Kansas, I ran it about eight or nine times in a row, but I really was unaware of what I was doing.

In the first game of my varsity career, we were playing Washington and I got kicked in the head, knocking me unconscious. I had played well to that point, but I sure don't remember it much. In the next game against Minnesota, I broke through the line of scrimmage in the third quarter, and somebody hit me as I spun into the end zone. Somebody then hit me after I got into the end zone, and I went flying to the ground. I was embarrassed that I got knocked down after I had scored, but we won 7–0 and that was the only touchdown. I knew one thing: you were supposed to be standing when you reached the end zone.

Later that season, I ran downfield against Missouri, and all I remember is a tangled mess of bodies. I was suddenly rolling backward, and as I came up to my knees, the official was standing over me with his arms raised. I don't know how I caught the football that day, but it was in my arms. We lost 10–7. The next day, the newspaper made a big deal about the fact that the touchdowns for each team were scored by "black sophomores." I really didn't understand that.

Joe Orduna follows fullback Dan Schneiss' block on his way to a big gain.

I never noticed any racial problems in Lincoln, though, and I was out speaking to people almost every weekend. I found the people there to be welcoming and wonderful to me.

I don't remember much about the 1968 season, other than the Oklahoma game. I took a helmet in the back and it broke bones in seven of my vertebrae. I was on the sideline, and one of the coaches said, "Get tough, go back in there."

I went to a doctor and they found out two weeks later that I had some broken bones. The coaches looked at the film, but couldn't see any hit that would have caused it. That was our 47–0 loss to Oklahoma, and let's just say that coach Devaney was not happy with that one.

In fall camp of 1969, I got hit on the left side of my knee and it stretched my ligaments. I tried to let it heal, but it wouldn't. I had to have surgery and they redshirted me that year. I had this cast from the top of my toes to the top of my hip. When they finally took it off, I came back for spring ball and got hit on the right knee, which tore a little bit of cartilage. I needed another surgery, but not as major as the previous one.

I was a little jealous of that 1969 team, because we had a good record [9–2] that year and went to the Sun Bowl.

When I came back in 1970, I had to share time with Jeff Kinney. My goal was to win, but I can't tell you any rhyme or reason as to how they alternated us. I never questioned the coaches' decisions when it came to playing time, but I wished I was in the game when Jeff was, and I am sure he would say the same. But it worked and I have no regrets about it.

Out at USC that year, I had the best game of my life with a 67-yard touchdown run in the third quarter, but we tied the Trojans 21–21. We missed a field goal in the final seconds, and I had fumbled inside the 20-yard line. I kicked myself after that game as much as anybody. I knew if I hadn't fumbled, it would have been a different outcome. Mom and Dad were at that game, and after it, Bill Cosby came into the locker room and asked, "Where's No. 31? I want to meet him."

Against Missouri, they came in with the great Joe Moore, but [Jerry] Murtaugh and our guys on defense put a real hurt on him. On fourth-and-1 in that game, I ripped off a 42-yard run, but I got caught from behind and was so embarrassed by it. You never get caught from behind!

I scored three touchdowns against Iowa State, and the next week I scored four touchdowns against Kansas State. I remember breaking a lot of tackles that day.

92

In the Orange Bowl against LSU, I did not start the game, and my girlfriend was annoyed by that. I guess I was, too. I did not play much that night and really do not know why. I know on one play I was one half inch from breaking a long run, but somebody barely caught my shoestrings and I tripped. That would have been about a 50-yard touchdown run. [Orduna led Nebraska with 63 yards rushing and scored on a 3-yard run in the Orange Bowl.]

After the game [a 17–12 Nebraska win], my teammates were extremely happy knowing we probably would be voted No. 1, but I wasn't. I realized it was my last game, and I always was very emotional that way. It was over and that made me sad. I got on a plane and we went to Hawaii for the Hula Bowl, and I never savored the moment like I should have.

We got to Hawaii, and I put my girlfriend up at one hotel while I was at another. One morning at breakfast, she told me, "I would marry you right now if I could."

I was speaking at a youth church meeting over there and met this pastor. I went to him and asked if he would marry us. So we got married on Friday, January 8, 1971, in a church in Honolulu. The Hula Bowl was the next day. When I walked my wife to her hotel room the night of our wedding, she stiff-armed me at the door and said, "The honeymoon starts tomorrow."

She was concerned about me playing in the game. So I went down to the lobby, and the trainer who knew us was laughing so hard when I told him that. He asked, "You want some sleeping pills or something?"

My biggest regret from my college days is that I feel I wasted five years of what was a free education. I left the university without a degree, and I was ashamed of that. Fortunately, my wife made me finish it by correspondence in 1974. Now I teach middle school and am on the verge of getting my master's in education administration—I plan to become a principal. I learned to love the joy of learning.

I had attended an FCA camp when I was in college, and I still think that camp changed my life. I played football, but I touched more lives by going out into the community and meeting people and giving speeches.

Since Nebraska, I have gone by the name of Joseph for a couple of reasons. When I was younger, I never liked "Joseph," but I got healed of all that. I realized that name has Biblical significance and I just started going by Joseph.

Nebraska nursed me and helped me through the formative years of my life. I figure that the experience at Nebraska shaped me in ways that I can't even imagine. I wish I could relive it now because I think I went through it numbly, almost blindly. I really did not understand the significance of what I was doing at the time. Playing football at a major university like that, people looked upon you as somebody special, and I didn't realize that until many years later.

I still root for Nebraska, and I really want Nebraska people to know how significant they were in my life. I don't think about what I did there, however, I think about what could have been. How could it have been better?

At the same time, I would never trade those experiences of meeting all the people I met. Those people in Nebraska really showed me a world that I never knew before. They touched me and helped make me the person I am today.

Joe Orduna rushed for 1,968 yards and 26 touchdowns in his career. He led the Cornhuskers in rushing in the 1968 and 1970 seasons. He also was named All–Big Eight and the winner of the Novak Trophy in 1970. He was selected in the second round of the 1971 NFL Draft by the San Francisco 49ers and played three seasons in the NFL. Orduna was inducted into the Nebraska Football Hall of Fame in 1990.

JERRY MURTAUGH
LINEBACKER
1968–1970

BEING FROM A FAMILY OF 10 KIDS—five girls, five boys—I learned to wrestle (I pronounce it "rassle") at a very young age. I had to because my sisters were always kicking my butt. It was a "rassling" family, you might say. Mom and Dad loved athletics. Dad was there for us athletically, and Mom stayed home and cooked for us. Because there were so many, she had to cook in shifts.

I went to school at Omaha North High and rassled at 180 pounds as a senior. On the football team, I was a fullback—all I ever did was block—and a linebacker. I had scholarship offers for rassling and football at several schools. Oklahoma, Oklahoma State, and Iowa State all wanted me. When I would visit these schools, the rassling coaches would say, "You can't play football," and the football coaches would say, "You can't rassle."

Anyway, I told Oklahoma I was coming. I was going to be a Sooner. They just kind of told me everything I wanted to hear. Things such as how good I was, how I would play as a sophomore, and all the opportunities I'd have after I got my degree. Then coach Devaney came to see me. He said, "I hear you are thinking about going to Oklahoma."

I said, "Yeah, how did you find out?"

"We have ways to find these things out," he told me.

He was very forward, but he was a real gentleman to my mom and dad. I had never followed college football much—Dad and I sat around on Sundays and watched pro football while I was growing up. But my parents got to like coach Devaney very well. He was a real talker and had a presence about him. It took about four or five visits, but coach Devaney swayed me and my father. He told my parents how they would get to see me play all the time at Nebraska because it was close. And I wanted my parents to see me play football. So I called Oklahoma and told them, and they were very upset with me. "You are backing out on your word," they said. I felt bad. I was 18 years old and they were upset with me, but I was set to become a Cornhusker.

I got to Lincoln, and the Nebraska coaches gave me the option—"Do you want to play offense or defense?" I decided on defense because I was too slow to carry the ball. When I got there, I didn't have any football accolades, and here were all these high school All-Americans. I didn't even get a vote for all-conference. I was pretty good, making tackles all over the field in high school, but my own coach didn't even vote for me.

As a freshman at Nebraska, there was an All-American here and an All-American there, and I wasn't even All-Metro. Larry Wachholtz, who was an All-American at Nebraska, was a graduate assistant (GA) coach during my freshman year. During one drill, he was showing us how to block and we had on helmets, T-shirts, and shorts. He told me to come at him. So I did, and I ducked my head. I looked up and Larry had both of his front teeth in his hands, and blood was gushing all over the place. I never saw Larry again that season—his GA days were over.

Monte Kiffin was our freshman coach, and he was a crazy, crazy individual, but I loved to play for him. We had four games that year, 1967, and won them all. That was a fun time. We played against John Riggins at Kansas and Joe Moore at Missouri. Then we would get to scrimmage against the varsity, and that was exciting. Before you got on the field with them, you felt a little intimidated, but once we started hitting, I thought, "This isn't so bad." Plus, we had Kiffin behind us yelling and screaming.

Nineteen sixty-seven was bad [a 6–4 record], and 1968 was worse [6–4] because it was two seasons in a row that Nebraska had subpar records. They were ready to run coach Devaney out of town on a rail. I remember the Oklahoma game in 1968 to end the season. We lost 47–0, and TV took the game off in the third quarter because it was such a blowout. Devaney came into the locker room following the game and blew up. "If I ever see you seniors again, it will be too soon," he shouted. "I will tell the rest of you coming back, God help you, because I will *own* you next season!"

But I had my best game of the year, making a lot of tackles against Oklahoma. Coach Devaney and I never talked much, but after that game when he was finished yelling, he came up to me and said, "You played a hell of a football game."

We weren't close friends, and I'll get into that later, but he recognized I had never quit during that game. I made a lot of tackles that year, but it was because we had such a great defensive line. No offensive linemen ever got to us linebackers because they kept them off of us.

We showed up for camp as juniors, and we could tell we had a good football team coming back. We were young, but there was a lot of enthusiasm. Devaney told the team, "Your soul belongs to the Lord, but your ass belongs to me this year. I will not go through another year like that!"

We really had a good defense [allowing 259.4 total yards per game], and we had young guys playing well. We lost a tough one at USC 31–21, but I think we were better than they were. By the time we played Oklahoma, we were 7–2 and Steve Owens had that 30-game, 100-yard rushing streak, or whatever it was, going. I had remembered the year before when they beat us so badly, I would tackle him and he would say, "Jerry, you having a good day?" So during our junior season, we held him to about 50 yards and beat Oklahoma really badly [44–14]. Every time I would hit him, we would be lying on the field, and I would say, "Steve, how's your day going?" He would say, "Murtaugh, you @#$%!"

Then we went down to El Paso, Texas, for the Sun Bowl, and I was married at the time, but the wives had not come into town yet. So we went out to Juarez and a few of the guys got thrown into jail. I was a bystander on this one, for once, but I went around and rounded up a lot of money to bail everybody out. We got them out of jail and on the bus and headed back to the hotel. As soon as the bus drove up to the hotel, Devaney was standing there. We got off and he started screaming and yelling.

"You're all done. You are done! You will never play for me again!" he screamed.

I went to my room and got a bang on the door. It was coach Devaney and three other coaches. He started screaming at me, "You started this, I know it, and you got everybody in trouble. You SOB!"

Then he came after me. He wanted to whip my ass, but the other coaches stepped in. I was screaming back at them, "Let him go! Let him go!"

Cocaptain of Nebraska's first national championship team, Jerry Murtaugh
still holds the school's career tackles record.

He was just a little guy, but he was an old boxer and a tough little shit.
Well, all the guys were scared that they were finished playing for Nebraska,
but I told them, "We are all starters, and there is no way we are done—he
wants to win this game too bad."

Well, we did play in the game and just ate Georgia up like a high school
team. After the game [a 45–6 Nebraska victory], Vince Dooley called us the

greatest team he had seen. Then we had another meeting, and Devaney said, "You will all pay when we get back home."

Let's just say that we knew every step of our stadium by heart. He got over it, but we ran a lot of stadium steps. I don't ever remember not running those steps. I got in a few fights on campus and a few fights off campus, and I got thrown in jail now and then. It always seemed I would go in some place and some guy would think, "That Murtaugh's not so tough, let's test him." And I could never walk away. I would be in jail for a few hours, then I would be up and down those stadium steps. I think they still have a cell with my name on it. So I ended up running up and down those steps all the time.

I remember one day before my senior season, we were standing on the field and I was looking up at the press box. "What are you looking at, Murtaugh?" Devaney asked.

"I have never been up to that press box," I told him.

He said, "Never in my day will you be in that press box! But you can get your ass up those steps and run."

So I headed up the steps running. And I have never been in that press box to this day.

On media day before my senior season, my big mouth got me in trouble again. I predicted flatly to the media, "We are going to win the national championship." Word got back to the coaches and Devaney asked, "He said what?"

He sent Jeff Kinney over to drag me out of there. Kinney comes over and says, "Keep your mouth shut!" But it was too late—I already had been quoted. My prediction started the year off.

We went out to USC and tied them 21–21. I think we fumbled three times inside their 10-yard line. They had a great football team, but we were disappointed because that game was ours. We just knew it was the last time that we wouldn't win a game. Dan Schneiss and I were cocaptains and we talked about it. We felt it. We would not lose. We rolled through the season and got to Oklahoma. We got lax, but still beat them 28–21. I knew they would be good the following year because they were young. But so would Nebraska, because only about five of us were seniors.

I have to tell you about Eddie Periard, our nose guard. Now Eddie was about 5'9", 195 pounds, and he was the meanest little guy in the world. He would make you laugh, though. He had been a walk-on and he never knew what the word "quit" meant. I remember in this one game, he got hit and he couldn't breathe. He was really hurting. I was standing over him, and I yelled, "Get him out of here! He's hurt!"

I looked down at him and he said, "Murtaugh, if you get me out of this game, I am going to kick your ass!" He had tears running down his cheeks and he screamed, "Don't you dare get me out of this game!"

On the very next play, I got the wind knocked out of me. Now I had tears coming out of my eyes. Eddie stood over me and asked, "Murt, you want out of the game?"

In that Orange Bowl game against LSU, Eddie should have been the MVP. He had about 15 tackles, and when we looked at the films the next week, he was just killing them. He was a great individual and he made second-team All-American as a senior. But sadly, Eddie was killed in a car accident about five years ago.

One of the days I always loved in practice was about once a week when coach Devaney would blow his whistle and we would go live and run isolation plays. There would be a center, two guards, a quarterback, and a fullback going against five defensive players. I would always have to meet that fullback head-on, and I got so sick and tired of seeing Dan Schneiss for four years. We just got nasty together. He was the meanest guy. But that was a fun drill. All the coaches would be yelling at each other. The offensive coaches would be screaming at the defensive coaches, and the defensive coaches screaming at the offensive coaches. [John] Melton would be screaming at [Carl] Selmer. [Mike] Corgan would be screaming at [Monte] Kiffin.

Coach Devaney would instigate it, then just watch and laugh. That was always fun.

99

We got to 10–0–1 and headed to the Orange Bowl ranked No. 3 to play LSU. On New Year's Day, we were very aware that the No. 1 team, Texas, had lost to Notre Dame and No. 2 Ohio State had lost to Stanford. We had the radio on in the locker room and we were saying things like, "It's our turn. Let's go do it."

Devaney came in and shouted, "Shut up! Sit down! Get your mind on this game. Just because those teams lost doesn't mean a thing to us. You haven't won a thing yet."

We had never played a Southern team like LSU. We were beating them, then we threw an interception and it got close at the end. Then they got to driving on us at the end of the game. Thank God for Bob Terrio, who intercepted that last pass to put it away for us.

After the game we were in the locker room and coach Devaney said something like, "Now, we have a chance at it—"

I stood up and interrupted him, "Where's the phone? Isn't the president supposed to call us after we win the national championship?"

But President Nixon never did call us or invite us to the White House that year. He later came to Lincoln, and Schneiss and I accepted the trophy from him. I went to say something to Nixon and the secret service guy told me, "Shut up!" and pushed me back. Everybody, even guys from outside the program, were always telling me to shut up. I was about to ask him, "How come you didn't call us? You called Texas the year before!"

When we got back from the Orange Bowl, I told the media, "I told you guys before the season what we were going to do." But I never brought up my prediction with coach Devaney, and he never said a word to me after the game. It seemed the only time he ever talked to me was when I was in trouble.

When they were planning coach Devaney's retirement party a couple of years later, Mrs. Devaney called me and asked, "Are you coming to his retirement party?"

I told her, "No, I will not be there."

She said, "You *will* be there, and I want you and Bob to stop fighting after all these years."

"No, I am not coming," I said.

"I am sick of this bickering between you two," she said. "I will get him next to you and you two will make up!"

So I was sitting at his party, and all of a sudden, I got my ear twisted. It's Mrs. Devaney. "Shut up and come with me," she said. Now the other Devaney was telling me to "shut up." Everybody around me was just cracking up. It felt like my mother was dragging me over there.

We went all the way over to the other part of the auditorium, and coach Devaney was sitting there by himself. There was nobody around him. "You sit down!" she ordered me. "Now I want you two to sit there to talk about this, work it out, and forget this. You heard me! Both of you!"

For about 30 seconds, neither of us said a word. Then he asked, "Want a beer?"

I said, "Hell, yes, I do."

So we were sitting there having a beer and he said, "Neither one of us has ever gotten along, have we? You think maybe it should end now?"

I just muttered, "Yep"

So we sat there and talked for about 30 minutes. He told me some great stories in that half hour, and he told me, "Look what you started here. You started a tradition of a winner. This is going to happen a lot around here now. There will be more championships on account of people like you. I really want to thank you and Dan Schneiss. But by God, I never could keep you out of jail, could I?"

Then he said, "I will leave you with one thing: I wasn't really a great football coach, but I was smart enough to hire great assistants."

I will always remember that.

Then we got along great over the years. I would go up to his [athletic director's] office just to say "hi" a couple of times each year. We would just sit and talk, and we really got to know each other. I was out of the state when he died and I didn't make his funeral, but I called Mrs. Devaney and we cried together.

You can ask, what is Nebraska football? It's tradition. It's family. It's pride. With my organization—GoalOmaha—I ask for help from former players all the time. They all do it because they know I played at Nebraska, even though some of them have never met me. I am 55 years old, and when I walk into a school nowadays, people will walk up to me and offer congratulations.

"For what?" I'll ask.

"For what you started here," they'll say.

If all of our starting defense from 1970 was right here right now, we could say, "We started this." We started a great tradition at Nebraska and that makes me very, very proud to say I am a Cornhusker.

101

Jerry Murtaugh, who holds the Nebraska career tackle record with 342 total tackles, was an All-American in 1970 and cocaptain of the Cornhuskers' first national championship team. He was inducted into the Nebraska Football Hall of Fame in 1987. He is the founder and president of GoalOmaha (Goalomaha.com), a nonprofit organization that places strength and conditioning coaches in Nebraska high schools.

BOB NEWTON

TACKLE

1969–1970

When I was being recruited by major colleges following my playing days at Cerritos Junior College in Southern California, coaches from Oklahoma, Kansas, and Nebraska all impressed me.

Barry Switzer was an assistant at Oklahoma, and Terry Donahue was an assistant at Kansas. They impressed me, but an assistant from Nebraska named Tom Osborne impressed me more.

The first impression I had of him was his sincerity and humility. I felt I could believe in him and trust him. Bob Devaney also had a huge impact on me during the recruiting process. When I first met coach Devaney in his office, he said, "Bob, we need help on our offensive line, and we need you to come to Nebraska." He was very up-front with me and very genuine. Plus he had a great sense of humor, which I liked.

Coach Osborne was very persistent in recruiting me, and that persistence paid off: I decided to transfer to Nebraska. My dad also encouraged me to make that decision because he liked coaches Devaney and Osborne very much.

Bob Terrio, a linebacker from Fullerton Junior College who was also transferring to Nebraska, and I drove back to Lincoln in Bob's Volkswagen Bug. The first day we arrived in Lincoln it was about 12 degrees below 0, and my mustache froze instantly. I had never been in weather below 50 degrees. I immediately thought I had made a mistake coming to Nebraska.

I remembered coach Osborne had a PhD in psychology, and I thought to myself, "He must have used all that psychology to get me to leave Southern California to come to Nebraska!"

A few days later, Bob and I reported to the field house to attend winter conditioning. In the winter of 1969, Nebraska implemented a winter conditioning program to "toughen up" the players. It consisted of 12 stations of about 10 minutes each of grueling drills and—let me tell you—it was pure hell. It was extremely difficult; I remember hearing someone throwing their guts up about halfway through the drills. It was my buddy, Bob Terrio, donating his lunch.

That conditioning program definitely toughened us up, and I bet we worked harder than any other team during that winter.

After my first spring practice session, I was on the third- or fourth-string, and I went home that summer intending to transfer again to another school. I had a very difficult time adjusting to the Nebraska system coming from junior college, and I admit that I was very frustrated.

When I told coach Devaney that I intended to transfer, he and coach Osborne called me almost every day and encouraged me to change my mind. I'm deeply grateful I did stay, because it would have been a huge mistake if I had left Nebraska.

103

By the end of summer camp, I had worked my way up to the second string. Then, about midway through the season, coach Devaney elevated me to the first string. My first start was on homecoming day against Iowa State, and we won 17–3.

The last game that year was against Oklahoma in Norman, and we had to win the game to be Big Eight champions. Remember that the year before, Oklahoma had beaten Nebraska 47–0. Plus, coach Devaney had never won before in Norman. Well, to put it mildly, we thrashed the Sooners, 44–14, with Jeff Kinney scoring three touchdowns.

I will never forget our locker room after that game. It was complete jubilation and we even tossed assistant coach Cletus Fischer into the showers.

I really believe that the Oklahoma game and our Sun Bowl victory over Georgia set the foundation for our championship run in 1970.

The 1969 season was also special, having a 9–2 record—especially after two previous 6–4 seasons. In fact, there were some businessmen who wanted coach Devaney fired after those two seasons. Thank God that did not happen because there would have been no national championships in 1970 and 1971.

Growing up, I had always wanted to play for USC badly because my idol was tackle Ron Yary, who played for USC and later for the Minnesota Vikings. I think every Southern California kid wants to play for USC. The coaches there called me once, but never followed up. When I called them later, they acted liked they had never heard of me.

So who did we play in the second game of the season during my senior year? That's right, USC—in the L.A. Coliseum. I had a special resentment against USC because I felt they slighted me during the recruiting process. So I had a special revenge motive that night, a game that ended in a 21–21 tie— the only blemish on our 11–0–1 record for 1970.

But even though we did not beat them, I felt I made my point and our offensive line had a great game against them.

The toughest opponent I faced during my senior year was Herb Orvis from the University of Colorado. One newspaper mentioned that we were a couple of Goliaths going after one another and that fans in the highest row in the stadium could hear our pads clash play after play that day. Herb was an ex-Marine and a few years older than me. (Herb and I continued our rivalry in professional football while he played for the Detroit Lions and I played with the Chicago Bears.)

Playing LSU in the 1971 Orange Bowl for the national championship will always be the most special memory of my football career.

It was a tough game, but we won, 17–12. LSU had the best defense in the nation that year and gave up only two touchdowns on the ground. We drove 80 yards on our first possession and scored a touchdown on a run by Joe Orduna. We wanted LSU to know we could run the football on anybody and no one intimidated us. It worked.

Ending my Nebraska career and winning the national championship in my last game was an incredible experience. I have a serigraph in my living room, painted by the famed artist Leroy Neiman, of Jerry Tagge scoring the winning touchdown. Winning Nebraska's first national championship was a great gift to the state of Nebraska.

I have to say that coach Devaney meant everything to me. He was like a father figure to me and I wanted to please him on that football field. He knew how to inspire us and he gave us confidence. I was insecure in many ways

Bob Newton (No. 74) leads Johnny Rodgers on a sweep against Oklahoma State in 1970.

when I was at Nebraska, but coach Devaney, coach Osborne, and line coach Carl Selmer worked with me until I developed my own confidence.

Coach Devaney also knew how to confront me to get the best out of me. I had a very poor game against Missouri my senior year, and after watching the films, he asked me, "Do you plan to play pro football?"

I answered, "Yes, sir."

He said, "If you ever have another game like that, you might as well forget pro ball."

The following week I was chosen Big Eight Lineman of the Week. (I later played 11 years in the NFL.) So you can say that simple talk from coach Devaney had a major impact on my football career.

Soon after my pro career was finished, I had to enter a treatment center for alcoholism in July 1983. I remember writing coach Osborne soon after I was admitted and telling him I had a severe problem, but I was trying to get help and do something about it. Coach Osborne immediately wrote me back with words of encouragement and support. In fact, he stated that once I got on my feet, he wanted me to come back and finish my undergraduate degree and work as a graduate assistant coach.

Six months later, I reenrolled at Nebraska as an undergraduate student at age 34, and two and half years later, I achieved my degree. Coach Osborne always put a high emphasis on education, and I think he was probably more proud of me going back to school at that age and achieving my degree than he was of all my football accomplishments. He has been very supportive throughout my recovery from alcoholism. He and coach Solich brought me back several times over the years to speak to Nebraska players about the dangerous effects of alcohol and other drugs.

My teammates were tremendous, and we had a very close team back then. We had great leadership from our cocaptains, Dan Schneiss and Jerry Murtaugh. I stay in touch with many of my former teammates at golf outings and alumni functions and phone calls during the year. I consider all my teammates at Nebraska to be family. And I remain close friends with Boyd Epley, who was a volunteer strength coach during my first year in 1969. Every Nebraska fan knows that Boyd later developed the best strength program in the nation.

Which brings me to the Cornhusker fans, who are fanatical in a good way. No matter where we played, we could always count on having thousands of our fans there with us. Nebraska fans are all over the world and they will let you know who the Cornhuskers are. The Nebraska fans have never forgotten the players on that first national championship team.

And as they say, "There is no place like Nebraska."

Playing football at Nebraska remains one of the greatest treasures in my life to this day.

Bob Newton was an All-American in 1970. He played 11 seasons in the NFL with the Chicago Bears and the Seattle Seahawks and was inducted into the Nebraska Football Hall of Fame in 1989.

The SEVENTIES

BILL KOSCH

DEFENSIVE BACK

1969–1971

Growing up in Columbus, Nebraska, my outlook as a boy was very simple—I loved sports. Almost all sports. And I still do. I went to Columbus Scotus High, a small Catholic school. We were a Class B school, and I played all the sports I could. I also played American Legion baseball in the summer. I still play basketball and slow-pitch softball to this day. But back to my high school days—our enrollment had dropped before our senior year, and they dropped us to Class C. It didn't look like we would have much in football because we were coming off an average season and lost some good players. But our team looked like a track team in shoulder pads—we were very small and very fast. We didn't pound on anybody, let me put it that way. We had about seven linemen and 25 backs on that team. But guess what? We ended up being state champs!

I was a typical small-town little guy, about 6'1" and 176 pounds, who nobody knew about. My high school coach put my name in for the Air Force Academy. And my only other offer came from Nebraska.

[Assistant coach] Clete Fischer showed up at my school, and we went back to the basketball coach's office to talk. We talked for about 15 minutes, and he asked me if I wanted to come to Lincoln to visit.

When I got there, I spent one hour looking at the stadium—I had never been there before—and I met with an engineering professor for a half hour.

I didn't know how good I was, and I didn't know how it would play out. But the Scarlet and Cream wanted me, and that's all that mattered.

I was still only 17 years old when I went to Lincoln as a freshman in 1968. I needed extra time to develop—psychologically and physically. We had about 42 freshmen scholarship players and another 20 or more walk-ons. It was obvious that we had a really good freshman team with such players as Jerry Tagge and Jeff Kinney. It was a special group. Monte Kiffin was our freshman coach, and he was such a fireball. His enthusiasm really spilled over onto us. We went 4–0 as a freshman team and then we were ready to compete for jobs on the varsity. Nebraska finished 6–4 in 1967 and 6–4 in 1968, and the coaches were under pressure.

I remember [assistant coach] John Melton telling a joke that, after Kansas State beat Nebraska 12–0 in 1968, a petition was going around Omaha to fire all the coaches. He added, "We signed it."

As a freshman, you were kind of kept away from coach Devaney. We were just dog food for the varsity. I never really met him until my sophomore year. But he was a very fair man. He never beat anybody up verbally; he attacked you on a team basis. Sometimes, he would pull you aside and tell you a joke. He always had a teacher's mentality, and what he told you lasted a lifetime. Bob really was the coach of the coaches. He was very well organized and scripted.

109

The angriest I ever saw him was during my junior year when we were tied with Missouri 7–7 at halftime The locker room was really quiet and all of a sudden, we heard something in the back of the room. It got louder and louder and it was like a crescendo building. Here's Bob walking from the back to the front, just patting guys and yelling, "Come on! Come on, we can do it!" He was really different during that halftime. I think he wanted to beat them so bad because they had beaten us the year before. I think we were so fired up that we ran out of the locker room before he was finished talking. We won 21–7.

Quite a few of our group began to make an impact as sophomores. I was a backup cornerback and safety, and I got a chance on some kickoff returns. I remember my first real action was at Minnesota [in the third game], and I felt like I was at the center of a bowl and everybody coming at me was running downhill while I was running uphill. I'll never forget that feeling. We started that year 2–2, losing to a great USC team 31–21 out in Los Angeles and to Missouri 17–7. After that, we never lost.

Bill Kosch (No. 24), here making an assisted tackle, anchored the free safety position for the Cornhuskers' 1970 and 1971 national championship teams.

You know how some teams don't have chemistry or don't gel at the right time, but have the talent? We were not that way—we were like a machine. All the parts came together and nobody worried if the other guy would do his job. He just did it, and we knew he would do it, whoever it was. We didn't celebrate our victories beyond reason, and it was just a given that we were going to win. We were so well prepared, and our coaching staff always did an excellent job. And we were well conditioned.

I worked hard as a football player. I worked hard in practice, and I felt like I was the quarterback of the defense. I could tell what a receiver was going to do from his stance. What we knew was that our second-string was better than most teams' first. If you handle practice, the games would be an awful lot of fun.

We had fun off the field, too. I got married after my junior season, stayed in Lincoln, and worked for the police department in the summertime. We had a program where the Lincoln Police Department hired a few players as patrolmen until fall camp started. We carried handcuffs, a gun, mace, the whole thing. We had one day of training and a couple of hours in the classroom, and then we were out there riding with other patrolmen.

I only had to unholster my gun once, and that was when an alarm went off at a store. We got the all-clear, and I put it back in the holster. I worked in the jail some days, and I probably looked like I was 15 at the time. When I served food to the prisoners, they let me have it verbally pretty good. I just kept my mouth shut and served their food. One time big John Adkins—we called him "Spider"—flipped on that siren and chased some guy down. We pulled up next to him, and it was the sheriff. We got into the station later, and there was the sheriff talking to some higher-ups. We kept our heads down and just kept walking, but Spider told him, "I clocked your butt doing 45."

Man, we were lucky we didn't get in trouble on that one. It was coach Devaney's program with the police, and we thought for sure he would be all over us, but nothing ever came of it. After all these years, it's pretty funny.

Now everyone always wants to know about the Game of the Century. I'll tell you about it. You know Oklahoma was always on our mind, and we were always on theirs. They loved to pound us, beating us 47–0 in 1968 when [Steve] Owens scored six touchdowns. And he was still in there at the end of the game. We loved to pound them, paying them back 44–14 the next year in Norman. We struggled to beat them in 1970 [28–21].

We respected them, but we didn't necessarily like them. So at the end of 1971, there we sat—No. 1 and 2 in the polls. We had 12 days to get ready for it, and that's all you heard about and all you read about.

Our defensive backfield—Jimmy Anderson, Dave Mason, Joe Blahak, and me—knew what each other thought all the time. Three of us were math majors, but Blahak was a physical education major, so we called him "airhead." But Joe could get beat and recover with his great speed. Jimmy was the slowest of us, but the smartest. He knew tendencies, down and distances, everything. We were a loose bunch, while the offense was more uptight. Coach Osborne was the receivers coach and he didn't like to screw around too much. He would give his receivers tests on the airplane on the way to road games while we would be joking around, having fun.

So on to the Game of the Century . . .

This is what many, many people never realized: I had played at free safety up until that game, and the coaches switched me and Joe for the Oklahoma game. I went to cornerback and he went to safety. We struggled all day, and unfortunately, that is why it became the Game of the Century.

For some reason, they had me playing 10 or 12 yards off the ball, head-up. I never felt good in that stance. I got beat twice for deep touchdowns. I kept telling them, "Let me play five [yards] off and jam him."

But they didn't. By the time the receiver got to me the way I was playing, I couldn't possibly turn and run with him. Now, I liked our quarterback Jerry Tagge, and I would take him over anyone, but [Oklahoma's] Jack Mildren would be second. I used to call him a grenade thrower, but on this day, he had a great game. Jack couldn't miss. My teammates never really said anything to me about the game and about getting beat so much, but Joe and I felt terrible about it. I am just so relieved we won. Can you imagine how I would feel if we had lost that game? I had nightmares about it, and we won the game!

112

I admit that it still bothers me to this day. When it comes to most touchdown passes, the fans see the result—which is a receiver scoring a touchdown and the number of the guy chasing him. Then they put their expletives on that number. People have kidded me about it, and I just try to laugh it off, but it hurt.

For years, [Oklahoma receiver] Jon Harrison said he had nightmares about the game because of a final bomb that went over his head. I remember that one because Joe came back to me and said, "I was beat." That was the play that Jon Harrison referred to that if he had caught one more pass, they would have pulled it out. Anyway, about 26 guys played really well, but Joe and I didn't. We were glad when it was over, but we didn't celebrate it much. Guys were going nuts in the locker room, snapping towels and shouting, but I just showered, dressed, and it was pretty cold. I walked back out onto the field as the sun was going down, looked around, and thanked God it was a victory [35–31].

Then I quietly got on the bus.

Joe and I lived in the same town, so over the years, we talked about it once in a while. The conversation I remember the most with coach Devaney was when he came up to me later and apologized for playing that defense that made me look terrible.

I just told him, "I accept your apology."

So we went down to the Orange Bowl to play Alabama for the national championship. Now earlier in the day, Colorado blew away Houston in a bowl game, and we had beaten Colorado badly [31–7]. Oklahoma made it look like a scrimmage against Auburn, beating them so bad. We said, "Man, Alabama had struggled with Auburn," so we wondered how good they were.

Then while we were warming up, I couldn't believe how small Alabama was. They seemed like our third-string practice guys. So the game starts and they weren't any faster than us, either. We were ahead 28–0 at the half [on the way to a 38–6 win]. It was easy. Bear Bryant said it best when he said, "That was absolutely the best team we have faced."

In the end, we had two national championship rings and had gone 33–2–1, plus those four freshman victories. We hadn't lost since the fourth game of our sophomore season, and I am highly proud of all of that. Our run was 31–0–1. Wow!

Once you play Nebraska football, it stays with you. It leaves an indelible mark on your life. We will go to our graves as Nebraska football players. The people here treat us like war heroes, and I feel very blessed to have experienced it all. I can still visualize myself as a little boy playing "kill the man with the football" in the front yard, making up names of the guys on the team. Something about this sport just makes you want to play. You find out if you are tough enough, fast enough, strong enough, and smart enough.

If Nebraska hadn't given me a scholarship, I don't know where I would have ended up. I don't feel like I am anything special and I don't act that way, but people still want to talk about my playing days. And I feel like I should share it as often as I can, because Nebraska is the fans' team. As the years go by, you see some of your teammates stricken with illness. You see coaches pass away. And with each one, it's no different than losing a family member.

Because Nebraska is our family.

113

Bill Kosch was named All–Big Eight in 1970 and 1971. His 95-yard interception return against Texas A&M in 1971 is tied as the longest in school history. Kosch, who had seven interceptions in 1970 and finished his career with 10, was inducted into the Nebraska Football Hall of Fame in 1997. His son Jesse punted for the Cornhuskers from 1995 to 1997.

JOE BLAHAK
DEFENSIVE BACK
1970–1972

I HAVE TO ADMIT THAT I WAS NOT A HUGE FOLLOWER of college football when I was growing up. I played sports and loved sports, but I wasn't much for watching them on television. At my junior high school in Columbus, Nebraska, we didn't even have a football team, but I ran track and played basketball. Then when I went to Columbus Scotus High, I started in football as a sophomore at running back and cornerback and played on all the kicking teams. I was pretty good in track, winning the state championship in the long jump at 23 feet. And I was fast. I probably could have received a track scholarship, but I had all the football schools after me.

I was about 5'9" and 172 pounds, but I could outrun almost everybody on the football field. My girlfriend was a year ahead of me, and she went to junior college for a year and had planned to transfer to wherever I went to college. So when Ara Parseghian of Notre Dame called me and offered a scholarship, I told him that he was offering it to the wrong person. I told him to offer it to my girlfriend because wherever she wanted to go, that's where I was going.

But I was from Nebraska and I liked the Nebraska coaches. Cletus Fisher was my brother's high school coach and he recruited me, and of course, coach Devaney was a genuine guy. He always had a smile on his face—well, almost always. I'll get to his other side later. So it was just a natural that I would go to Nebraska.

I never made any visits to other football schools, but I was in Lincoln quite a bit for our track meets and saw enough of the university to know it was the place for me. I remember my first experience at Nebraska in an early freshman practice. Our locker rooms were on the east side of the north end, while the varsity was on the west side of the north end. We were waiting for practice one day, and the varsity was walking through. I saw Larry Jacobson and Dave Walline—they were just huge guys—and I thought, "Oh my God, what did I get myself into? Is this really for me?"

We had a lot of great talent in my class. Guys such as Johnny Rodgers, Richie Glover, and many others who were high school All-Americans. What is amazing is that freshman team lost a game—and it wasn't to Kansas State or Iowa State or another Big Eight program. It was to McCook Junior College. That is unbelievable when you think back on it, but upsets happen. What I had going was my speed—I was faster than Johnny in straightaway speed, although he won't admit that. He was quicker laterally. I ran a 40 in about 4.4, and I settled in at cornerback.

Going into our sophomore year, 1970, I had a gold shirt, which was the second-team defense. Everybody in the state knows the first team wears the black shirts. Our first game was against Wake Forest, and I found out later that I would have started from the beginning, but I broke curfew. It wasn't by accident—my brother had been in the service and I hadn't seen him in years. I asked for permission to break curfew and go home to see him, and the coaches said no. So I just left and accepted the punishment when I got back—it was extra running.

115

The starter at cornerback was John Decker. I didn't start the first game, but I had a great game in relief of John. I was quicker and faster than John and I was a hitter, and I think the coaches knew it and could see it in that first game. Coach Devaney believed it didn't matter what class you were in—if you were a better player, you played. As we went to practice on Monday to prepare for our game at USC, coach [Warren] Powers told me, "Go get a black shirt." I just said, "Cool, this is the greatest thing in the world!"

So there I was, starting against O.J.'s school and Mike Garrett's school. I mean, this was USC! And it would be in the L.A. Coliseum. I remember that day at the hotel in California: I was nervous as heck. I was actually only nervous in two games in my whole life. They were this game at USC and the Game of the Century, which I will get to later.

For the USC game, we came out of the locker room first and walked down the ramp that leads to the field at the L.A. Coliseum. I really had a case of the nerves, and I could just feel the ground shaking. Here came USC, and they were huge. I turned to Dick Rupert, who was standing next to me, and I told him, "We are going to get killed!" There was this big roar as USC ran out, and then we ran out, and I heard it get even louder. There was red everywhere and that's when I learned how well Nebraska fans travel. I thought, "This is just amazing." After the game started, I settled down and soon got my first career interception, but I returned it 12 yards and fumbled. We should have won that game, but we had a bad snap on a late field goal attempt and it ended in a 21–21 tie. A lot of the seniors considered that a loss, and we really should have beaten them that night, but the younger guys felt pretty good about it.

As the season wore on, we didn't lose. I remember Dave Walline knocked out Missouri's Joe Moore with a huge hit that separated his shoulder. Against Kansas State, I had three interceptions of Lynn Dickey. We beat Oklahoma and went on to play LSU in the Orange Bowl. As it turned out, it would be for the national championship since Stanford had beaten [No. 2] Ohio State and No. 1 Texas had lost. It was in this game that I got to see Bob Devaney's other side. And man, I will never, ever forget it.

LSU had Buddy Lee as the starting quarterback and then Bert Jones came off the bench. I don't remember which one was in at quarterback at this time, but we had them in a third-and-33 hole. I was pretty aggressive at times, and they ran a route in which the outside receiver ran a hook, and the inside receiver ran an out-and-up. We were in a three-deep zone at the time, and I jumped the short route. I was thinking "interception return for a touchdown, game MVP" and all that, and all of a sudden, the quarterback pumped it once and lobbed it over my head. The guy caught it, and Billy Kosch tackled him after they had picked up about 34 yards. We later stopped them on that drive. When I came off the field, I ran a long way down the sideline so I wouldn't have to go near the coaches. [Linebacker] Jerry Murtaugh just scared the hell out of me—I mean, he still does—and he came over to me and screamed, "Don't ever do that again!" But as I sat there, if you ever watched *The Ten Commandments* when the sea parts, that is what happened next. Out of the corner of my eye, I could see the sea of players on our sideline parting. Down the middle came that small, angry Irishman, otherwise known as coach Devaney. He came up to me, grabbed my facemask and put his face right

Joe Blahak (No. 27), here making a tackle against Minnesota, was one of the fastest players in Nebraska history.

down in front of mine. "You #$&★@!" he screamed. "If you ever do that again, you will never touch the football field again!"

I wish I could tell you what he called me, but it would be unprintable. Coach [John] Melton then came by and said, "He meant it, Airhead!" That was my nickname—"Airhead." Let me just say that I never got beat on that route again.

I had gotten married the week after the Oklahoma game, so our honeymoon was that Orange Bowl. Several of the players were married, and we hung out together with our wives. John O'Connell, John Kinsel, Phil Harvey, and Donnie McGhee were all married at the time and had their wives there. Here we were in Miami, with two extra days after the game and we were national champions. Nebraska fans were everywhere. You can say that we just had a blast. We went down to the Fountainbleu Hotel to see the Temptations play, and we got seats right near the stage. I remember when they brought the mike down to us and we sang "Psychedelic Shack" with them. We were having the time of our lives. We were up all night after the Orange Bowl, having a few drinks—we even had a beer or two with the coaches, and you could never do that today. Then we had a fishing trip the next day. As soon as our boat got past the jetties and into those waves, guys were hanging over the boat. I think we caught one fish.

As 1971 started, we never thought about losing. Ever. It just never entered our minds that we would even lose one game. We just went out and did our jobs and moved forward. We won all of our games and so did Oklahoma.

By the time it got down to the Game of the Century, it was billed as the "immovable object" versus the "irresistible force." They had the leading offense in the nation. We had the leading defense. I admit that when we got to that game, a lot of us were nervous. I know that I was. The weeks leading up to it—that's all you heard about. On that day in Norman, it was overcast and cool. It was my kind of weather. We had noticed that Missouri had made a switch on their defense when they played Oklahoma and had some success with it, so the coaches decided to switch me and [safety] Bill Kosch. They thought I was a better tackler than Billy and that it might be better against the wishbone. I wished it would have never happened that way, but Billy really had a rough day. The switch wasn't fair to him because he was out of position. And Jack Mildren threw a lot of ducks up there, but guys were running wide open.

That game had probably the greatest punt return in college football history, and everyone has seen it on film about 100 times by now. I remember it this way: Johnny Rodgers caught the punt and made Greg Pruitt miss right away—just put a move on him that made Pruitt look like an idiot. I go up through the hole with Johnny and I take off. Johnny cuts to his left, and I saw that Jon Harrison was going to catch him and tackle him. I peeled back, blocked Harrison squarely from the side, and fell on top of him right in front of the Oklahoma bench. They were all screaming, "Clip! Clip! Clip!" I got up and asked, "Did they throw a flag?" Somebody answered, "No." I said, "Well, it wasn't a clip then." It was the most phenomenal runback I had ever seen.

After we won that game, it was like a huge weight off our shoulders. It was amazing—just like we had dreamed about. When we came back to Lincoln, the plane couldn't even land because fans had knocked down a fence and were running around out there. I was just trying to find my wife after we landed, and there were so many people there. It was wild. It just seemed like the entire city was at the airport.

Then we went to the Orange Bowl to play the next No. 2 team, Alabama. That game wasn't played against Alabama, it was played against Bear Bryant. That game was payback for coach Devaney, who had lost to him a few times [1966 Orange Bowl and 1967 Sugar Bowl]. We just dominated them from start to finish [a 38–6 Nebraska win] and won our second straight national championship.

I really think the 1971 team had more talent up and down the line than the 1970 team. But the 1970 team probably had more experience. Let's put it this way—those were two great football teams.

And we had lasting friendships. After games, we would get together and play charades with the married crowd. I mean, we didn't have any money, so we had to have some cheap entertainment. That was the best part of being on those teams and something that I will never forget. But it would change.

In 1972, we had a pretty good team, but we had a change in leadership. To put it bluntly, we just didn't have the leaders we had had before, and as a senior, I was as guilty as anyone. We had Dave Humm at quarterback, but he was inexperienced, so it wasn't his fault. But we had little chemistry and we had issues that tore the team apart. All the players on that team know what they are to this day, but I won't name names. It was kind of disappointing, not because of our record [9–2–1], but because we didn't have the camaraderie and friendship we had before. We didn't do things together as a team, either. I was disappointed for coach Devaney, because we didn't send him out the way we would have wanted. Coach Devaney had been passing hints about retirement, and when he did announce it, I don't think we were surprised.

There is no more coach Devaney, no more coach Osborne. The game of college football has become a business, and I truly regret that. Something has been lost. I see guys standing over other players and taunting. I see too much celebrating. Coach Devaney taught us, "If you knock them down, help them up!" There always will be that tradition, but I don't see it as a game any longer.

Nebraska football became a family for me. To experience the success we had—that's what made it really special. How many teams can say they won back-to-back national championships? And we played in one of the most monumental games in football history. It was great and was something I will always cherish. Pro football was a business, but college football was family and it was fun. Because of that, I love Nebraska and always will.

Joe Blahak was named All–Big Eight in 1971 and 1972. He had three interceptions against Kansas State in 1970—one of three players to hold the Nebraska single-game record for interceptions. He played for five seasons in the NFL and was inducted into the Nebraska Football Hall of Fame in 1990.

LARRY JACOBSON
DEFENSIVE TACKLE
1969–1971

I WAS FROM THE BIGGEST CITY IN THE STATE OF SOUTH DAKOTA—Sioux Falls—and anything that happened in the state happened there. I played football and basketball at O'Gorman High School. I was 6'6" and about 220 pounds, so naturally I played center in basketball, and we were first in the state my junior year. I had started from my sophomore season, and most of the state schools like South Dakota and South Dakota State wanted me for basketball.

In football, I made trips to visit Minnesota, Iowa, Kansas State, and one of the western schools, I can't remember which one. I signed a Big 10 letter of intent to go to Iowa, which meant that locked me into the Hawkeyes if I was to end up in the Big 10. But it wasn't binding nationally. It turned out that Nebraska was recruiting a kid from another high school in Sioux Falls, and I blocked a punt and had a bunch of tackles in the game against that school. I guess that must have gotten their attention.

When I visited Lincoln, I'll never forget that coach Devaney gave me his wife's car for the weekend. It was a 1968 red Bonneville convertible with white leather. Another time, I came down with a Nebraska booster who lived in Sioux Falls, and when we were driving back home, I was calling people on his car phone. You know, there weren't many of those back then, so that was amazing to me. I was from a small school, so all of these things during recruiting were pretty overwhelming.

The night before national signing day, [Nebraska assistant coach] Monte Kiffin came up to see me at my high school. We left from the back area of the school and drove around the corner where we saw one of the assistants from Iowa sitting there in his car waiting on me. He spotted us, then followed us in traffic in Sioux Falls, until Monte drove down in the snaky places of town and lost him. The Iowa coach then went out to the house to talk to my mother. When we got home, coach Kiffin went out back to play croquet with my sister while I talked to this coach from Iowa.

Kiffin told me, "Coach Devaney says I can't go back to Lincoln until I have your name on the line." It's about a three-and-a-half hour drive to Lincoln, so I signed with Nebraska.

I admit, I didn't realize what the hell a Cornhusker was.

Nebraska wasn't that big to me back then. Seeing the stadium and locker room was pretty tame to what the school has now. But playing at a big school like Nebraska was what I wanted to try. I thought, "If I don't try the big time, I will never make it in the big time." I just figured if I didn't make it, I could go somewhere else later.

But right away, I liked the coaches. Coach Devaney was very easy to get along with and all the coaches were always cracking jokes, having fun. That is the biggest reason players pick where to go to school—do they like the coaches? I did. And they made it fun for us.

It was fun learning a new system in college and practicing on those nice grass fields. It was always fun being around Monte Kiffin, who coached the freshman team. He would be practicing us at a normal pace, then they would bring high school coaches in to watch practice, and he would work the living crap out of us. As soon as they left, he would go back to a normal practice. Our class got along really well, too. It was not a team of stars, and we didn't have any cliques on that team, but we always got a great team effort out of everybody. There was John "Spider" Adkins, whose dad was a garbage collector, but I think John is a doctor now. There was Bill Janssen, who was from North Dakota, so we got along really well.

In my sophomore year, I became a starter [at defensive tackle] after Dave Walline got hurt—he blew a knee out against Kansas State with just a few games left in the season. I remember at the end of the season, Devaney came in and said we could play in the Liberty Bowl or the Sun Bowl. He asked, "Is there anybody here who doesn't want to go to Memphis?" All the black players put their hands up. Not many people wanted to go to the Sun Bowl, either, but Larry Frost, who is Scott Frost's dad, said he wanted the coaches to leave so he could talk to the team. So Larry got up and gave this really emotional speech that went something like, "Let's go to a bowl and be proud of Nebraska and be proud to go to a bowl game and play well and win the game!"

After that, everybody voted to go to the Sun Bowl [El Paso, Texas] to play Georgia. We get down there, and they didn't have one black player on their team. They had made a few comments about the state of race relations, you could say. We got to a function with both teams, and Georgia was all dressed up in their little sports coats and ties. We were dressed in just regular clothes. One of the Georgia players got up and said, "We hope you have a good game and we wish you a lot of luck" and so on—all the usual, polite stuff. Then Bob Liggett, one of our defensive tackles, got up and held his thumb up. He just said, "You know where that's at!" We were just howling with laughter.

A few of our guys happened to go over the border to Juarez and got in trouble for peeing in the street. The cops picked them up and threw them in jail, which sent Devaney into a rage. I didn't play much in that game because I had gotten hurt, but I remember after the game [a 45–6 Nebraska win], the coaches bought a keg of beer and put it by the pool. We sure had a lot of fun on that trip, and you could say we were all glad we voted to go down there.

As a junior, I became a full-time starter. I remember we were playing at Minnesota [a 35–10 Nebraska win] and they ran a play around end, right in front of our bench. I missed the tackle, and Devaney jerked me right out of the game. My high school coach and my parents had made the trip to the game, and boy was I hot. But he put me back in, and I didn't screw up after that. Later that season, I intercepted a screen pass against Iowa State and ran it back a long way.

We ran the table down to the final game, heading into the Orange Bowl against LSU. I know we expected to win that game, especially after the teams above us [Texas and Ohio State] had lost. Bert Jones had a pretty good game for LSU, but it came down to Jerry Tagge sticking the ball over the goal line for us. And then Bob Terrio, whose father was a pit boss in Las Vegas, made the big interception to secure the game for us. After the game, we were all holding our fingers in the air to signal we were No. 1. And that's the photo of me, Bill Janssen, and Bob Terrio that appeared on the cover of *Sports Illustrated* the next week.

Following the 1970 season, I got a job as a roughneck on an oil well in California, a place called Geyserville. Let me tell you, that is a hard way to

Larry Jacobson, who won the Outland Trophy in 1971, bears down on the quarterback.

make a living. We were drilling 7,500 feet down. I was a worm. It was all physical stuff. You put pipes into the hole, took pipes out of the hole, changed the drill bits, and drilled. . . . It just made me realize how important it was for me to get my accounting degree. After that type of work, it was good to get back to Lincoln for fall camp.

In 1971, we were coming off our first national championship, and we knew we had a good nucleus of players coming back. There weren't too many seniors from that 1970 team who had left and we had Johnny Rodgers coming up, so we just had a feeling we would win them all. We were justified to think that way because nobody came close to us until we got to the Game of the Century. The whole thing, the whole season, was just a massive build-up for Oklahoma.

The week before the Oklahoma game, Monte Kiffin called me and said I won some award called the Outland Trophy. I said, "What the hell is that?" He tried explaining it to me. I even told him to spell Outland and he did. I knew I had a good season—I had made All–Big Eight Lineman of the Week two or three times, but the year before I didn't even make all-conference.

The thing is, it was a team effort. We had a heck of a line—Rich Glover, Bill Janssen, Spider Adkins—just a heck of a defensive line. We had some real characters on that team, guys from all over and from all different backgrounds. For example, Jimmy Branch, our middle linebacker, was from a gang in Chicago. And all together, it was a great, great defense.

So everything had built up toward that one game. We knew Oklahoma was rolling. They knew we were rolling. We were both rolling toward each other. We were confident and well prepared for that game, it was just a question of whether we could execute or not. There was so much build-up and so much publicity for it that our legs were like rubber in the first quarter. There was just so much emotion. My shoulders were heavy. You just wanted to play the damn game and get it over with.

We were so worried about their running game, and all they did was pass the ball all day. I think Rich had 22 tackles and I had about 16. After a while, they couldn't run to my side, so they quit trying. On the option, we would just grab the fullback and throw him down every time. Rich was so quick that he would catch the option from behind. So they had to throw the ball, and [Oklahoma quarterback Jack] Mildren just got several passes off right before he got hit. I remember we ran Jeff Kinney so much that he didn't have any jersey left by the end of the game. Then Jerry [Tagge] made that great play on that third-and-13 throw that kept the drive alive. As our offense was driving for the winning touchdown when we were trailing [31–28], I was just thinking, "Don't get it done too quick." But our offensive line played so well, Oklahoma couldn't stop them.

On Oklahoma's final possession, I got one sack, and then on fourth down, I got right by my guy and I went flying at Mildren. He gave me a little juke and side-stepped me, and my momentum took me by him—but Rich knocked down his pass. All I could think about was recovering the ball. I was trying to find the ball, but of course, it was an incomplete pass! I should have had a sack on that damn play! I missed him, but it forced him to take some extra time, which allowed Rich to get free and knock the pass down. Poor Bill Kosch—Bill and Joe Blahak had switched positions. It really wasn't his fault, but he had a rough day covering people. I remember after the game, Devaney said he was happy we won the game for the team, but he added "thank God we won the game for Bill Kosch." It was really a relief not only to beat Oklahoma, but to have the game behind us.

It is really too bad everybody doesn't get to experience that feeling at least once in their lives. It was such total elation. Everybody got thrown into the showers after the game, and then the plane couldn't even make it into the terminal [in Lincoln] because there were so many fans there. It seemed everybody came to the airport. We went to Little Bo's that night, and let's just say that we didn't have to buy any drinks all night.

After an easy game and fun trip to Hawaii, we went to the Orange Bowl to play Alabama. I remember they had a guard named John Hanna, who later played a long time in the NFL. Hanna just tried to cut me [block below the waist] on every damn play. He was a great player, but I could get by him pretty easily, and we beat the hell out of them in that game [38–6] to win the championship again. It wasn't even a game.

Earlier, Rich and I had to fly to New York to appear on the *Bob Hope Show* for All-Americans, and nobody was there to pick us up at the airport. So Glover's dad had to pick us up. Then we got to the show, and we were supposed to bring our jerseys and helmets, but nobody told us. So they hustled to some shop, got two jerseys, and put some tape on them for our numbers. Then they got two white helmets and put red tape to make the N on them.

Later, some of us got to fly to Washington to meet with President Nixon. The day we were flying to D.C. was also the day of the NFL Draft. As we were on the way in to meet Nixon, Jerry [Tagge] found out he was drafted by Green Bay. Then they would pass us notes during the meeting with Nixon. They passed Jeff Kinney a note that he got drafted by Kansas City, and I got a note I was drafted by the Giants. Devaney stayed over in Washington, and when we flew home in this private plane, we raided the bar on the way back to celebrate our arrival into the NFL. Now that was a great time.

Bob Devaney was a great, great guy. He loved to have fun, too. He loved to have a beer. During practice, he would take his little golf cart around the field and check in, and he would let his assistant coaches coach. But on Saturday, there was no doubt who was in charge. He made all the decisions.

I have so many fond memories of Nebraska, but a lot of my mementoes didn't make it with my memories. During the 1996 Fiesta Bowl, while Nebraska was whipping Florida for the national championship, a fire started at my cabin. I had put some ashes in a garbage can that day at about 4:00. At about 10:00, they caught fire and then my sauna caught fire. Then it got my house, which was cedar. I was at home watching the game at the time, and after I called 911, they put me on hold. I then called the operator, got through, hung up, and waited for the fire department while my house was burning. I couldn't do anything about it, so I went next door and watched the game with my neighbor as my house burned. I tried to get out what I could, but I lost my Outland Trophy and my jersey [No. 75], which Nebraska had retired. Fortunately, my national championship rings survived. And fortunately, I had good insurance and now I have a really nice house on the lake here in South Bend, Nebraska. Later, I got my Outland replaced.

It was an awful night, but at least we whipped Florida to win another national championship.

As I look back on my time at Nebraska, I ask, "What more could I have done?" As an athlete, my dream was to play major college football on a winning team. It may sound conceited to say this, but we won two national championships, I won the Outland, and I was the 23rd overall pick of the NFL Draft. I am the only national award winner ever from South Dakota.

Like I say, what more could I have done?

127

Larry Jacobson was an All-American and won the Outland Trophy in 1971, becoming Nebraska's first major award winner. As a senior, he recorded 73 tackles, including 12 for losses. He also was an Academic All-American in 1971. Jacobson, who played four seasons with the New York Giants, was inducted into the Nebraska Football Hall of Fame in 1979.

DAVE HUMM

QUARTERBACK

1972–1974

I WAS BORN AND RAISED IN LAS VEGAS and grew up on the west side, when there were twenty-five thousand people here, and now it has grown to a major city of 1.5 million, so I have seen a huge change in my hometown. I went to 12 years of Catholic school and played sports at Bishop Gorman High School. I played baseball, and they tried to make me a wide receiver in football, but then the coaches asked about what other sports I played. I told them I was a pitcher. They said, "Well then, try out for quarterback." My first dream was to go to UCLA and play quarterback for the Bruins because, while living in Las Vegas, UCLA was the team on TV all the time.

I have to say that I really enjoyed my recruiting process, except for maybe the trip to Notre Dame. Getting recruited when you lived in Las Vegas was a great thing because you got to see a lot of great shows when coaches came to town. We were going to a different casino and a different show every night with whatever coach came to town. For example, I went to see a show with Bear Bryant and Joe Namath. My dad worked 25 years at Caesar's Palace, and when he got off work, coaches would be lined up to have coffee with him.

Now, about that Notre Dame trip: we flew into Chicago and it was snowing. Then we got to South Bend and got snowed in at the dorm. I saw Ara Parseghian for about 15 minutes, and then we got snowed in again before we could leave. I said, "Lord, you have to be kidding—all this snow? And they want me to come here?"

The next week, my trip was to Lincoln and it was 70 degrees. Coach Devaney said, "Don't believe what other people tell you about Nebraska weather—the weather here is not that bad."

I went to Alabama and Joe, right after he beat the Colts in Super Bowl III, was one of my hosts there, and he has been a good friend since. But I said, "Alabama is too far from home." Then I considered Colorado and Kansas State, where Lynn Dickey was my host. Coach Devaney told me, "Those are two wonderful universities, and there is only one downside to them—they each play us once a year!" I thought that was great. I visited UCLA and my host was [Heisman Trophy winner] Gary Beban, who was one of my idols when I was growing up. But UCLA had no training table, and you ate in a cafeteria.

All of those schools had great facilities, but Nebraska had a great training table, the weight room, and the trophy rooms, and you can see the stadium from about anywhere in town. When you went to Lincoln, all the restaurants had Husker signs and players' pictures on the walls. Coach Devaney and [assistant] coach [John] Melton came to my home and never talked to me— they recruited Mom and Dad. Mom would always say, "Coach Devaney and coach Melton are so nice!"

129

The people, the facilities, the coaches—Nebraska just won me over. It was the place for me.

When I got to Nebraska, I remember that first orientation when the coaches talked to us. Coach Devaney told us, "Now all of our phone numbers are in the telephone book, so if you need to talk to us, give us a call anytime." I thought that was tremendous.

Back then, you could sign 40 freshmen and there were about 125 freshmen total with all the walk-ons. Coach Devaney had told me I was the quarterback of the future. What he didn't tell me was there were six other quarterbacks of the future in my class. I asked coach [Jim] Ross if I could talk to coach Devaney and he said, "Yeah, you can talk to him . . . in two years." That was the life of a freshman. We played four freshman games and I passed for something like 900 yards in those four games, and we won them all. We were wide open, running three wides [receivers], and we threw it a ton. In 1971— that was my redshirt freshman year—I dressed and was on the sideline for every game, which included the Game of the Century against Oklahoma. It was an amazing thing, and you didn't realize until it was all over, but history has shown how great that team was.

That is when I got the feeling of how Nebraska fans are, to see them stand and applaud just the effort from football players—not the outcome, but the effort. It is too difficult to describe what it is like to run onto field at Memorial Stadium for the first time.

After the 1971 season, Jerry Tagge was gone and the [quarterback's] job was mine to have. And guess who we started the 1972 season against? That's right—UCLA. In Los Angeles. But it was a killer for me because it was my first start, and I didn't play that well [a 20–17 loss, ending Nebraska's 32-game non-losing streak]. We had entered the game ranked No. 1 and we lost right out of the gate.

I knew then it was time to buckle up and go play. It was a rough week back in Lincoln, let me put it that way. When you play this game, you are not going to win them all, but back in Nebraska, you think about winning them all. But the next week, I had a good game against Texas A&M [a 37–7 win] and from then on, I felt comfortable. We had a pretty good year and then beat Notre Dame [40–6] in the Orange Bowl. I still have people in my church upset, first, for not going to Notre Dame, and second, for beating them so badly. It would turn into coach Devaney's final game.

130

He had told me when he recruited me that he would be there for my four years. He called me into his office when he announced his retirement and said, "Now I know I told you I would be here for your entire career, but I really want to step down right now. The time is right." I told him, "What am I going to do, tell you that you can't [retire]?" I thanked him for what he did for me, and I loved that man so much. He did so much for me and he taught me so much. Bob even said, "I will lose Tom if I don't step down now." He knew coach Osborne was young enough that he was ready for a head coaching job and he probably would have taken one somewhere. He wanted him to stay at Nebraska. It was a shock to me that coach Devaney retired, but Tom Osborne was my position coach and I had spent more time with him. So when he was promoted to head coach, I already knew the man. I just didn't know the offense would change that much.

I knew from the time I saw coach Osborne drawing the line [of quarterback movement] sideways, instead of straight back when he drew up a play, that it wouldn't be the wide-open offense we had before. He was drawing up option plays, saying, "Dave, you can do this." I would say, "I am not an option guy." I just wanted to toe the rubber and drop back five or seven [steps] and let it fly. But coach Osborne had a different offense in mind. But

Dave Humm, here running the option, holds most of Nebraska's career passing records.

remember, I always had the audible available to me! I would audible to a pass and come over to the sideline, and coach Osborne would get so mad at me. He would say, "Dadgummit!" shake his head, turn, and walk away.

Even though our offense changed, I never really thought about transferring. My little brother had come to Nebraska and—NCAA rules allowed this then—we had "Husker families," and I was very, very close to mine. I was happy in Lincoln, so why would I go anywhere else? In Lincoln, they called me "Dave the Dealer." I mean, I was from Las Vegas. My hair touched my collar and I wore different colored pants and my shoes weren't always black. Come on, a kid from Las Vegas playing quarterback in the Midwest? They never mentioned my name without my hometown. My hair would just poke out of my helmet a little and they would say, "Another completion from that long-haired kid from Vegas."

We had lost a lot of seniors from that 1972 team, guys like Johnny Rodgers, Rich Glover, and our center, Doug Dumler, so we didn't know what to expect. I had a knee injury in camp before the 1973 season and missed the opening game [a 40–13 win over UCLA]. I came back for the second game and we beat North Carolina State, and then Wisconsin and Minnesota. In the next game, we trailed Missouri [13–6] and scored a touchdown at the end of the game to make it 13–12. We went for a two-point conversion to win the game—I rolled out, but we didn't complete it, and we lost by a point.

It was a tough media town. Nebraska had won back-to-back national championships in 1970 and 1971, and then we went 9–2–1 in 1972 and had two losses in 1973 after Oklahoma shut us out [27–0]. The Oklahoma defense was unbelievable. All I can say about Oklahoma is I was tired of seeing Lucious, LeRoy, and Dewey—otherwise known as the Selmons—by the end of my career.

Early in my senior year, we went to Wisconsin. Tom had called an option, and like a dope I ran it and got a bad hip pointer. I was out in the second quarter [of a 21–20 loss], and I remember Tom telling me, "You ran it to the wrong side." We won seven of our next eight and got to Oklahoma at the end of the season as usual. They were ranked No. 1, but we were leading them 14–7 at halftime. But they took over in the second half and beat us. Again. This time the score was 28–14. We had our chances to beat them, but just didn't. There is no feeling like losing to a rival like Oklahoma, and we never beat them in my three years of playing quarterback. You don't understand what it did to the state when we lost to Oklahoma. It was depressing. It is still depressing. It doesn't get any easier with time, either. It is with me right now.

I have to say that of all the football I played, including all those years in the NFL, there are two guys who could come up with a game plan and make adjustments and study film and so on above all the rest: Tom Flores with the Raiders and coach Osborne at Nebraska. Coach Osborne was just a great educator, a brilliant guy. He was better than any of those coaches in the NFL. He really was.

Anyway, we went down to the Sugar Bowl to play Florida in my final game, and I just didn't play well [2-of-12, 16 yards]. My whole senior year was an emotional time for me, but that game really was emotional. At the end of your career, it is an emotional time for every player. When it was all over and we beat Florida [13–10], coach Osborne came to my room and he said, "I love you. We have been through a lot together and I really want to thank you." We are good friends to this day.

When the Southern Nevada Sports Hall of Fame formed, they made me the first inductee and they called Al Davis and Tom Osborne to be presenters. The chairman said, "You have good friends. We called each, and in seconds, they said 'We'll be there.'" Well, on the day of the ceremony, coach Devaney died. But Tom got up and spoke and Al Davis got up for me—that's the kind of loyalty those people show.

I just loved playing this game of football. I played 19 years at all levels and in those 19 years, when I walked into the locker room and saw my jersey and shoulder pads hanging there, I never once was not in awe of what I was doing. I would think, "OK, don't let them see your smile." I never took it for granted.

Likewise, my memories of Nebraska are so great. I still talk to a ton of guys I played with there. Just look at the tradition. Look at the 40 years of nine or more wins each season. Look at the Heisman winners. Look at the national championships. My whole experience there was so incredible. Knowing I was a part of the whole deal makes me proud. Very proud and humbled.

Let me end it this way: if I had to make the decision of where to attend college all over again, I would be back at Nebraska before dark tonight.

Dave Humm, a cocaptain in 1974, was an All-American and finished fifth in the Heisman Trophy voting during his senior season. He holds Nebraska school records for passing yards (5,035), attempts (637), and completions (353). His 15 consecutive completions against Kansas in 1974 also remains a school record. Humm played 10 seasons in the NFL, including seven with the Oakland/Los Angeles Raiders. He is a member of the Nebraska Football Hall of Fame. Humm, who was diagnosed with multiple sclerosis in 1988, currently works on the Oakland Raiders' radio network as an analyst.

JUNIOR MILLER
TIGHT END
1977–1979

ONE OF MY FIRST MEMORIES OF COMPETITION while growing up in Midland, Texas, was racing in the streets with no shoes. If you got beat, you got talked about, and I didn't want to be talked about for getting beat. I played basketball and football at Midland Lee High School, and it seemed everybody wanted me to stick with basketball in college. Paul Stuckler was our basketball coach, and when the football coach asked me to come out, coach Stuckler was mad about it. He didn't want me to get hurt playing football. We went 33–3 in basketball my junior year and went to the state tournament. I was 6'4" and weighed about 215, playing in the post, but I had a football-type of attitude. I pushed and shoved in there and was very aggressive. I could go outside and shoot, too.

Mom worked for Mayflower, the moving company, and I had this Mayflower box filled with recruiting letters from basketball programs. I wouldn't open them, I would just look at the envelope and throw them into the box to show the other kids. I was getting letters from basketball programs like UCLA, Kentucky, everybody.

In football, I played tight end on offense and linebacker on defense, and I began to get noticed when we played Odessa Permian and their star was Daryl Hunt, who went on to play at Oklahoma. In that game, I started making tackles sideline-to-sideline. One time, when I was a junior, Nebraska assistant coach Jerry Moore, who recruited the state of Texas, came to town to see Keith Bishop, one of my teammates who was a year older. [Keith signed with Nebraska, but later transferred to Baylor.] When he watched film of Keith, he accidentally saw me. "Who is this big kid?" coach Moore asked.

Coach Stuckler wanted me to go to college on a basketball scholarship and I liked basketball. But I loved football. I loved the physical part of it. Gosh, man, I loved to hit. I loved to get hit. I loved to run over people. I loved to tackle people.

So it came down to three schools. Texas Tech and Kentucky wanted me to play both sports. Nebraska wanted me for football. I first visited Texas Tech and loved it. The people were awesome. It was a beautiful campus, full of colors, and it was right down the street from home. Mom wanted me to go there really bad. When I came home from my visit, there was this big businessman in Midland who was a Texas Tech man. He called me and invited me to his office. As I stood there in front of his desk, he pulled out the letter of intent and 10 one-hundred dollar bills.

He looked up and told me, "Junior, if you sign this letter, you can walk out of here with this $1,000."

I looked at the paper and then I looked at the money. You know, that was a lot of money back then. My mom was raising seven kids by herself and she never made much money. I don't know what made me say it, but I told him, "I have two more visits to make and I really want to wait to make my decision."

135

I got home and told Mom about it, and she said, "Boy, why didn't you take that money?"

Then I visited Kentucky and I loved it. It was a beautiful campus and the people were nice. There was an older guy there associated with the program who went by the name "the Colonel." I can't remember his real name. So "the Colonel" took me out to his house, this big, beautiful house. He pulled out the letter of intent, and asked, "Have you made a decision?"

I told him I hadn't. He said, "See this big old house you are standing in? You can stay in this house and you can drive that fancy car in the driveway if you sign this letter." I told him, "I have one more school to visit and I am not ready to make a decision yet."

Then I went to visit Nebraska. Just like the other two schools, I loved it, too. The people were great. It was obvious to me from the beginning that they loved their Husker football. I loved everything about it, but more important, they didn't offer me anything. They didn't even tell me I would play. They offered me a scholarship and they offered me the opportunity to

Tight end Junior Miller cuts upfield after hauling in one of his 55 career receptions.

play. That impressed me so much. They wanted me for who I was and it was up to me. I really appreciated that. I told my mom I had made my decision, but she didn't like it.

When coach Osborne came down to visit me earlier, I remember it like it was yesterday. He wasn't the first white guy who ever had been to our house, but he was the first one to sit down and talk. The others had been service men and people like that who would come, fix something, and go. It was strange, seeing this big, tall white guy with red hair and his red face. It was different than seeing the white guys in the South, who are all tanned. The first thing I noticed about him was how slowly and eloquently he talked. I could tell that he was talking from the heart. The first time I met him, I really liked him. I liked his honesty. He was very sincere and I could tell he was real.

So I passed on the money, passed on the house and the car, and I became a Cornhusker.

I had worked some in Midland, so I had money to buy this Chevette—a three-speed with big ol' wide tires. I loaded that car up and took off driving to Nebraska by myself. When I got to Lincoln, I hadn't experienced one-way streets before. All of a sudden people were honking and hollering at me because I was headed the wrong way on one street. Then I couldn't get in touch with anybody that day and had nowhere to sleep. I pulled the car behind a building, rolled up the windows, locked the doors, and slept in my car that first night. The next day, I called coach Moore and he got me into the dorm. When it snowed later, I remember me and that car were sliding all over the streets. It wasn't equipped for the snow. And the first couple of days in the winter were tough. My clothes were from the South—the cold air and wind ate me alive.

But for the first time, I had that freedom, and it was awesome. I was making a lot of friends, and I was starting to do things I shouldn't. I had smoked some cigarettes in high school, but now I was moving on to weed.

As a sophomore, coach Osborne came to me and said that he noticed I had a lot of ability and talent, and he thought I would become a great player. But he had Kenny Spaeth and Mark Dufresne at tight end. He told me, "I want to be honest with you—you are not going to get to play that much at tight end. Will you move to linebacker? You will play more if you do."

137

He said I could switch positions or I could redshirt. I didn't want to redshirt because I wanted to play in the NFL, and I knew I needed only two years of playing time to do that. But I wanted to remain a tight end. For the first time, I found myself sitting on the sidelines, and I hated it. I was a better athlete and a better football player than the other two—I knew it and they knew it—but it was the commitment that coach Osborne had for those two players who had put in their time.

I called home to talk to Mom and told her I wanted to transfer to Texas Tech. She said, "Oh no, you big-headed boy. You made your decision. You keep your butt there and stick it out!" So I told myself, "OK, that is that. I guess I am staying."

A few weeks before we were going to play in the Liberty Bowl in Memphis, a friend of mine was trying to date this one girl. I was dating another girl at the time, and he brought this new girl over to my house. I saw her and said, "Whoa, that is a beautiful girl." Her name was Carol and right away, she thought I was the biggest jerk in the world. She turned my friend down flat and he left the house, so I started to talk to her and realized she was a good Christian, and I soon fell in love with her. What a special woman. Sometimes in life, you meet people and you instantly know they are good and special and all those things. If I had left for Texas Tech, I never would have met my wife, and it would have been the biggest mistake of my life. Mothers know best, I guess.

As I said, I had been experimenting with weed and drinking, and I was smoking cigarettes. I was living the type of life that I knew was wrong and I wasn't raised that way. Things always came to me so easily as an athlete that I didn't work out as hard as other kids did. I wish I had. But once I met Carol, she talked to me about the Lord and then one night, we went out to Creek, Nebraska, to have dinner with her parents. After dinner, we sat around and talked about the Lord. Being from a Christian family, Mom had preached to us all the time, but when Carol's parents talked to me, it really touched me. I said I wanted to change. I started to read the Bible. And I began to change.

As a junior, I also started to play more. Coach Osborne saw the things I could do, and he always was great at taking your ability and creating something to take advantage of that ability. He did that for me. Kellen Winslow was the tight end at Missouri, and I always kept an eye on him. I thought I was better than him. That year, he was the first-team All-American and I was on the second team.

We had beat Oklahoma 17–14 when they were ranked No. 1 late in the season, and all of a sudden, we were talking national championship. We were 9–1 and on a big roll, and the next week, Missouri and Winslow came to town for the final game. Then started the offensive explosion. We couldn't stop them and they couldn't stop us. We went up and down the field. So did they. Finally, they won 35–31. We were so, so up, and then we came crashing down. I still remember that game so well. It was a horrible feeling. It still hurts. I was mad at the defense because they couldn't get them off the field. Then after the game, we got hit with a wet towel in the face when they announced we had to play Oklahoma again in the Orange Bowl. Oklahoma got revenge on us, 31–24.

During my senior year, 1979, Mom decided to come to a game for the first time to see me play. It was against Penn State, and they had those two big, bad defensive linemen [Matt Millen and Bruce Clark] and the great Joe Paterno. Early in the game, I had cut a route short and it was intercepted. The guy ran it back for a touchdown and we were behind 14–0. So here we are in the first game with my mom in the stands, and we're getting beat bad. I remember running a drag-and-out, and the ball was underthrown. I was talking to the ball, "Come down! Come down!" I caught it and just knew I was going to score. I was running down the sideline with the fans going crazy, and I knew Mom and my cousins were there watching me. After I scored, I was jogging back to the bench and I saw coach Osborne, who had never been that emotional before. But he had this big smile on his face and he came over and hugged me. I'll never forget that. I scored two touchdowns that day and had one called back by penalty. We won 42–17.

We were undefeated when we went to Norman to play Oklahoma at the end of the season. It was the first time I had played there, and I remember how hard their turf was. It was like Astroturf on cement. I don't understand it, but we lost to them again, 17–14. It was another nightmare. They always had a tendency to beat us in the last seconds of a game. Barry Switzer called it "Sooner Magic," and it seemed like he always had a play up his sleeve. For coach Osborne, it was another tough loss.

I got married to Carol right after the game, December 1. We were headed to the Cotton Bowl to play Houston, and we lost that one 17–14. Then I went on to play in the Hula and Japan Bowls. That was our honeymoon.

Carol and I have two grown kids now and one of the reasons we came back to Lincoln to live was the people. The people are really good people here. These people are honest, hardworking, respectable folks. You don't run into racism here. It's been more than 20 years, and when the fight song plays and I see that *N*, I feel that spirit in my heart. Nebraska is a big family, and we all love our family. Becoming a Cornhusker, and remaining one, were two of the greatest decisions of my life.

Junior Miller finished his career with 55 receptions for 1,045 yards and 12 touchdowns. He was an All-American in 1979 and was selected in the first round of the 1980 NFL Draft by the Atlanta Falcons. He played five seasons with the Falcons and two with the New Orleans Saints. He also was named to Nebraska's All-Century Team. Miller was inducted into the Nebraska Football Hall of Fame in 1988.

TOM RUUD

LINEBACKER

1972–1974

Gᴿᴼᵂᴵᴺᴳ ᴜᴘ ɪɴ Bʟᴏᴏᴍɪɴɢᴛᴏɴ, Mɪɴɴᴇsᴏᴛᴀ, the Big 10 and the Minnesota Golden Gophers were what I knew when it came to college football. It was just natural: when you grow up somewhere, the local or state team is the team you follow. But at the time I was being recruited, Minnesota was not doing well. They had been to the Rose Bowl and had been a great program in the early sixties, but had dropped off some by the time I was a high school senior.

I began looking around. I wanted to play for a team that would go to bowl games and compete for national championships. And I wanted to stay close enough to home so I could get home if I needed to. I wanted a place where I felt I belonged, and where I liked the city and the campus and the people were friendly.

I guess all of that describes Lincoln, Nebraska.

In my first two years of high school, I attended Bloomington Lincoln before the city expanded to three schools. I finished high school at Bloom- ington Jefferson and was an all-state running back and defensive back. At the time, I was just shy of 6'3" and weighed about 205 pounds.

I took 8 to 10 recruiting trips because there was no limit then and signing day wasn't until May. And coming from a middle-class family, I was excited to see the country, eat steaks, and have a good time. I thought it was a neat deal that you could just jump on an airplane and see different campuses around the country, so I visited such schools as Wisconsin, Iowa, Colorado, Missouri, Florida State, Nebraska, and, of course, Minnesota.

The week I visited Lincoln, in early January of 1971, there had been a major, major snowstorm that brought about 24 inches of snow. That didn't bother me—I was from Minnesota. I didn't make up my mind right then, but I knew that Nebraska would be hard to beat. The people were impressive, the coaches were impressive, and I felt I belonged there. I knew that Big Red Mania was there for a reason. And Lincoln is far enough south of Minnesota that there is a lot less winter, and it is slightly warmer—despite that huge snowstorm.

One of my high school teammates, Monte Johnson, who was two years ahead of me, went to Nebraska, and I kept notice of him. And Bruce Haugie, who also was from Bloomington, was about four years ahead of me, and he played at Nebraska. Locally, there was pressure for me to stay home and play for the Gophers. Sid Hartman, a sportswriter in Minnesota, had lunch with me a few times, and he was a diehard Minnesota fan. To this day, Sid still thinks I should have gone to Minnesota. But Nebraska was coming off their first national championship, the fan base was second to none, and when it all added up, I decided I should go play with the best.

And that's how I became a Cornhusker.

141

From the beginning, I could tell that Bob Devaney had an aura about him. He was usually in a good mood, and when he smiled, he would light the whole place up. When he came up to the Twin Cities to visit with me, he took me and my parents out to a high-end steak house. It was the first time I had been in a place that nice, but coach Devaney was right at home. He was eating and drinking and telling stories, keeping the whole table entertained for a couple of hours. That was his forte. He could get along with anybody—from top-shelf people and dignitaries to lower-income workers. I liked him right away.

When I got to Nebraska, there was a group of freshmen that came in early to take some tests. There were three guys from New Jersey—Richie Costanzo, Jeff Patuto, and Tom Coccia—and they were Italian guys who were used to the big city. They were always telling us stories about how crazy it was back East. Bob Nelson, another linebacker who was from Stillwater, Minnesota, and I were used to being around pale people with Scandinavian backgrounds, and we looked at these guys like they were from another planet. These guys decided they all wanted Mohawks, so here are these good-sized,

18-year-old guys with dark complexions and Mohawks and heavy beards—let's just say it was funny. The great thing about a football team at Nebraska is that when you come in as a freshman, you are around people you are not used to being around. We had cowboys from Nebraska and Montana, kids from the Deep South, inner-city kids, and just a mix of different backgrounds and races. We were all teammates and the mix worked.

The coaches asked me where I wanted to play. I wanted a shot to play running back, and they said they would give me that opportunity, even though I knew all along I was better on the defensive side. I just thought toting the ball was always fun to do, and I played fullback and linebacker on the freshman team. But I figured out really quickly that I liked linebacker, and that that's where my future was.

I think the highlight of my freshman year was simulating Oklahoma's offense for the Turkey Day Shootout down at Norman. It is now known as the Game of the Century. Anyway, the coaches figured the freshman team could put together a backfield that simulated the Sooner wishbone because the scout team didn't have the speed that was needed to do it. Our freshman team was a lot faster, with a few sprinters at the halfback positions. I think the slowest guy ran a 4.6. I simulated the fullback, and Terry Luck would have simulated Jack Mildren. Well, we put the Sooners' numbers on our uniforms, and taped up our shoes like they wore those white spats back then. We had our helmets looking like theirs and the whole deal. In the end, I think we really helped the varsity win that game. I remember watching it back in Lincoln, like millions of others. If there was a more exciting game, I don't know what it would have been. It was definitely an exciting time in Nebraska football history.

As a sophomore, Bob Nelson and I were backing up seniors in the middle at linebacker. We got to play a fair amount, and I was on special teams for the entire season. The first game I ever played in was at the Los Angeles Coliseum at night against UCLA, and the crowd was unbelievable that night. It was a lot of fun running around in front of a crowd that big for the first time, but we had a real disappointing loss that night [20–17]. That team went on to a 9–2–1 record, and there was a lot of disappointment after two straight national championships. I really feel there was probably more talent on the 1972 team than on teams prior to that, but the chemistry wasn't good at all. Maybe we had a little loss of focus, and Dave Humm was a sophomore quarterback who had never started before. It wasn't his fault—he would become a good player, but he was just inexperienced at that point.

Tom Ruud (No. 45), here standing over a pile of Blackshirts, recorded 104 tackles in 1974.

Then coach Devaney retired. I was 20 years old, and more than anything, I just wondered what was going to happen. Devaney was a god, and now Tom Osborne would be taking over. We didn't know him that well because he was an assistant on the offensive side of the ball. He was more serious, while coach Devaney was always joking around. I remember one of coach Devaney's funnier lines. He would be screaming and hollering at us and then when it was over, he would gather everybody around him to close practice. Then he would say, "All right, everybody take a lap around coach Melton!"

That would break everybody up because coach Melton was a bit on the portly side, and he was the butt of coach Devaney's jokes.

In 1973, coach Osborne had a lot of pressure on him to duplicate what coach Devaney did. Fans weren't happy unless you won the Big Eight championship—or the national championship, in some cases.

In the spring of 1973, there was no doubt in my mind that I would be starting. Bob Nelson was back too, so we both were penciled in as starters at linebacker. We all felt it was very important to play well in coach Osborne's first game, and we were facing UCLA, which had beaten us to open the previous season. This time they came into Lincoln, and it was one of those very hot, summer-like days. We had been practicing in the heat for a month, and we just took them apart [40–13]. After the first quarter, I don't think I saw an offensive lineman. We got coach Osborne his first win, and it was a great way to start a new era. The year was marred by the 13–12 loss at Missouri and the 27–0 loss at Oklahoma to end the season. I don't think the offense crossed the 50-yard line that day. And against their wishbone, if you gave them the short field too much, you were just looking for trouble.

That is the one thing that still bothers me. We never beat Oklahoma in my three years, and they had been a thorn in our side for years. It took coach Osborne until 1978 to get a win over Barry Switzer, and it was hard to take. They just had better talent than we did in my junior and senior years. We couldn't move the ball on them at all. But yes, there's no doubt about it—that still bothers me.

I remember I had a few speaking engagements scheduled as a senior and I wasn't very comfortable with it, but coach Devaney [then the athletic director] took the time to help me. He spent 30 minutes with me, talking about how he had handled it in different situations. He gave me a number of jokes, and different things to use. He was very sincere, and he was always there to help. I really appreciated that. I was not very good at asking for help, but he was there for me when I needed him. I'll never forget his personality. He would just come into a room and the whole place would light up. It seemed everybody was in awe of him.

The staff that Bob Devaney put together there, and when Tom Osborne became a part of it, made Nebraska football special in my opinion. The one thing I know is that Nebraska football players always played hard. Even when they weren't successful in the early days, they played hard in every game. It is because hard work is the staple of the state of Nebraska. Nobody works harder anywhere than the farmers and the ranchers in this state. All you have to do is see a calving session at 2:00 in the morning during a spring snowstorm. Farmers are out there working because they either work to save that calf or it dies.

That is the basis for the tradition here. It is hard work and dedication. I have to say that I think the world of the University of Nebraska and the city of Lincoln and the entire state. I was fortunate enough to meet my wife here and raise a family here. This is my home—I am a Cornhusker and I always will be.

> Tom Ruud was named All–Big Eight and a team cocaptain in 1974. That same year, he was awarded the Novak Trophy. He finished his career with 202 tackles and was inducted into the Nebraska Football Hall of Fame in 1997. He played three seasons with the Buffalo Bills and two with the Cincinnati Bengals. His sons, Bo and Barrett, are current Cornhuskers.

JEFF KINNEY
RUNNING BACK
1969–1971

IT'S BEEN MORE THAN 30 YEARS AND EVERY YEAR that has passed since Thanks-giving Day, 1971, somebody interviews me about the Game of the Century. It really amazes me that we are still talking about it, but it's fun to reflect on. It really does become more special as I grow older, and the main thing I remember is how much fun it was. It was so much fun playing football at Nebraska. I would have to agree with those who say it was the best time of our lives.

I grew up in McCook, Nebraska, and I admit I was a football nut. I was a quarterback, defensive back, and linebacker at McCook High. On Saturday mornings, I would watch film, go pheasant hunting, and listen to Nebraska football on the radio, or watch them if they were on television. In fact, I watched all the football I could. My biggest thrill of the week was the Sunday sports page. I couldn't wait to get up and get the Sunday paper and see how they showed the sequence of a big play from Saturday's game. I remember all the big names from Nebraska—like Harry Wilson, Bobby Hohn, Bob Churchich, and Dennis Claridge.

By the time I was a senior at McCook, Bob Devaney was like the president of the United States to me. He was very popular and worshiped around the state—even though the Cornhuskers were going through a 6–4 season.

I did visit Kansas State, just because they told me I could play basketball, too, but I knew in the end that I could never leave Nebraska. I couldn't wait to be a part of coach Devaney's program.

When I arrived in 1968, there were about 45 freshmen on scholarship. There were about seven quarterbacks there, and that is where I started off. I made the mistake of scrambling around too much, and the coaches must have thought, "Hey, he would make a good running back." So they moved me there during my freshman year. I went to wingback and blocked and caught passes. I was about 6'2" and 198 pounds at that time.

I went into the 1969 season battling Larry Frost for a starting position at wingback, and all of a sudden a couple of running backs got hurt, and I ended up as the starter. Near the end of the season, I was alternating back and forth with Joe Orduna, but then I hurt my shoulder pretty bad near the end of the season.

Before the 1970 season, the biggest feeling we had was that we could compete with anybody. We had finished 9–2 the year before and had beaten Georgia pretty bad in the Sun Bowl. Before the next season, that's when Jerry Murtaugh made his prediction that we would win the national championship. Coach Devaney did tell me to go get him away from the media, because we didn't do much trash-talking back then. That was a pretty brash statement for the time, and it wasn't like Jerry because he was always sort of quiet. But he believed it, and we felt good about what was to come.

It is true that we should have beaten USC, but came away with that 21–21 tie out in Los Angeles. Even though it was a tie, that game really gave us the confidence we needed. And we didn't lose again. The first thing I remember about the Orange Bowl against LSU was that before the game, we realized we had a chance to win it [the national championship]. The other teams [Texas and Ohio State] in front of us got beat that day, but we knew LSU was a great team, too. They had allowed only two or three rushing touchdowns that season, and they had great players like Andy Hamilton, Bert Jones, and Tommy Casanova. One play I remember is on that final drive, we had a critical third down. I was lined up in the slot, and they had called an under-pattern and Jerry [Tagge] hit me with it for the first down. Then we went in and scored [to lead 17–12]. After the game, I don't think anybody figured we had the national championship won yet because we had to wait for the final poll. I know Bob [Devaney] was doing some lobbying for us, though. I remember that a former player, Rex Lowe, was dying of Hodgkin's disease and Johnny Rodgers took him a game ball. That was a special moment.

The next season, 1971, was one of those years where we always would get a good lead in the first half. It seemed we were ahead 28–0 or 31–0 at halftime

148

Jeff Kinney cuts through the hole on the way to some of his 1,037 rushing yards in 1971.

during every game. At the half, coach Devaney would come up to the starters and say, "Let's go score on the first drive of the second half and then take the rest of the day off." And that was what we did. We scored and that was it. But I think that was good for team spirit and very good for morale that everybody was getting to play.

In practices, coach Devaney never worked us too hard. In fact, I remember, going into my senior season, I told him, "Coach, somebody has got to hit me. I have to get some shots in to be ready." We just didn't have contact that much. He believed in saving it all for the game, and it really worked out well for us.

What can I add about the Game of the Century? It's hard to say anything that hasn't been said or written already. We had great leadership as we approached that game, but you could tell the coaches were getting a little uptight. They were yelling and screaming more. Going into it, we knew our business wasn't finished, and anything less than winning would have diminished what we had accomplished to that point. Then we got behind in the first half [Oklahoma led 17–14 at the half].

Oklahoma was known for its offense, but it had a good defense, too. They pretty much shut us down in the first half. But we made one adjustment at halftime that made a difference for us on offense. We had been running the isolation play where the fullback reads the guard's block, and I would read the fullback's block, and we were attacking the guard hole. They were stopping that play pretty well. In the second half, we moved it wider and we had our linemen block down, so we started to attack the tackle hole instead of the guard hole. That enabled me to take it inside or out, depending on what I read on each play.

After that adjustment was made, we started to move the ball on them.

As the offense stood on the sideline that day, we knew we would have to outscore them. We had the No. 1 defense in the country, but they were hitting some passes, and as it went back and forth, it was becoming a shootout.

Everyone always wants to talk about our final drive. After we fell behind [31–28] late in the game, it was pretty quiet in the huddle. We just said, "We got to go down and score," but there wasn't a lot of yelling and screaming in there. It may sound boring, but we were very methodical and business-like—that's the way that team was. I remember that I had a long run early in that final drive, and after I got tackled, I cramped up and had to come out for a couple of plays. We knew in the huddle that every play was critical, but we knew what we had to do. I just got into one of those grooves. It seemed to me like the more I carried the ball, the stronger I felt. At that point, I just wanted the ball on that final drive. I really wanted it. And I wasn't tired at all. I think our offensive line wore them down some, and we just executed better that entire second half. It's a hard thing to describe, but I ran as hard as I could, and each of the offensive linemen blocked as hard as they could, and we never thought of making a mistake or having a fumble. Jerry may have said something like, "Wrap your arms around it," but I don't remember it. On that final touchdown [2 yards], it was the same play and same adjustment we had made earlier—I just read the fullback's block, I think it was Maury Damkroger, and ran it off left tackle until I hit the end zone [with 1:38 remaining]. Then the defense held them and we won the Game of the Century [35–31].

149

The interesting thing is, everybody remembers my jersey being ripped apart. It was the first time we had worn the tear-away jerseys, and I think I went through three of them that day.

Since that day, it seems like every year I give an interview or two about that game or we talk about it with somebody. It still amazes me that people want to talk about it. I guess the game has become bigger with age.

Heading into the Orange Bowl against Alabama, we really didn't know what to expect. We knew this: coach Devaney had never beaten Paul "Bear" Bryant before, and he meant so much to all of us that we wanted to win it for him. We didn't know what their talent level was, because it's always tough to tell by watching film. But we saw Oklahoma blow out Auburn that day [in the Sugar Bowl], and that gave us some indication. Our defense really got after Alabama that night and it was 28–0 at halftime. It was over.

I guess when it was all over [Nebraska won 38–6], we didn't realize what we had accomplished: two national championships and 32 straight games without a loss. But when you are 22 years old, you don't have a perspective for it. Now I look back on those years with a great sense of pride because of what our teams accomplished.

It becomes more special and now it's fun to reflect on it.

As I do, that's the thing I remember the most. It was just so much fun to play for Nebraska and for Nebraska's fans. They really got behind you, and you could always feel the excitement of the crowd. Being part of it was so special for me, and like I said, it was the best time of my life.

In the end, I can summarize it this way: Nebraska is a very, very special place for me and it always will be.

Jeff Kinney led Nebraska in rushing and receiving in 1969 and in rushing in 1971. He finished his career with 2,244 rushing yards and 29 touchdowns and ranks third on the school's career receptions list with 82 for 864 yards and three touchdowns. In 1971, he was named an All-American and an Academic All-American and was awarded the Novak and Chamberlain Trophies. In the Game of the Century, a 35–31 win over Oklahoma in 1971, Kinney rushed 31 times for 174 yards and four touchdowns. He was inducted into the Nebraska Football Hall of Fame in 1981. Kinney played four seasons with the Kansas City Chiefs and one season with the Buffalo Bills.

VINCE FERRAGAMO
QUARTERBACK
1975–1976

I DIDN'T TAKE THE USUAL ROUTE TO NEBRASKA by any means, but as they say, better late than never.

I grew up in Wilmington, California, and played football for my brother Chris at Banning High School. He always had a great little passing attack, and that's where I learned to play quarterback. We had a drop-back, pro-style, play-action passing offense, and that was unique for high school teams back then. In fact, after I left, Chris' team won seven straight state championships. Chris was 15 years older than me, and growing up, I knew him more as a coach than I did as a brother.

When it came time to be recruited, I considered Washington, Stanford, USC, Nebraska, and Cal. My dad loved Bob Devaney when we met him, but my brother thought Cal was the best place for me at that time. He was looking strictly at what would be the best system for me as a quarterback. UCLA was running the wishbone at the time, and USC had Pat Hayden, who had a firm hold on the starting job there. I just wanted an opportunity to play.

Once I got to Cal, I played freshman ball and then started the last three games of the 1972 season. In my first game, against Oregon State in Corvallis, Oregon, I broke the school's all-purpose yardage record. Then I threw a last-second touchdown pass to beat our rival, Stanford, in the rain, in the final game. I went into 1973 as the starter because Steve Bartkowski went exclusively to play baseball. After the finish of the 1972 season, all of the other quarterbacks on the roster didn't even come out for football the next spring. After the season started they needed a backup, so they persuaded Bartkowski to come back. He arrived after about the fourth game, and then we split time for the rest of the season.

After my sophomore year, the coaches then wanted me to redshirt, and I said, "No, I am going to transfer." Now, I wouldn't advise anybody to transfer. But originally, I wasn't in charge of my decision to go to Cal, and I learned a very important lesson in life right there—decision-making in important matters should be yours alone. I wasn't extremely happy at Cal. I wasn't keen on the whole hippie movement there, and it was a very liberal campus life.

Coach Devaney had recruited me two years earlier, but he had retired at Nebraska, so I called coach Osborne and also wrote him a letter to find out if they were still interested. I always wanted to be a part of a winner, and Nebraska certainly offered that. San Diego State got involved then and wanted me, but coach Osborne got back to me and was very cordial and very receptive to the idea. There was nothing promised to me at all, but he said there was an opportunity if I wanted to come to Lincoln. So I made the move, and they put me on a baseball scholarship because there were no football scholarships left. I went to the first baseball practice to fulfill my end of it, then went into training for football.

I realized I had to prove myself all over again, but I was used to that. At first, I had to prove myself in high school to the people who may have thought I was playing just because I was the coach's brother. Then I had to prove myself at Cal and then at Nebraska. And I was excited about that because I was confident in my ability as a quarterback. Looking back, I wish I had had more influence from my dad because like I said, he liked coach Devaney, and I probably would have ended up at Nebraska in the first place, but he stayed out of the recruiting process.

My brother had a motor home, and he drove me to Lincoln in the summer. There was an old house where I would be rooming with Larry Mushinskie, a tight end, and Mark Heydorff, a safety. Both were also from California. This place was like an old rooming house they lived in, and we just swung by, I grabbed my suitcase, and my brother dropped me off. I got in there, and they told me I was staying on the top bunk. So I walk up three flights of stairs, and there was this small attic way up at the top of this old house, and that's where my bunk was.

Vince Ferragamo, an All-American quarterback in 1976, was one of the few successful transfer stories in Nebraska history.

On that first night—and I'll never forget this—Lincoln had the worst thunderstorm I've ever experienced. There was lightning, thunder, and all kinds of noise. It just shook this old house when the thunder hit. Having grown up in Southern California, I never experienced anything like that, so I was literally shivering. It was the most god-awful thing. I kept waking up in the middle of the night. But finally, when the next day came, it was one of those perfect, blue-sky, sunny days. I asked those guys, "Did you hear that last night? How did you sleep through it?'

The thing I noticed at Nebraska right away was there were guys from all over the country. There were guys from California like me, from Texas, from New York, from Kansas, from everywhere. And as soon as I hit the practice field, I was happy. I knew I had to redshirt that season, but I really needed a redshirt season to learn the system and develop a camaraderie with my teammates.

We redshirts went to the Sugar Bowl at the end of the season, and that turned into a mistake that we really didn't know about at the time. Jim Lampley of ABC was interviewing me on the sideline during the game, and the NCAA rule at that time prevented redshirts from being on the sideline of a bowl game. I was told later that Oklahoma had blown the whistle on it, and I was suspended for the first game of the next season.

I had won the job in the spring of 1975, after Dave Humm left, but Terry Luck was playing the first few games of the season. He had been elected captain that year. We were losing at halftime to Miami in the fourth game, and coach Osborne told me, "Loosen up, you're going in for the second half." I played well, we came back to win, and then I started the next game against Kansas. That was a very good team, because we won our first 10 games, but Oklahoma beat us pretty badly [35–10] at the end of the season. Then we went to the Fiesta Bowl to play Arizona State. I started, threw an interception, and after three plays, coach Osborne jerked me and put in Terry. I think he wanted to showcase Terry for the pros because it was his final game. I never got back into that game and we lost 17–14. I always wondered, "Why start me if you are going to pull me after three plays?" But I think he was just being loyal to Terry.

The next year we had a good team, but we just had some slip-ups along the way. I remember in that Missouri game I threw some picks, and No. 41 got most of them. Years later, I was the guest host on a football show and one of the guests was a guy named Larry Fredrickson. He was the guy in the old Budweiser commercial who would shout, "I love you, man!" This was the guy who was No. 41 for Missouri and intercepted my passes that day. After football, he became an actor. Anyway, his appearance brought back some bad memories from that Missouri game.

We lost to Iowa State, and then Elvis Peacock scored late as Oklahoma beat us 20–17. Our bowl was the Astro-Bluebonnet Bowl in Houston, and it turned into one of the better games of the bowl season. We beat Texas Tech 27–24, and guess who the defensive coordinator was for Texas Tech that night? Bill Parcells. I remember that his defense took away the run, and the only way to beat them was by throwing it. [He passed for 183 yards and two touchdowns.]

Looking back on it, it was a quick two years, but I was very thankful for the opportunity to play at Nebraska. It was a great time in my life there. I met my wife at Nebraska, and I made several lifelong friends. The people at Nebraska gave me a second chance and welcomed me as if I were a hometown boy. Hopefully, I gave them something in return, too. I just wish I had given them more years, but all in all, it worked out very well for me.

Vince Ferragamo was an All-American in 1976 when he completed 145 of 245 passes for 2,071 yards and 20 touchdowns, which remains a single-season school record. His 8.31 yards per attempt remains a Nebraska school record. He also was an Academic All-American in 1976. Ferragamo played 10 seasons in the NFL, including eight with the Los Angeles Rams. He was inducted into the Nebraska Football Hall of Fame in 1984.

JIM ANDERSON
DEFENSIVE BACK
1969–1971

BORN AND RAISED IN GREEN BAY, WISCONSIN, on the same street as Lambeau Field, I was a big football fan from the beginning. We could walk right down the street, get a ticket for 50 cents, and see the Packers play. We often rode our bikes to Packers practices to see players like Paul Hornung or Bart Starr as they walked off the field.

We played sports in the park while growing up. Whatever the season was, that was the sport we were playing. I didn't play organized football until the ninth grade when I started out as a quarterback and a defensive back. I was the quarterback for Green Bay West High School through my junior year, before I moved to halfback for my senior season. They felt they had an up-and-coming quarterback who was better. His name? Jerry Tagge.

But I liked playing halfback more than quarterback, and the fact is, I wasn't a very good quarterback. I played every down in high school—at halfback on offense, at safety on defense, on kickoff returns, punt returns, and I punted, too. I don't think I ever came off the field.

Still, I wasn't very heavily recruited. My home-state team, Wisconsin, didn't do a very good job recruiting me, and they weren't winning at the time, anyway. Back then, you could sign up to three conference letters of intent. I signed a Big 10 letter of intent with Northwestern and a Big Eight letter of intent with Nebraska.

Coach Devaney was a great recruiter. He was really smooth, very pleasant, and had a great way about him. Plus, he was winning almost all of his games. Northwestern had a been a little successful at the time, but the great fan support at Nebraska was very attractive to me. It reminded me of the Packers, because they had the support throughout the community. Also, Nebraska was going to bowl games almost every year.

When I made my decision based on those factors, I picked up the phone and called [Nebraska assistant coach] George Kelly at his house and told him I wanted to come to play for the Cornhuskers. He was all excited, and Jim Ross, then the defensive backs coach, happened to be over at his house that night.

Coach Kelly handed the phone to coach Ross, who said in this stern, gruff voice, "I don't want you coming out here chasing girls and getting yourself into trouble!"

Coach Ross, I would come to find out later, had a great sense of humor. But I thought, "Well, the recruiting honeymoon lasted about 15 seconds."

When I finally got to school, my folks dropped me off in Lincoln and I got the classes I wanted. I showed up for practice, and there were about 50 full scholarship players and at least 100 walk-ons—and that was just the freshman team. Luckily, I didn't calculate all that when I was making my decision—and I ended up as a math major!

157

The coaches put me at cornerback right away, and I stayed there for the next five years.

When our freshman team played down at Missouri, my dad drove with some friends down from Green Bay through a snowstorm to watch the game. I got hurt on the opening play of the game, when I got flipped over from behind and landed on my knee. I had to have surgery to repair the cartilage, and it took a year or so to recover.

I ended up redshirting in 1968, and it was a fortunate thing for me. I wasn't disappointed at all, so I just kept plugging away in practice, but you always think you can play.

In the spring of 1969, we had some cornerbacks graduating and a couple of us were competing for an open job. The coaches put Bill Kosch and me at that spot and said, "Let's see who comes out as the starter."

I think they were fully expecting Bill to become the starter at that corner, but I ended up with the job. They switched Bill to safety, and Dana Stephenson was to be the starter at the other corner.

Jim Anderson started every one of his 36 games, from 1969 to 1971, at cornerback, setting a school record until Johnny Rodgers broke it a year later.

After I won the job, I didn't plan to give it up. As it turned out, I started against USC in the season opener, and that was the first of my 36 consecutive starts, which set a Nebraska school record [until Johnny Rodgers broke it with 37 starts].

My foremost memory of my sophomore year was the bus ride over to Missouri to start off the Big Eight Conference. Monte Kiffin was our new defensive coordinator, and it was his first conference game, too, because he was replacing George Kelly, who went to Notre Dame. Monte sat down next to me and was trying to calm me down. I think he was worried I would get beat deep.

I think he was right to be worried: on the third play of the game, they threw an 80-yard touchdown pass right over my head, and we were down 7–0. That was my baptism into the Big Eight.

When I look back at it, I think the real turning point of the program was the game against Oklahoma that year. The year before they had beaten us 47–0 on national television. But we went down to Norman, and Steve Owens had this long streak of 100-yard games going. Our defense stopped that streak cold and we beat them 44–14 that day.

We had a lot of fun down at the Sun Bowl after that because none of us had been to a bowl game yet. El Paso had had a freak snowstorm the previous week, when they were hosting the state high school playoff game at the Sun Bowl stadium, but when they plowed the snow off the field, they plowed the grass off with it. So we played the game on dirt painted green. And I think I had my first interception in that game.

I don't think any of us had any great aspirations that we would be national champions in 1970, but we had some confidence because we finished the previous season with seven straight wins.

It was a big thrill to play in the L.A. Coliseum in the second game that season. USC had such a great team and players like Sam Cunningham and Bobby Chandler, but we missed a field goal that would have won the game. It was 21–21 and they threw a long pass into our end zone on the final play of the game toward Ron Dickerson, but I knocked it down to prevent a loss.

In the final game of the season, we were leading Oklahoma 28–21 when they had two plays left in the game. They ran a counter play with Joe Wiley, and he broke through the line and it was him and me alone in the open field. I made the tackle at about our 40-yard line. On the next play, Jack Mildren dropped back and threw into the end zone for Greg Pruitt. The ball got tipped up into the air and it was about to land in Pruitt's lap, but I came over the top and snatched it with one hand and made the interception.

I ran over to the sidelines after the game and I threw the ball into the stands, but I wish I hadn't done that because I would like to have that football today.

There was a picture of me during that play the next week in *Sports Illustrated*.

Before the Orange Bowl, we entered New Year's Day as the No. 3–ranked team, but Notre Dame beat No. 1 Texas [in the Cotton Bowl] and Jim Plunkett led Stanford over No. 2 Ohio State in the Rose Bowl. All of a sudden, we were playing for the national championship.

I had a big play in the Orange Bowl, too, but it isn't one that I am proud of. We couldn't get anything going on offense for most of the game, but we were ahead 10–6 in the third quarter when LSU faced a third-and-long. I was covering their fastest receiver when they ran an out pattern and I jumped it, but he cut it up, and they completed it for a touchdown to go ahead. When I came off the field, I headed for the sideline to get as far away from coach Devaney as possible.

Fortunately, Jerry Tagge led our offense back down the field and scored so we could take the lead and win the game 17–12.

As everyone knows, when all the voting was finished, it turned into Nebraska's first national championship.

The next year was different because we were ranked No. 1 from the start, rather than finishing No. 1 at the last minute. We really felt good going into

1971 because we had a good veteran team that already had been successful. Plus, Johnny Rodgers was another year older. That was a big plus.

We rolled through the season until all the build-up and the hype for Oklahoma, which really was unbelievable. I was watching *Monday Night Football*, and there was Howard Cosell on television hyping the game. From my standpoint, I couldn't wait to finally play the game.

When I look back on it, one of the biggest keys to the outcome of that game was Johnny's punt return. Normally, most of the classic plays in college football—Flutie's Hail Mary or Cal running through the Stanford band—happened on the final play of the game. But Johnny's return was in the first half, and it set the tone for the second half.

On punt returns, Johnny and I were always the two guys back, but we worked it out so he would catch most of the punts. I would be the upback in front of him after he caught it, and my job was to block that first guy down. It isn't an exaggeration to say I just tried to stay out of his way.

The first guy down for Oklahoma was Tom Brahaney, and I just shielded him off to the left, and Johnny took it from there. Then came the classic confrontation of him going against Greg Pruitt. He juked Pruitt aside and got started and basically did the rest himself. I think their fans were stunned by the time he ran into the end zone.

I have seen it on tape a million times, and I am still amazed at how great a play that was by Johnny Rodgers.

The thing you have to remember is that Oklahoma was so awesome on offense that they rarely punted, so I don't think they had much experience at covering punts.

When we got ahead in the fourth quarter 28–24, they got down to our 30-yard line, and we finally got them into a passing situation, about third-and-6. I was thinking, "The game's on the line on this play," and I knew they were going to pass. My responsibility on the play was the tight end, and sure enough they threw that way and I almost intercepted it. Then Mildren threw a touchdown pass on the next play to go ahead.

I got to the sideline, and now we're behind, and all I am thinking about was that missed chance at the interception.

But fortunately, our offense marched down the field in that classic drive to win the Game of the Century 35–31.

I think everybody in our locker room sensed something special had just happened for all of us. I showered, got dressed, and went back into the stands.

It was totally empty and quiet and I sat down and looked out at the field and just soaked it all in. That was probably the most satisfying moment of my career and I just sat there reminiscing. It was really a neat moment for me.

We played in Hawaii next, a game that some people forget because of all the hype over Oklahoma and the upcoming Orange Bowl. Most of us were country bumpkins, and here we were hanging around the beach and seeing Don Ho in concert. We also saw Pearl Harbor and had a great time [a 45–3 win over Hawaii].

Alabama was also undefeated, but we were pretty confident heading into the Orange Bowl after watching all the other bowl games. Oklahoma just ripped Auburn earlier in the day, and we were pretty confident because of that, but we were confident anyway. Well, we dominated Alabama as expected, and on the final play of my college career, I intercepted a pass and ran it back something like 50 yards. I had never scored a touchdown—and I was going down the sidelines heading toward the end zone. But I got cut off, caught up in this tangled mess, and got tackled at the 1-yard line.

No touchdown for me, but we won 38–6 for another national championship.

When I stop and think about it, I couldn't have written a better script for my college career if I tried, and I couldn't have picked a better place to play college football. I think our teams during those three years really set the foundation for Nebraska football for the next 30 years.

161

I want to mention Jim Ross, who was my defensive backs coach in 1968 and later became the freshman coach when I came back as a graduate assistant coach. He really meant a lot to me, and so did Don Bryant. Both of them became great friends after my playing days, and when I was inducted into the Nebraska Football Hall of Fame in 1999, coach Ross was seated there with me, and Don Bryant presented me.

I know other schools have great tradition, too, but Nebraska's is as good as any. Being part of that means a tremendous amount to me, mainly because Husker football is so important to the people in the state of Nebraska.

Jim Anderson started 36 consecutive games at cornerback from 1969 to 1971. He was named All–Big Eight in 1971. He led the team in pass breakups for three straight seasons and finished his career with nine interceptions. He was inducted into the Nebraska Football Hall of Fame in 1999.

JOHNNY "THE JET" RODGERS

WINGBACK

1970–1972

MORE THAN 30 YEARS SINCE MY DAYS at the University of Nebraska, I like to think I brought about some positive change and made a difference through my words and actions.

But playing for the Cornhuskers, I have to admit, wasn't even my first choice when I was thinking about where to play college football. I had always been a big fan of the USC Trojans, but that wasn't meant to be.

I played all the major sports—football, basketball, and baseball, and I also ran track—at Omaha Tech, which was a predominantly black school. I was always all-city, all-state, and All-American. I was a wingback and linebacker in football, and I dove over the top to tackle the quarterback and ran around and made plays on defense. I played shortstop and centerfield in baseball and had a very good career ahead of me in that sport if I had wanted it.

In the spring, I would go to a track meet, take my turn at the broad jump and the triple jump, and then leave the meet to go play baseball. I would read in the paper the next day whom I had beaten in the track meet. I always won the events, but didn't stick around long enough to see the finish.

The next year, they passed the "Johnny Rodgers Rule," which prevented kids from playing two sports at the same time.

I got offers from all over, but I made my mind up to go to USC. I just figured that playing at USC would be my automatic ticket to the pros, and also, my father lived in L.A. I had visited their campus earlier, but it wasn't by invitation. The problem was, [USC coach] John McKay didn't think I was big enough to play for them. I was about 5'10", 155 pounds, coming out of high school, but my size didn't prevent me from doing anything I ever set out to do. I knew I was going to be a success in whatever sport I picked and I was going to make it big, so I figured it was USC's loss.

After that, I didn't really consider anybody else but Nebraska.

Nebraska, though, didn't have many black players before my class, and when I met with coach Devaney, he told me he would start signing more minorities. I think my class had the most blacks ever signed by Nebraska and I hoped it was a sign of things to come.

We also had an agreement that I would be able to play baseball, too.

Bob Devaney was a good, fatherly type of guy to me, although I never considered him to be a good football coach. His strong point was that he was smart enough to go out and get the best coaches he could hire for each position. Then he let them do the coaching. He concentrated on befriending the players and going around the state raising money for the program. But you still knew coach Devaney cared about you and got the most out of you.

I was very close with coach Devaney, and we got much closer as the years went on after he retired. Bob was always very decent to me and we never had many run-ins. In the later years, Jerry Tagge and I would pick him up and take him to our autograph signings.

Bob made one deal with me, though. He told me if I gave up playing baseball, I would become the first player he would ever endorse for the Heisman Trophy. I really thought I was in a position to become what now would be considered the first Bo Jackson—and I didn't think playing baseball in the spring would ever hurt my football ability. But reluctantly, I gave up baseball.

I wish we would have been able to play on the varsity back in 1969 when we were freshmen, but the NCAA rule prevented it until a few years later. We just killed everybody with that freshman team we had. I had an illustrious year, and there was a lot of notoriety on me heading into my sophomore season.

People always talked about my speed, but the truth is that I didn't have the top sprinter's speed. I probably ran the 100 in 9.7, but it was my quickness that was better than most. I always thought I had an advantage over other guys because of my quickness. I was never going to win the 100-yard dash, but I wasn't going to get caught from behind on the football field, either.

In 1970, I started to make a name for myself on punt returns and kickoff returns, but we never had plays actually designed to get me the ball. When you look at my stats, they are good only because of my playing on special teams. If I touched the ball 10 times a game, that was a lot. We had quite a few plays for the wingback to run the ball, but we didn't call them a lot. We did get the ball to Jeff Kinney as much as we could.

Yes, I can say that I wanted the ball more, but I never griped about this because we were winning so much. It was a team sport, and I made my contributions.

We came into the Orange Bowl that year ranked No. 3 in the country. We came to win the football game, but we certainly didn't come to win the national championship. Somehow with other teams losing, things fell into place and that's what we did.

After that game [a 17–12 win over LSU], I thought we needed to honor Rex Lowe, a former player who had been in our receivers' club. Rex had Hodgkin's disease, and he was getting worse and worse by the day. We couldn't do anything for him, but I thought it was fitting that he should get a game ball, so I gave him one.

I remember the days when Rex was as healthy as I was, and his disease got me to thinking. Why was I one of God's chosen people and given the abilities I was given? I didn't know why, but seeing Rex go the way he did really humbled me. He died shortly after the Orange Bowl, and I will never forget him.

After that game, we all felt it was so important to come back and do it decisively the next season. We knew we could beat everybody, but the entire season was a build-up for one game: Oklahoma.

We didn't know if we would beat them, but we knew we could if we played like we should. What I really liked about this rivalry was that I think we made each other great. It wasn't a mean rivalry full of hatred, I can tell you that. We had high respect for each other. Greg Pruitt and Jack Mildren were friends of mine.

You hear so much about the Game of the Century. We knew that was the national championship game. Forget about the following game at Hawaii or whatever the bowl game would be, this game was our national championship game. If we won it, we were national champions. It was that simple.

I was never the type to get too emotional or worked up before a game, and I never had trouble eating or sleeping before a game. All I hoped for before that game was to get the ball enough to make a difference in it. And my punt return set the stage.

Greg Pruitt and I had some bets going—who would make the big play?

So when I caught that punt, I knew Greg would be the first Oklahoma player I would see when I looked up because he told me he would be. I believed him. And he was. And he was the first one to get shook. I knew Greg wanted to plaster me because we were so competitive with each other. He was just too close to me when I caught it.

When you watch the tape of it, you can tell that return comes from instinct because if you have to think about it, or think what move you are going to make, it is too late. You have to feel it, and that's how I handled most of my moves during returns.

The fact is that the call on that play was for a punt return right, but I ended up going to the left. Cletus Fischer was our special teams coach, and he always gave me that freedom. We would call for a punt return right and I would go left or we would call one left and I would go right. Cletus never told me to call for a fair catch, either. My teammates knew I was going to do my own thing, too. I just told them, "Whatever way I go, just meet me at the goal line."

165

After I shook Greg, I went to the right and there was a guy across my face, so I cut back left. There was a guy there, too, and then the referee got in my way, but I broke to the sideline and it was clear. I knew I was gone [for a 72-yard touchdown].

People always remember that play. It never ceases to amaze me the recognition that comes up with that punt return. Remember that on Thanksgiving Day back then, there were only three major networks, and only one of them had a football game that day. So at that time, everybody in the country was watching that game.

In the second half, it became tit for tat. We moved the ball and scored. They moved the ball and scored. I thought it would come down to who had the ball last.

On that final drive, we were down 31–28 and faced that crucial third down. It was one of the few times in my life when I was not trying to score a touchdown. We had to have that first down to keep the drive alive. I ran the route beyond the first-down marker and thought, "Just catch it."

Johnny Rodgers (No. 20), Nebraska's first Heisman Trophy winner, may have been the best punt-returner in college football history.

When Jerry [Tagge] released it, I just reacted and went down and got it. That play, when it was all said and done, was just as crucial as the first-half punt return.

That huddle was very business-like on that final drive. It always was that way. None of us ever talked but Jerry. That drive was all about ball control and first downs. What I love about that game is that we didn't make any mistakes. Jeff [Kinney] was the workhorse, and our plan down the stretch was to give it to Kinney, give it to Kinney. And when we got in trouble, they came to me. I remember that [fullback] Billy Olds was a wild man, taking on their linebackers with great blocks.

We knew we could score, but looking back, yes, we might have scored too quickly. They had been throwing all day and completing them. They just ate Bill Kosch up with their passing. But in the end, they couldn't score on their final possession, and the Game of the Century was ours.

In the aftermath, we were celebrating the national championship. We knew then we had Hawaii and Alabama [in the Orange Bowl] left, but we knew we had just won it all. Neither one of those teams was going to beat us. In Hawaii, we partied a little bit, and I figured Alabama would be no tougher because we didn't even want to practice in Hawaii [a 45–3 Nebraska win].

When we got to the Orange Bowl, we had a vendetta against Alabama because Bear Bryant had been named Coach of the Year. That was an insult to us because we felt Bob deserved it. Plus, Bob had never beaten the Bear before.

I was told later that as I ran back that 77-yard punt return down the side-line in front of Alabama's bench, the Bear decided right then and there to start recruiting more black players. It was very satisfying to beat them [38–6].

In 1972, they used me more at running back [58 carries for 267 yards], and I really thought we could make it three straight national championships. The difference was that coach Devaney had announced he would retire at the end of the season and coach Osborne would take over. We really had two head coaches that season, and it didn't work. We had two guys making decisions, and we needed only one.

We had those three-point losses to UCLA to start and Oklahoma to finish the season and that [23–23] tie to Iowa State in between. It was frustrating because, the way I saw it, one head coach wanted to do one thing and the other wanted another thing that whole season.

I really did want to win the Heisman, but I didn't expect to win it. I was a controversial person to the media because I was outspoken. There was little doubt that I wasn't nearly as popular as I was talented. I remember a lot of media types lobbying against me because I did some things and said some things they didn't like. I really expected Greg [Pruitt] to win it—Oklahoma had beaten us and had had a very good season. Greg had that HELLO on the front of his jersey and GOOD-BYE on the back, and the media loved that. Plus, he was getting the ball more than I was that season.

When they announced my name at the presentation, it brought me to tears. I vowed at that time that I would reach out to help other people, and I have tried to live my life that way ever since that night. I was fortunate enough to get into that Heisman group and to find out that all the past winners felt the same way.

When we got to the Orange Bowl to play Notre Dame, it was Bob's idea to put me at running back. I thought if I had been there to begin with we would have beaten Oklahoma and won those other games, but we really wanted to make sure we won this game to send Bob out a winner. [Rodgers scored four touchdowns and passed 52 yards to Frosty Anderson for another touchdown in the 40–6 win over Notre Dame in Devaney's final game.] If we had taken that attitude for all of our games, we never would have lost.

My whole life has been a blessing. I know that if I had not won the Heisman Trophy, my life wouldn't be the same, but not because of the reasons you may think. It was joining that fraternity of men who are very special people and who have taught me so much. I have never, ever felt out of place in that group.

Believe it or not, one honor means more to me than the Heisman Trophy.

Nebraska fans voted me as the Husker of the Century on Nebraska's All-Century Team, and I can't tell you what that means to me. But I will try: it is a very special honor to me because it comes from our great fans.

Playing football at Nebraska changed my life. I really do love being a good part of that history and tradition at Nebraska, and I am very proud of being a part of those teams that started a tradition that has carried on for 30 years. I feel I was part of the integration of more blacks into the system, too.

I would like for all of Nebraska's football players—past, current, and present—to feel a sense of family. And I always have wished for our university to remember more of our rich tradition and to look after our family, and that is why I participated in this project.

After all, I can never go out and get another university, like you can a car or a house or a job. I was a Husker, I am a Husker, and I will continue to live and die as a Husker.

168

Johnny Rodgers is widely regarded as Nebraska's greatest player. He was the first of the school's three Heisman Trophy winners. He was named All–Big Eight from 1970 to 1972 and All-American in 1971–1972. He finished his career with 6,059 all-purpose yards and scored 44 touchdowns. He is Nebraska's all-time leading pass receiver with 143 receptions for 2,479 yards and 25 touchdowns. He also holds 41 school records. Rodgers was inducted into the Nebraska Football Hall of Fame in 1973 and the College Football Hall of Fame in 2000. He played four seasons in the Canadian Football League and two seasons in the NFL with the San Diego Chargers.

The EIGHTIES

BRODERICK "THE SANDMAN" THOMAS

LINEBACKER

1985–1988

B<small>EING FROM</small> H<small>OUSTON</small>, T<small>EXAS</small>, and with my family background—Mike Singletary is my uncle—you could say I grew up with football in my blood. But at times when I was young, I was hanging with a rough crowd and I was starting to get in trouble. I went to spend a week or two with Uncle Mike during his off-season and he set me straight. One day, he said, "Let's go work out," and we worked out with guys like Earl Campbell, Lester Hayes, and Darrell Green. My uncle pointed to the parking lot and told me, "You see these cars here? See these Mercedes and BMWs and nice cars? Do you want to earn this kind of living, or do you want to keep doing what you are doing?"

That set me straight. From that point on, I started working out and playing hard because I wanted to make it big in football.

I became a high school All-American at Houston Madison, and I could have gone wherever I wanted to go for college. I grew up as a big Oklahoma fan and loved Barry Switzer. I followed Texas some. Baylor, where my uncle played, wanted me. So did Miami and Jimmy Johnson, and Texas A&M, and just about everybody else.

Then Tom Osborne came to Houston to see me. My high school defensive coordinator, George Dearborn, told me, "Tom Osborne ain't ever been down here. When somebody like that comes to see you, that's where you need to be."

Then my mom told me, "Broderick, I really trust him. I think he will do what he said he will do," which was to give me a chance to play and to get an education.

One day I was watching Alabama play, and I saw Cornelius Bennett and said, "I want to be like that. I want to play as a freshman."

I knew I wanted to play at a place that was on national TV so people could see what I did. At one point, I even committed to Texas, but took it back a few hours later. But I liked [Texas coach] Fred Akers. I admit that I always was a big dreamer and that I ran my mouth at times, but that's who I am. I just didn't want to redshirt. I thought I was good enough to play right away, and I told people that. I was so loud and confident. I was just boiling with confidence, and I probably was a difficult person to like at times. In my heart, I just knew that nothing could stop me from being successful. And I wasn't afraid to leave Texas.

Uncle Mike told me one thing: "It's your choice. You have to go there, not me. You need to go where you are happy, and once you make your decision, don't be calling me back saying you are unhappy and you want to transfer."

But a year later, that's exactly what I was doing.

I told coach Osborne that if I came to Nebraska, I wouldn't be redshirting. I would be playing. He said he would have no problem with that. When I heard that, I was headed to Lincoln.

When I got to Nebraska, I roomed with Pernell Gatson, a wingback, and we used to sit up all night talking. I would tell him all the things I was going to do on the field, and he would tell me, "Broderick, just because you are a blue chip and an All-American this and that, it doesn't mean you will be owning this place. There are high-school All-Americans all over the place here."

I would tell him what I was going to accomplish, and he would just say, "OK, Broderick. OK, Broderick." He was always saying that to me.

Then *Sports Illustrated* came out with an article titled "Just Another All-American at Nebraska," and it had this picture that was an overhead view of the whole team stretching, meaning all of the Nebraska players were All-Americans. I thought, "That sounds just like what Pernell was saying."

One of my most embarrassing moments came in the weight room when we had to test out before we put on the pads. You were supposed to bench 225 pounds as many times as you could. Here I am a big, bad All-American, but I was nervous because I had to do it in front of everybody. All of a sudden, the 225 fell on my chest, and I couldn't get it off. All of my teammates were laughing at me. I got off that bench, got the bar off my chest, and just went irate. I yelled, "Wait till we get on the field." I was screaming and cussing and that opened up a whole can of worms. I'll never forget that.

That freshman year, I wanted to show them all. I wanted to play right now, and I thought I was better than the linebackers who were playing ahead of me. I just didn't get along with the linebackers coach, George Darlington, at all. I thought I should be starting, but he would tell me, "You don't know the defense."

I told him, "I don't need to know it, and I can still run around and make plays better than the guys ahead of me. I make plays and they don't."

He would say, "That won't get it around here. You need to know the defense."

I was learning the position on the run because I had been a defensive end in high school and now I was an outside linebacker. I was young for my class, too, still 17 years old. I just thought, "This coach is crazy."

I am sure coach Osborne looked at me at times and just thought, "Oh my God, what have we got ourselves into with him?"

I guess that I was angry my whole freshman year. I started to threaten to leave toward the end of the season, and I was very close to leaving. I just didn't want to take a backseat to anybody, and I know a lot of my teammates didn't like me. I spoke my mind, and I was different from what they were used to at Nebraska. I would call my mom and my uncle and I would tell them I wanted to leave. Everybody told me to be patient, that things would work out.

But I was on my way out, and I told coach Osborne I was leaving. But apparently, all along he had been making some moves. Coach Osborne called my room one morning at about 7:00. Now Coach never called your room at that hour unless you had done something wrong. I thought, "Damn, what did I do now?" He just said, "Come over to my office before you go to class."

I walked in and he said, "We're making a few changes; we got you a new coach." It was Tony Samuel, who would be the new linebackers coach. Right away, coach Samuel told me, "I don't pick the starters—you decide who the starter is."

"Let's go," I said.

Right away, that calmed me down. I knew then that I didn't make the wrong decision by coming to Nebraska.

A native Texan, Broderick "the Sandman" Thomas made plenty of noise on and off the field while becoming a two-time All-American.

From that point on, coach Samuel said, "We're getting you ready to play Florida State in the opener next season."

One of my proudest days was becoming a Blackshirt at the beginning of my sophomore year. Before that Florida State game at 8:00 on national TV, I had to bend down to get in the stadium. I just told everybody back home, "If y'all got regular TVs—you don't need cable—turn on ABC Saturday night, because I won't be hard to find."

I started that night and made a few plays in the backfield, and I knew then that that was what the "Sandman" came to Nebraska for. (I got that name when I was throwing offensive players around in high school. A teammate, Joseph Green, just started calling me "Sandman," and it stuck). At that moment, everything changed. I think they all thought, "Maybe he really can play like he says."

One time that season, coach Devaney [then the athletic director] came out to watch practice and said, "We are very lucky to get a guy like Broderick. He's an Oklahoma-type guy in a Nebraska uniform. He's brash and confident and he can play."

I think I really was misunderstood more than anything.

After my sophomore year, the offense was getting so much publicity that it angered me. I began to become very difficult to deal with when it came to the media, and I hated the perception that Nebraska was all about offense. We had one of the top defenses in the country for four years in a row, but all you read about was offense, offense, offense. I was very rebellious about it, so I fired off even more than normal. I kept saying, "We play defense around here, too! Has anybody noticed?"

I guess it was always something with me. I had to have something to be angry about. I was just fired up about something every day of the week.

At the end of my sophomore year, Brian Washington called my room and asked me to come down to his room. I walked in, and there were mostly Blackshirts in the room. "What are y'all doing?" I asked them.

They said they just wanted to talk. One of them said, "As a group, we want you to know that we accept you. Whatever you say from this day on, we are with you." I figured before that 85 percent of the defense didn't like me, but now I thought, "This is one less fight I got."

By the time I was a senior, I already was an All-American and people knew I had backed up what I had said. We lost at UCLA early in that season because we took them lightly. We had beaten them badly the year before and thought it would be easy. Everybody else—we blew them out of the game, and I played about half of the games because they weren't close.

I used to plead with coach Osborne to let me play more, but he didn't want the starters to get hurt. I think I played only five full games in my senior year because of all the blowouts. By the end of the season, at my last home game, when they called my name before the game, it just seemed like everything slowed down. The four years had gone so fast, but I could see everything so clearly in that final home game. Now, everything was moving in slow motion.

I thank God that He sent me to Nebraska, I really do. In Texas, I am a stepchild to this day. I thank God for Jack Pierce, who came and recruited me. I want to thank two of my best friends in the whole world—Neil Smith and Lawrence Pete. They were great teammates and are great friends. I remember when Neil and I started to become close. Neil is from New Orleans, and we were in study hall one day, and he said something to the tutor that she didn't understand.

She asked, "Will you say that again?"

He said it again and she still didn't understand. So I said, "Excuse me, let me tell you what he just said."

175

I told her and he said, "Yeah, that's what I just said." We were Southern folks, and we talked fast and talked different, and she didn't understand Neil. But from that point on, we became very close.

I want to thank Charlie McBride—he was the greatest defensive coordinator. And Bob Devaney was the greatest athletic director. Coach Osborne always said, "We are a family." It was our Husker Family. My teammates always will be part of the family, but I am not for what they did at Nebraska recently. I figured coach Devaney would be kicking in his grave when he saw what they did to coach Solich. I was not for it at all, and I am very disappointed with the way it happened.

On the other hand, the Nebraska fans are the best. Fans love our Blackshirts, and I feel blessed to have played in front of that Big Red crowd. There is no place like it. In the NFL, I remember Sterling Sharpe once told me, "I have never been to a place like Nebraska in my life. We got beat and they gave us a standing ovation!"

Nebraska fans just appreciate good football, and they show good sportsmanship.

It was the people at Nebraska that made my time there so special. I want to thank Don "the Fox" Bryant; the current sports information director, Chris Anderson; the McGowan family for being such a great family to me; the Misle family; the Semrad family; Doctor Garcia and his family; Dave and Bonnie Martin; the football secretaries, Mary Lyn Wininger and Joni Duff; and trainers George Sullivan, Jerry Smith, and Jerry Weber.

After the NFL Draft, I'll never forget the time my agent and I were riding to Tampa, and I started to cry. He said, "What is wrong with you? Do you realize what you are doing? You are about to sign a $4.3-million contract with a $1.7-million bonus, and you are crying?"

I just said, "Man, things will never be the same."

I was about to get all this money, and all I was thinking about was leaving Nebraska and how bad I felt. People always welcomed me there. In Nebraska, there is no "black and white." It is all red and white. It is literally home for me. Nebraska is where I can be me and be comfortable. As soon as my son graduates from school, I would like to move back there and build a house. I have to admit that Nebraska spoiled me for the NFL. I played for one of the finest coaches to ever walk the sideline, in front of those fans, and then I got to the NFL and played in half-empty stadiums.

I was proud to be a Buccaneer, a Lion, a Viking, and a Cowboy, but there is nothing I am more proud of than being a Blackshirt for the Nebraska Cornhuskers.

Broderick Thomas was a two-time All-American and three-time All–Big Eight linebacker. In 1988, he was named the Big Eight Defensive Player of the Year and was a team captain. He finished his career with 242 tackles, 39 tackles for losses, and 22.5 sacks. He was inducted into the Nebraska Football Hall of Fame in 1994. Thomas played 10 seasons in the NFL, including five with the Tampa Bay Buccaneers.

DAVE RIMINGTON
CENTER
1979–1982

AS A LITTLE KID, I WOULD PLAY FOOTBALL IN THE YARD with other kids and pretend to be a Nebraska player. We would listen to the radio on Saturdays, and when you heard Lyle Bremser's voice, it was as if you were at the game. That's how I became attracted to Cornhusker football—through the radio. I think my first memory of it would have been the 1969 Sun Bowl when Nebraska beat Georgia easily. All those names—like Rich Glover, Johnny Rodgers, Larry Jacobson, Jerry Tagge—I thought those guys walked on water. And believe it or not, back then I wanted to be a quarterback like Jerry.

In high school, at Omaha South, I wasn't towering and the way my body was built, I thought I had better concentrate on the center position. I was about 6'2", and put together about perfectly for the position. So I played center and linebacker, and my weight was up to about 245 by the time I was a senior. I really was a better defensive player in high school, but I knew I wouldn't be fast enough to stay on that side of the ball in college, so center just seemed more of a natural position for me.

I visited Colorado, Iowa State, and Nevada-Las Vegas, but there was no doubt about where I would wind up. Nebraska really didn't have to sell me when it came to recruiting because I was already sold before I ever took my visit. I just knew, after I got to Lincoln, that this was where I wanted to be. Nebraska had a great reputation—a great tradition and I knew they graduated

Shown here preparing to snap to Turner Gill, Dave Rimington is one of the most honored centers in college football history.

a majority of their players. I saw the Alabama game in 1977 on my visit, and seeing Bear Bryant on the opposing sidelines, seeing the stadium, seeing the crowd—I just thought to myself, "I want to be a part of this."

From the beginning, I could tell coach Osborne was a class act. First of all, when he talked to your parents when he was recruiting you, you never had to worry about a lot of double-talk. He told them I would get a good education, and if something happened to me injury-wise, I would still have a scholarship to go to school.

And I already had my share of injuries: as a junior in high school, I broke my femur, and then I blew out my left knee in a high school all-star game.

From that point on, I played without a cruciate ligament, and then the cartilage came out. Back then, you either played with that injury or you didn't play at all.

As a freshman in 1978, I got into a few games right away. I'll never forget going to Alabama. When we were running out onto the field, a whiskey bottle flew over my head. I thought, "Wow, I am not back in Omaha anymore." I knew right then that college football was played at another level.

I got hurt a few games later, and that dictated that it would become my redshirt year. I got my knee rehabbed, and the trainers took care of me very well. I was behind Kelly Saalfield in 1979 and I really learned a lot by watching him. I used to go 100 mph straight ahead when I played, but I learned finesse from watching Kelly.

I then became the starter for the next three years.

That summer before the 1980 season, I stared at this promotional photo of an opposing nose guard just to motivate me when I was working out. It was Ron Simmons of Florida State. Ron was, in one word, huge. As you may know, he later became a professional wrestler. They had made this PR poster of him wrestling an alligator, and you could tell that he was a full-grown man. In the third game, we faced Penn State. They had Matt Millen and Bruce Clark on the defensive line, and I did OK against them. The next week, we played Florida State, and I have to admit that Ron scared the hell out of me at first. I really thought he was going to rip my head off. But I did OK against him, too, and blocked him some.

179

I thought to myself, "Maybe he's an All-American, but I blocked him, so I must be OK." That really boosted my confidence for the rest of the season.

That year, we went to the Sun Bowl and beat Mississippi State pretty badly [31–17], but we all knew that that type of bowl game wasn't what we were used to at Nebraska. We were there in Texas on Christmas Day, and a lot of people wanted to be home that day. At Nebraska, we were meant to go to Orange Bowls, and it served as an awakening for everyone to work hard to get back there.

The big thing in my era was playing, and beating, Oklahoma. Coach Osborne had never beaten them until that 1978 game in which they came in ranked No. 1. I really think it was the most excited I ever saw a Nebraska football team. They really had twice the team we had that year, but we ended up beating them, and it was coach Osborne's first win over them, so it was very special for all of his players as well.

We beat Oklahoma again in my junior and senior years, so we finally got that Oklahoma thing off of coach Osborne's back. The fact is, our team was put together to beat Oklahoma. We ran the I [formation], but we had a lot of option in the offense, and our defense was geared to face Oklahoma's offense. That was the next step in coach Osborne's career—to beat Barry Switzer and get that monkey off of his back. And we did that.

After my class was gone, they would say that he couldn't win the big game, so I was ecstatic when he did that to win three national championships in the nineties.

As I look back, I really believe our 1982 team was as good as any. We were just a couple of plays away from winning the national championship. But at Penn State, we were winning the game with a minute to go, and they got a couple of calls go their way, and they ended up winning the national championship. We were pretty good, finishing 12–1, with that last-second loss to Penn State the one thing that kept us from a national championship. They always talk about the 1983 team and how it was one of the best teams ever, but we were right there the year before. I would have put us against anybody that year. (I still think the 1995 team was the best Nebraska ever had, though.)

People always ask me about my awards, and fans remember you because of that. But honestly, all of that happened so fast, you just can't absorb it all when you are in college. I was worried about the day-to-day things, like getting ready for the next practice, the next play, the next game. It was an exciting time for me, but those awards are even better when you get older.

I'll always remember being in that foxhole with my fellow linemen because we were like a family: Randy Theiss, Jeff Kwapick, Mike Mandelko, Dean Steinkuhler, and a few others. If they needed something, they could call on me, and I always could call on them. It's that type of relationship with your teammates that I will always remember the most.

The wins and losses, because we played so many games, I don't remember as well. But all that hard work toward a common goal, with those people who become like brothers to me—that is what I'll never forget. In reality, that's what made you work so hard—I never wanted to let down the guy next to me. It was a fear. A good fear.

It really was a dream for me to go to the university in my home state, with great tradition, great players, and great people—and we did everything the right way. We were competitive in every game—I don't think Nebraska had ever been blown out of a game back then, and we had a lot of fun, too. There was a sense of purpose, knowing what you were there for.

The coaches pushed us, but they never used us. I loved Cletus Fischer and coach Osborne. I mean, what can you say about him? He's a class act. What you see is what you get with him. I couldn't ask for anything more from my experience in college. I have no complaints at all.

After I got into pro football, I was with a franchise [the Cincinnati Bengals] that didn't exactly have great facilities. In fact, they were the worst I had ever seen. That made me appreciate being a Cornhusker, and how good we had it, even more. And I got a great education, as promised.

The tradition we have at Nebraska is very special. I have to say that you really appreciate it more as you grow older, and to leave a mark on that tradition and add something to it is a very exciting thing for me.

Dave Rimington is one of the most-honored players in college football history. He won the 1981 and 1982 Outland Trophies, becoming the only player to win the award twice. He also won the 1982 Lombardi Award. Rimington, who was inducted into the College Football Hall of Fame in 1997, played seven seasons in the NFL, including five with the Cincinnati Bengals. He was recently voted as the center on the Nebraska All-Century Team. He currently works for the Boomer Esiason Foundation, which sponsors the Rimington Award given annually to college football's best center.

STEVE DAMKROGER

LINEBACKER

1979–1982

My father Ralph played football at Nebraska from 1947 to 1949, and my older brother Maury played from 1971 to 1973, so that worked against me when it came time for other schools to recruit me. I am sure that coaches at other schools thought, "Why waste time recruiting him because he will probably end up at Nebraska?"

I still wanted to be pursued by other schools, just for my own personal satisfaction, but they were probably right. I probably would have ended up a Cornhusker no matter how hard they had recruited me.

When I was growing up, I sold programs and Cokes at the games at Memorial Stadium. And being around my brother, I got to know all the Nebraska stars in the early seventies. I was hanging around with guys like John O'Leary, John Dutton, and Tom Ruud. I remember seeing all their bowl rings and being impressed with how big they were. Some kids have all the Nebraska players memorized and all that, but I actually knew them personally.

At that time, I was more into pro football. I was a fan of guys like Dick Butkus, Chris Hanberger of the Redskins, Ray Nitschke, and Mike Curtis. You might notice they were all linebackers, too.

Cletus Fischer recruited me to Nebraska, and coach Osborne was very professional and a class act right from the beginning. Nothing changed as the years went on and you played for him. You could tell from his message when he recruited you that he wanted you to get an education and that he was not using you as a football player. I could tell that he wanted to take care of us down the road. He always told us, "Playing pro football is a nice goal to have, but it is not a realistic goal for everyone." He always stressed that in all of our meetings.

I wish back then that I had a clearer picture of planning for the future. I just really loved the game of football, and that was one of the main reasons I went to Nebraska. When you are 18 or 19 years old, though, you don't think 20 years down the road. I just knew I wanted to play football for Nebraska and get some sort of degree.

After I signed my scholarship, I went to the spring game and I thought, "Geez, these guys are big." I saw Barney Cotton, Mark Goodspeed, and Kelvin Clark, and they seemed huge to us. Here we were, 18-year old, skinny little weenies, and we all wondered how we would play against guys that size.

I redshirted in 1978, and that became a great thing for me later because it allowed me to play varsity for four years. I remember the first action I got the following year was running down the field on the kickoff coverage teams in front of eighty thousand screaming fans. You feel like you are on top of the world and it is the best time of your life.

In my sophomore year, Steve McWhirter and I felt we should have been playing instead of the starters who were in there. Steve and I were both line-backers, and we were good buddies. Both of us were a bit unhappy with a lack of playing time, and I think coach [John] Melton got word of it through the media that we were unhappy and had our transfer papers in hand.

It was routine that coaches felt that you had to pay your dues before you played, but I always believed the best player should play, no matter how old or young he was. I just wanted a chance to prove myself. I wasn't too fast, I wasn't really strong, and I wasn't very smart, but I thought I should have been playing. I loved the game of football, and I always tried as hard as I could at every aspect of the game. Well, coach Melton got word that we were unhappy, even though we never did have our transfer papers in hand.

At that time, I don't think the coaches were really happy with the line-backers in front of me. I started the second half of the Kansas game and had a really good half with about six tackles and a knocked-down pass. After that, I became a starter.

To start off my junior year, we went over to Iowa and got beat. Then we lost to Penn State two games later, and we were 1–2. We were really down in the dumps. I remember my brother told me at that time, "To be the best,

Steve Damkroger (No. 35) was one of the most intense linebackers in Nebraska history.

you have to be good—and lucky." And we weren't having much luck then. But we started to gel right after that and won the rest of our games to get us to the Orange Bowl.

When we played Clemson in the Orange Bowl, Turner Gill was hurt, and they hung on to beat us [22–15] to win the national championship.

The next season, we were one of the better, if not the best, clubs in the nation. But we went to Penn State and really got hammered on a bad call.

That Penn State game sticks in my craw to this day because of a play that I did not make.

We were leading them late in the game, and they were driving when they faced a third-and-10. I came clear on a blitz, and I had [Penn State quarterback] Todd Blackledge in my sights. Just as I got to him, he ducked underneath my arms and then got off an incomplete pass. On the next play, he completed a fourth-and-10 pass. A few plays later, they scored and benefited from that poor call on a pass reception in which the guy was out of bounds.

But I will *always* remember that one play. If I had sacked him, it would have been about fourth-and-18, and they wouldn't have picked up the first down. I just felt like I had let everybody down.

That is the one thing that really bothers me: we never won a national championship when I was there. If I had made that play and we had beaten Penn State, we would have finished 13–0 instead of 12–1, because we won the rest of our games and beat LSU in the Orange Bowl.

I am very glad that I followed my dad and my brother and went to Nebraska. I would do it all over again if I had the chance. It really was the best time of my life, and I did get my degree in natural resources. All these years later, I have to consider my college career a once-in-a-lifetime opportunity.

I am sure that most schools have some sort of tradition, but at Nebraska, we had a special tradition. I have always appreciated the effort that the older guys put forth to build it into what it is today. I realize that it took a large commitment and the loyalty and effort of those people who came before me. I have to thank all of them for making Nebraska what it is today.

Steve Damkroger was a cocaptain, along with Dave Rimington, in 1982 and also was named All–Big Eight that season. He ranks fifth among Nebraska's career tackle leaders with 269. He was inducted into the Nebraska Football Hall of Fame in 1995.

DERRIE NELSON
DEFENSIVE END
1978–1980

MY FOOTBALL BEGINNINGS WERE SOMEWHAT HUMBLE because I was from the small town of Fairmont, Nebraska, which had a population of about 760 at the time. When I was a freshman and sophomore, my school played eight-man football because there were so few kids on the teams. Then we turned to 11-man football by my junior year. Our school, Fairmont Public, was a Class D school, but we had a great defense. We played a 3–4, and I played inside linebacker, which was great for me, because we blitzed a lot. My head coach let me call the defenses, and I made sure that we went after them.

But I suppose my best sport was baseball. I was a left-hander, and I could bring it at about 90 mph. I had the Cincinnati Reds looking at me pretty hard. I think I threw three or four no-hitters in high school and had several 20-strikeout games. My uncle—my mom's brother—was Bob Cerv, who roomed with Mantle and Maris on the Yankees, so you could say I had good baseball bloodlines.

Despite all that, when I came out of high school, all I had offered was a track scholarship to a small college. Arizona State and Oklahoma State wanted me to try to walk on in football, and I didn't want to go to either school.

I had only one real dream—and that was to play football for the University of Nebraska.

I was 6'1", 195 pounds, but I really couldn't believe that those guys who were receiving scholarships and playing at big schools hit any harder than I did. I just had to go check, to find out, to see if I was right. I didn't want any regrets as I grew older, so I headed to Lincoln to walk on for the Cornhuskers.

When I first got there, there were about 140 guys at that first freshman practice. They asked me, "There are the defensive ends and there are the linebackers, which group do you want to go to?"

I looked at the defensive ends, which were actually stand-up outside line-backers in Nebraska's defense, and decided that was my place. I think there were two scholarship [freshmen] players ahead of me. The one thing that got my attention right away were the pink slips. Every day you would come into the locker room, and the pink slips would be everywhere. Coaches would leave pink slips in the lockers of the walk-on guys who were being cut. If you got a pink slip, you knew you were going home. We were on one side of the stadium, and the scholarship guys were on the other side. In the end, after the pink slips were given out like candy at Halloween, it was me and one other guy left.

187

The freshman game that sticks out in my mind was up at Iowa State. My position coach grabbed me on the sideline and said, "Nelson, get in there and sack the quarterback!"

I said, "Is that what you want?"

On the first play, I sacked him. On the second play, I sacked him again and caused a fumble. I came off the field, and coach said, "We pretty much know where you will be now, don't we?"

Having avoided the pink-slip parade, I knew just being involved with the program was huge for me. I came from a small town as a walk-on, and now I was part of the pride and tradition that is Nebraska football. It was over-whelming at times, but once I strapped on a helmet, I felt I could do any-thing. I just had peace of mind once I put that helmet on.

I had to take financial aid as a walk-on to pay for school, but it was a known thing that if you cracked the two-deep chart that you were automatically on scholarship. So I didn't worry when they would tell me, or if they would tell me, that I received a scholarship. I just knew if I could get to second-team, I would have one.

Going into my sophomore year, I figured they would have to throw me out of the program to get me out of there. I knew the seniors that were leaving at my position, and I figured I had a good chance to move up the depth chart. The position was wide open and I had a great spring game. I knew our [offense's] audible system pretty well, so I knew what the offense was going to do. I would think to myself, "Just run the ball to my side!"

So after the spring of 1978, I was on scholarship. It was a huge thing knowing I didn't have to pay for school or books or whatever. I had made it.

Heading into camp, it was me and L. C. [Lawrence] Cole battling it out to start. I remember running out onto Memorial Stadium for that first game [against Alabama, 1978]: I was totally engulfed by the emotion. It was something you just dream about. It was a sea of red, and I just soaked it all in. It was the whole reason and purpose of all the hard work I had put in. My first action would have been on kickoff coverage. I was to the right of the kicker—"R1"—and as I ran down the field, it was as if my feet didn't touch the ground.

Later in the season against Oklahoma State, I was spread way out toward the sideline on one play in which they ran a screen pass. It broke wide open on the opposite sideline. I ran the guy down 50 or 60 yards downfield from the opposite sideline and knocked him out of bounds. On the next play, I sacked the quarterback, caused a fumble, and recovered it. After that, I had cemented my position. It was a huge confidence-builder, and I took it for all it was worth. You could say that I knew the power of emotion, because I played with total controlled rage.

On the kickoff team against Oklahoma that year, I witnessed the hardest hit ever. I was trying to get through a wedge, and all of a sudden, my roommate John Ruud somehow sliced through and hit this guy—and I swear I thought he had killed him. It was the biggest hit I had ever seen, and they still show the highlight of it here in Nebraska. Anyway, the guy fumbled, but the officials called it dead. I remember Barney Cotton, our big guard, saying, "We just got f***** on that call and we are not going to take it! We are going to beat their asses"—which we did.

Oklahoma was the most talented team I ever saw on a football field. They had two first-rounders and a second-rounder in the backfield, including Billy Sims, and we held them to 14 points [a 17–14 win]. The next week, we hadn't quite gotten over beating Oklahoma, and Missouri came to town and ruined our national championship dreams. Missouri wasn't chump change, either. They had Phil Bradley at quarterback, James Wilder, and Kellen Winslow.

Derrie Nelson, here taking on a blocker, went from walk-on to Big Eight Defensive Player of the Year in 1980.

They beat us in a track meet, 35–31, and then we had to play Oklahoma again in the Orange Bowl.

That was a meaningless game to us because we already had beaten them. How can you have two teams in the same conference play in a bowl like that? It was terrible.

It seemed every year we were in the national championship race till the end. In 1979, we had won 10 in a row to start the season and couldn't beat Oklahoma. But that year our defensive line was full of studs. Dan Pensick—man, I wouldn't have wanted to fight him. Rod Horn was a [third]-rounder with the Bengals. Kerry Weinmaster—we called him "Wine-o"—and Oudious Lee, Bill Barnett, and David Clark, who was a Golden Gloves boxer. That was a great defensive line.

My senior year was totally different for me. I knew how I had played as a junior, and I knew I had to up the ante, so to speak. I was voted captain by my teammates, which is the highest honor I ever received. Back then you only had one captain on defense and one on offense. Randy Schleusener was our offensive captain. To be voted captain was a neat thing—I just always felt that you put it on the line and led by example, not with your mouth.

We really went at it in practice, though. We had one-on-one drills with the tight ends, and going against Junior Miller and Jamie Williams would have been worth paying to see for the fans. Junior was big, fast, strong, and everything you wanted a tight end to be. I used to watch him catch one over the middle and just run away from defensive backs. And Jamie played more than 10 years in the NFL, so we had great tight ends.

Jamie once told me, "Those one-one-one drills got me ready for the NFL."

We won the first three games of 1980, and then we were down 18–14 to Florida State. Our offense was going in for the winning touchdown, but our quarterback, Jeff Quinn, dropped the ball on the 3-yard line. That one really hurt, because we were better than them that day. That was about the time that Bobby Bowden and Florida State were just getting started.

We may have lost to Oklahoma again [21–17] in our final home game, but I still to this day say that the 1980 defense was the best that Tom Osborne ever had. Look at the statistics: we gave up only 8.5 points per game [fifth best in Nebraska history]! We used to say, "It's up to us—if they don't score, we won't lose." All the offense needed to get was 17 or 21 points and we would win the game, and we knew that.

Back then we had so much pride, and we had only 11 Blackshirts. If one got hurt, then we had 10. We didn't give them out to just anybody. Later on, they had something like 14 or 15 Blackshirts, and I always thought that wasn't right. You had to battle to get a black shirt, and there was major pride in wearing one.

I always liked Charlie McBride, our line coach at the time, but I couldn't stand our defensive coordinator, Lance Van Zandt. He would make me the angriest I had ever been in my life. I just hated that man. He used to try to intimidate players by pushing them and kicking them. I told him, "If you ever do that to me, we will have it out." I saw him once at a Super Bowl in New Orleans years later, and my feelings for him had not gone away.

Coach Osborne, however, was a great, caring individual. He had great wisdom and my biggest regret to this day is that we never got him in our captains' photo. It was tradition for the head coach to be pictured with the captains, but our photo is just Randy and me.

I still have my jerseys and my helmet, and I just recently put all my Nebraska memorabilia on the walls. The camaraderie from Nebraska was unbelievable to me. Sometimes, I feel sad at what I see there now. I don't know if they play with the same emotion or fire that we played with on defense.

I have to say that my career was a field of dreams. I got a shot, I took it, and things fell into place at the right time for me. It was a blast, too. We were like a big family, and we all had heart. That's why I had hoped they wouldn't eliminate the walk-on program, because it is where I had come from. You have to recruit the heart, not just the size and speed and those things.

I guess that was what drove me—how far had I come? How far could I go? Nebraska was the only place for me to make it happen.

Derrie Nelson had 21 tackles for loss in 1980 and was named the Big Eight's Defensive Player of the Year. He also was an All-American and team cocaptain that year. He finished his career with 145 tackles, including 30 for loss. Nelson played five seasons with the San Diego Chargers. He was inducted into the Nebraska Football Hall of Fame in 1998.

JOHN MCCORMICK
GUARD
1985–1987

WITH A NAME LIKE MCCORMICK, IT WAS NATURAL for me to be attracted to Notre Dame—and I was when I was a kid. I remember on Sunday mornings when I was growing up, I would always watch the Notre Dame replay show, you know, "Later, in the same series of downs . . ." Notre Dame was the big thing when I was younger, but when it came time for me to choose a college, that changed.

I was always a pretty good-sized kid—so big in the seventh and eighth grades that they didn't even let me play football. They had a weight limit and I was over it. It was frustrating for me because I loved football, but I stayed involved and helped the team out on the side. I still wrestled and played basketball and baseball, but I wanted to play football.

By the time I got to high school, Daniel J. Gross High in Omaha, I was playing guard on offense and noseguard on defense. I was named all-state for my junior and senior years. We had quality teams, losing only two or three games each season.

I was pretty highly recruited, and I had to visit Notre Dame just to see what it was like. I liked the campus, but Gerry Faust was the head coach then, and he seemed a little bit too hyper for me. He was like a pep-rally type of guy. He reminded me of a high school coach, which he was before getting the Notre Dame job. I visited Duke, too, but I wasn't really serious about them. I went to UCLA and really enjoyed that visit. That was right before the 1984 Olympics in Los Angeles, and they had all this new stuff—weight rooms, upgraded facilities.

I remember when Nebraska was playing in Hawaii during my senior year [1982], coach Osborne called me from there. At first I thought it was one of my friends joking around, so I didn't say anything on the phone. Finally, I realized it was coach Osborne actually calling from Hawaii. I thought that was pretty cool.

I realized that Nebraska was right in my own backyard, it was a quality program, and in the end, my decision had a lot to do with proximity. I was always close-mouthed about things like that, so Dad asked me, "What do you want to do?"

It came down to UCLA and Nebraska, but I knew that I really wanted to play football at Nebraska. How could I go somewhere else?

When I got to campus, I had the usual worries. You worry whether you are good enough, and like most freshmen, I was in awe. You wonder if you fit in, and then you get some practices in, go to classes, make friends, and realize that you do fit in. I liked it in Lincoln right away.

At that time, I know I was very tired. I had played in a high school all-star game right before fall camp, and we had two weeks of two-a-day practices. Then I got to campus and we had two-a-days at camp, so I had more than a month of two-a-day practices.

I redshirted in 1984, and by fall camp of the next season, I had become a starter—and I would start for the next three seasons.

People always ask me, "What was coach Osborne like to play for?"

I answer, "What you see with him is what you get with coach Osborne." He's a good Christian man with good values. What people don't realize is that he is actually kind of funny. He has that dry humor.

I'll never forget the hardest I ever saw him laugh. We had two streetwise guys on the team, Willie Griffin and Tyreese Knox, who were both from California. These guys bought what they thought were VCRs on the street, but after they opened the box, there were nothing but some bricks in there. Well, Chris Drennan, our kicker, drew this big cartoon on the chalkboard one day after that and he wrote something like, "It hits you like a ton of VCRs." Coach Osborne walked in and saw that cartoon and just started laughing out loud. I had never seen him laugh like that.

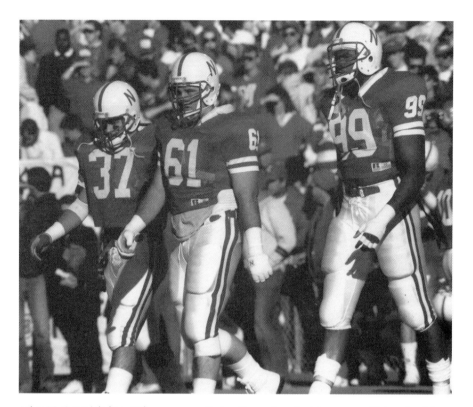

John McCormick (No. 61) grew up a Notre Dame fan, but became a Nebraska All-American.

In 1986, we were getting beat by Iowa State at the half, and he was really yelling at us. There were "dadgummits" flying left and right, and he kept hitting his hand. And when he would hit his hand each time, his watch would come undone. I was thinking, "What a cheap watch." I couldn't even concentrate on what he was saying because I was paying so much attention to that cheap watch.

But even when he got mad, it wasn't too mad. "Dadgummit" and "gosh darn it" were his cuss words. He had such great self-control.

We had some great teams in my years at Nebraska, but we could never run the table to get that national championship. We never beat Oklahoma, but we came so close. In 1985 and 1987, they outplayed us. But in 1986, we should have beaten them. I thought we had their number that year, but it just didn't work out [20–17 loss in Lincoln]. Then in 1987, we flip-flopped in the polls the week before and we entered the game No. 1 while they were No. 2. They probably had more talent overall in those three years. We were kind of a bunch of overachievers, and they were always very talented. But what did Barry Switzer always call it? Sooner Magic? I never thought it was a mental thing with us, though. They were just our nemesis and seemed to make one more play than we did.

I always said it was a great honor to be named an All-American, but I would have traded it for a win over Oklahoma.

We had a great lineman tradition at Nebraska, and the best thing when you were younger was getting to learn from the older players. We always helped each other, and we had great camaraderie. We always felt that pressure not to be the team that broke tradition and not to have a really terrible season. That's why I felt so badly for those guys a few years ago who went 7–7. We always said we didn't want to be that team.

All those years since the sixties and seventies, we didn't have the peaks and valleys like a lot of programs do. We were a consistent winner, and now we all realize how hard that was. The older guys helped recruit us, and we helped recruit those guys who came after us.

When Nebraska won the three national championships in the nineties, I was so happy for coach Osborne. He finally got that thing off of his back. We weren't there to play in it, but it was great to see our Nebraska family win it all.

195

John McCormick was All–Big Eight, an All-American, and team captain in 1987. He was inducted into the Nebraska Football Hall of Fame in 2002.

TONY FELICI
DEFENSIVE END
1980–1982

If it wasn't for my job working at Ak-Sar-Ben, the horse racing track in Omaha, I probably would have never ended up playing football at Nebraska.

I played at Omaha Central High, but I wasn't a great high school football player by any means, and I had no intention of playing college football. I was just a middle-of-the-road player, and I wasn't exactly an academic type, either.

But our team had a great running back named Danny Goodwin, and Nebraska came to recruit him, although he ended up going to Iowa State. [Nebraska assistant coach] Cletus Fischer had recruited him, and Cletus loved going over to the track to bet the horses when he was in Omaha. I would be out there selling race programs and see Cletus. "What horse do you like?" he always asked me.

I got to know him and really liked him, and he started talking to me about Nebraska's walk-on program. He tried to talk me into coming down and walking on.

The problem was, I think I had a high school GPA of about 1.9, and it had to be higher than that to get on scholarship. I had just never applied myself in school. I had played one year of midget football, and our school didn't even have a freshman football program. When my friends talked me into going out for football at Central, I broke my ankle in the third week of practice.

The next year, I came back and started at quarterback, even though I never had any experience playing quarterback. We had some great athletes, but we weren't well coached at all. It was kind of a hodgepodge team.

I remember playing Dave Rimington's school one season, our linemen were the same size as me, and I was getting killed at quarterback. They would snap the ball and I would get tackled. They would snap the ball and I would get tackled again. After this happened on one particular first down, I called time-out and walked to the sidelines. I told the coaches, "You got the wrong guy at quarterback. I am not doing quarterback anymore."

And I didn't. They told me, "If you are not playing offense, you are not playing at all."

I said, "OK."

But they finally switched me to the defensive line, and I enjoyed it there. I was strictly a playground-type of kid, and we never had a structured defense. If the other offense ran the ball, you yelled "run," and if it was a pass, you yelled "pass." But I was always around the ball, and if a college coach would turn on our film, he probably saw me near the football.

I guess Cletus had watched a little film, because he tried to talk me into the Nebraska walk-on program. Finally, he talked me into trying it.

I had never really talked about it much with my family that summer, and one day I just told everybody that I was going to go to Nebraska to try out for the football team.

"You've got be kidding me," one of my brothers said. "Have you lost your mind?"

They all felt that way.

I was about 6'1" and 180 pounds and I wasn't fast, but I think the coaches probably looked at me as a special-teams guy. They always took about 50 walk-ons each year, and if 10 of them worked out, that would be great.

On that first day of practice, there was one kid at defensive end on scholarship, and he was my roommate. All he did was cry about missing his girl-friend. Finally he quit and I suddenly had my own room.

In the first few practices, Junior Miller was an All-American tight end, and I was holding my own against him in those one-on-one drills, and I started to think I could fit in and play college football. About 10 practices into fall camp, they handed me a letter to go see coach Osborne. I met with him and he told me I was academically ineligible to play that year based on my GPA.

But he said, "We think you can play at this level and we still want you, but you need to prove you can handle the academic side of college."

So I redshirted and really applied myself to school. I took a heavy load of classes and ended up with a B average. I really thought college was easier than high school, but it was probably because I was applying myself.

198

Tony Felici is introduced at Memorial Stadium before the Cornhuskers' final home game of 1982.

In my second year, they put me on the freshman team. I learned the system and played in all of the freshman games. Coach [Frank] Solich was the freshman coach, and I got to know him really well, and Tony Samuel was my position coach. After I received some coaching from those guys—which I never had before—things came a lot easier for me. After I was taught things like footwork, the angles, reading offensive linemen, and knowing the details of my position, everything just clicked for me.

I went through winter conditioning in 1980, and my goal was to make the traveling squad during my sophomore year. I admit that I wasn't the consummate practice player as far as grasping all of the details like I should have been, but I could make plays. I always think the coaches had a fear of putting me in there because of my unreliability.

In our first game that season against Utah at Memorial Stadium, it was awesome for me. My family showed up with their red jerseys with my number on it and the whole nine yards. I have four brothers and three sisters, and I was the only one of the family to go to Nebraska. I got on the field as a wedge-buster on the kickoff team.

But in that first road game, against Penn State, I didn't get to travel, and Dave Rimington had to calm me down. "Don't worry, man, it will work out," he told me. I did get to play on special teams at home and on some mop-up duty that year.

By the next spring, I reached one large goal: they put me on scholarship. Just the little things of a scholarship, like switching from eating dorm food to getting to eat at the training table, was such a luxury. Before, after practices, the guys you practiced with and sweated with every day would go eat at the training table, and I would have to hustle back to the dorm and hope the cafeteria was still open. Now I got to eat with the guys, and that was one of the best parts of being on scholarship.

One of my first goals was to earn a scholarship, and I finally did that. But once you get a taste of being on that field, you want more playing time.

In 1981, I was probably third-team going into camp because the guys ahead of me were more focused, but I think I may have had more athletic ability. The coaches never knew what I was going to do on the practice field. They always felt that if you practiced well, you would play well in the games. And like I said, I wasn't a great practice player.

In the opener, the starter didn't play that well, so they put in his backup. He didn't play that well, either, so I think they figured, "Well, we have one more straw in the basket, so let's try this guy." I went in and played pretty well.

Then against Florida State, Mike Knox just drilled a guy on a kickoff return and the ball flew up into the air. I caught it and ran about 20 yards into the end zone and scored. On the next series, they told me to go into the game, and I had a couple of sacks and made some big plays. Now did I grade well from a coach's perspective? Probably not. But it seemed that I was always making big plays, so they started me the rest of the season.

I turned into an all-conference player that season, but if they really had gone by how I graded out, I would have been at the bottom of the Big Eight. I was perceived as a dumb kid, like I never knew what was going on—and I admit now that I played into that perception. Coaches would ask me questions like, "What color was George Washington's white horse?"

I would say something like, "Don't ask me. I don't know anything about horses."

But Cletus always thought I did, or he wouldn't have asked me for tips way back when.

200

It was kind of a joke, but it made things easier for me because they didn't expect much. On game days, if I thought they would be passing, I would rush the quarterback. If I thought it was going to be a run, I would play the run. It drove the coaches crazy because I may not have been following the specific defense we had called, but they would just say, "Well, let's play him another game."

I did get in much better shape working out with Dave [Rimington], because he was the consummate workaholic. I would spot him when he lifted weights, and spotting him was a workout in itself.

In 1982, we had one of coach Osborne's best teams ever, but we barely lost that game at Penn State that later cost us a national championship. Winning games was fun, of course, but for me, the camaraderie of being around the guys was the best part of it all.

Off the field, we had a blast—a real riot. And I was always organizing something.

We were at the Orange Bowl to play Clemson my junior year, and they gave us tickets to the NFL playoff game between the Dolphins and somebody. I wanted to get a group together and go up to Fort Lauderdale to have some fun, but none of us had any money. I told everybody, "Give me your tickets. We'll have money real soon."

So we were just hanging around outside the stadium and we made a lot of money selling our tickets. Then one of the coaches walked by and said, "What are you guys doing out here?"

"Well, we forgot our tickets," we said.

So the coach called security to get us in the gate, and they took us to our seats, where the people we had just sold our tickets to were sitting. I think security kicked them out of our seats as they protested, and we felt really bad about it. Then we bolted early in the game and headed up to Fort Lauderdale for some fun. We had a riot—we went to some disco and then went to the dog track.

I remember I got in trouble with coach Osborne one time over working a deal to get a few of us some new shoes. They were called "Kangaroo" shoes, which Walter Payton was wearing at the time. Our team had a deal with Nike, so coach Osborne called me in and said, "You can't be doing this. Nike gives us a great deal to wear their shoes."

Mike Rozier was about to break the career rushing record at the time, and I had told this guy for Kangaroo that he would wear his shoes as he broke the record. They really were terrible shoes, but we had a deal with this guy. So Mike wore the Nikes in the first half and the Kangaroos in the second half when he broke the record.

Like I said, I was always organizing something.

To have the opportunity I had, to play at one of the top programs in the country for one of the greatest coaches of all time with the players I played with, I can't imagine it being any better than it was.

Look at where I came from: I was a walk-on with poor grades, a guy who nobody really wanted. If I was in this generation today, I would have been kicked aside as small, dumb, and too slow. But the main thing is that I persevered and things fell into place for me.

I feel so much gratitude for all the people at Nebraska that made it happen for me, and the memories I have from it are priceless.

Tony Felici was named All–Big Eight in 1981 and 1982, becoming one of only four players in school history to begin as a walk-on and later earn all-conference honors twice.

MIKE ROZIER

RUNNING BACK

1981–1983

P EOPLE ALWAYS LAUGH AT THIS, BUT MY DREAM wasn't always to be a professional football player—I wanted to become a trash man when I was growing up in Camden, New Jersey. Sometimes even today, I still do. You are probably laughing now, but it's true. Back then it was all trash, but now it's a lot cleaner with all the recycling bins, but football took me away from those dreams. The thing is, I never had a problem with hard labor. My dad had worked two jobs, and my mom worked at the school because there were six boys in the house to feed.

Dad worked for the U.S. Pipe Company and Mom was PTA president, so she was always very involved in the school programs. I grew up with five brothers and it was just natural for us to play sports. I started playing football when I was very young in the 80-pounders league, and I can remember our team name—the Vikings. By the time I got to high school, I had started all four years at fullback, and because we ran the wishbone, I was in a three-point stance, but I still got plenty of carries. I don't want to brag, but I was the man in high school. We had a powerhouse of a high school team, but I think it took another player for the Nebraska coaches to notice me.

They were looking at film of Billy Griggs, who later played with the Jets. They saw me playing against Billy's team, and asked, "Who's the kid from Camden?"

When I was being recruited from Woodrow Wilson High, the only head coach to come visit me was Tom Osborne. Ever since that day, I have so much respect for that man. I like to think that we became close from that day forward. Penn State recruited me. Arizona recruited me. It seemed every big football school wanted me, but he was the only head coach who ever came to my house. Frank Solich was the Nebraska assistant coach who also had been recruiting me at the time.

My grades were borderline when I came out as a senior, and at that time, there was a teachers' strike going on at my school. My mom had a lot of boys to support, so she crossed the picket line to go to work. My history teacher didn't like that and took it out on me by giving me a bad grade. How did that affect me? It prevented my GPA from being where it needed to be for me to go to a four-year college and play football.

So the Nebraska coaches recommended me to Coffeyville Junior College in Kansas, and I hopped on a Greyhound bus and headed to Kansas. Man, that was lonely. I didn't know anybody, and I was traveling halfway across the country to a place I hadn't been before. It was a scary time. It was my first time away from home, and I had grown up as a mama's boy. I wanted to quit a few times that first year, but my mom told me to hang in there, that things would get better for me.

203

At Coffeyville that year, we only lost one game. Dick Foster was our head coach, and we were running the wishbone, but I had moved to halfback. Mel Gray [who later played a long time in the NFL, including five years with the Detroit Lions] was on the other side of the wishbone opposite me. Let's just say that I called home a lot that year. I had lived in East Camden and South Camden growing up, and I had not spent that much time with white people. But Kansas was all white—the only black people on campus were the athletes. It was good for me because my teammates took me home to their farmhouses and their country neighborhoods, and people treated me really well.

The important thing was that I got my grades up. Back then you only had to play one year of junior college if you got your grades up. They changed that rule later, making it so that you had to play two. When I came out of Coffeyville, everybody wanted me once again, but I felt loyal to Nebraska because they were the only school that stuck by me the first time. Other schools even offered me money to come, but I wanted to go to Nebraska because of coach Osborne and the way he treated me from the beginning.

When I got to Nebraska, I was really homesick and tried to quit there a few times, too. We were always a close-knit family, and I missed everybody and missed being home. Coach Osborne talked to me, and Mom talked to me often. I agreed to stick it out—Mom always knows what's best. And my Lincoln parents, Mike and Maggie McGowan, helped me a whole lot. I would go over to their house and watch TV, and they made me feel right at home. I got through that homesick period and felt much better after that.

Roger Craig was at I-back when I got there, and coach Osborne had to figure out a way to get us both on the field at the same time. He moved Roger to fullback, and Roger was cool with that. I give him a lot of credit because he really took it well and we still talk to this day. It worked out for both of us, as far as the NFL goes, so there are no hard feelings.

When I think of games, that loss at Penn State in 1982 was a tough one because we all felt that we got screwed up there with the officiating. If not for that game, we would have won them all that season and had a national championship.

But we got back at them the following year. By the time we played them in the Kickoff Classic in the Meadowlands, we were so mad that they had cheated us the year before, we were ready to kill them. I think there were three bus-loads of my friends and family in the stadium that day because it was only an hour's drive from home. And we did kill them [Penn State] that day [44–6].

We did that to everybody that year, but the thing about coach Osborne was he was so classy that he didn't want to run up the scores, so we played only about half of each game.

We always beat Oklahoma in my three years, and that being our rivalry game, I always felt good about that. I got to know coach Switzer later and still see him from time to time. He really is a good guy.

By the time we got to the Orange Bowl to play for the national championship against Miami, we were hungry for that title. I had about 150 yards [147] by the time I got hurt in the second quarter. I still don't know the guy's name, but it was No. 5 for Miami. He tackled me and my ankle twisted. It wasn't a dirty play—just a part of football. But I was done for the day with a bad sprain, and it was very tough to be on the sidelines for the second half of that game.

Jeff Smith came in and did a great job, and we scored the touchdown at the end of the game to make it a one-point game [31–30]. At that point, I remember everybody huddled on the sideline trying to decide whether to

Mike Rozier, Nebraska's all-time leading rusher, sizes up a cornerback before making his move.

kick the extra point or go for the win. We would have been national champions with a tie, but we had played to win every game that season, and coach Osborne wasn't going to change now. They just got a finger on that two-point pass, or we would have won.

All these years later, I still think it was the right thing to do. I have no problems with coach Osborne's decision. I know another thing—there is no doubt in my mind that if I hadn't gotten hurt, we would have beat Miami and won the national championship that night. It wouldn't have even come down to that final play.

But as the years pass, that game doesn't haunt me like it does some people. It was played and over with, and I don't look back on it now. We lost only

[five] games in my three years, but I don't dwell on them. I never did. I had won the Heisman Trophy already, and I ended up giving it to my mom. She still has it in her living room. It would have been nice to add a national championship to that, but I guess it just wasn't meant to be.

People ask me about my records and the Heisman and all those types of things, and I really have never been into all those things. I don't even remember my first touchdown at Nebraska and I don't remember my first 100-yard game, but the truth is that we had a great offensive line at Nebraska. You can't gain yards without the offensive linemen doing their job in front of you.

Those awards get a little more special as the years pass, and the memories of Nebraska are so good for me. I try to go back to Lincoln a few times each year because the good people there always treated me well. They love their football. As for me, I can't watch football anymore. I don't know how people do it. I can't imagine going out to a stadium and sitting in the cold or the rain or bad weather to watch somebody play football. I just turn on *Sports-Center* to see the quick highlights and that is it for me. It is too boring to watch a whole game.

When I look back on my days at Nebraska, if I had to do it all over again, I would make the same decision and go there all over again. Coach Osborne helped turn me from a boy into a man. He kept my head on straight and helped me do the right things. I think I would give a kidney to that man if he needed one. I played a long time in the NFL, but I can say that my college days were the best times of my life.

Mike Rozier was Nebraska's second Heisman Trophy winner. His 2,148 rushing yards and 29 rushing touchdowns in 1983 remain a school record. He also won the Maxwell Award, the Walter Camp Award, and was named Big Eight Player of the Year that season. He is Nebraska's all-time leading rusher with 4,780 rushing yards and second on the career touchdowns list with 52. Rozier also was a two-time All-American. He was a first-round supplemental draft pick of the Houston Oilers in 1984 before playing two seasons in the USFL and seven seasons in the NFL. He was inducted into the Nebraska Football Hall of Fame in 1984.

MARC MUNFORD

LINEBACKER

1984–1986

I WAS BORN IN LINCOLN, BUT OUR FAMILY MOVED AWAY when I was five, and I grew up in Littleton, Colorado. My brother and I always followed Big Red football. We would play in the yard, and I would be Jeff Kinney and he was Jerry Tagge. I always loved to play running back, and that is basically why I didn't play any football in junior high school. They had a weight limit, and the only place I could play was on the line. They would put a patch on your jersey and make you a lineman, but I didn't want to play on the line so I quit for three years. I really loved basketball and I loved baseball, but I just tolerated football.

By the 10th grade, I was about 6'1" and 155 pounds then, really skinny, and I got to play running back and linebacker at Heritage High.

However, baseball was my best sport. As a catcher, I was entertaining offers from baseball schools like Wichita State and Arizona State. I had gone to the Nebraska football camp in the summer of my junior year, and that's how I got on their radar screen. Toward the end of my senior year, they offered me a football scholarship.

When that happened, I just said, "Screw baseball. I am going to play for the Big Red."

Others, like Colorado State, Colorado, and Wyoming, had offered me scholarships, but after I accepted Nebraska's offer, Colorado coaches said in the Denver newspaper that I wasn't smart enough to be admitted into Colorado. You can imagine that that didn't sit too well with me. Bill McCartney was in his first year, and you can say I am not a real big Bill McCartney fan.

When coach Osborne walked into the room when he was recruiting you, he certainly received your attention, although he didn't demand it. He came to Littleton to see me, and Dad knew him from when they used to play basketball together in a town league back in Lincoln.

When I arrived in Lincoln for my freshman year, I had never been in the military, but that's how I envisioned it would be. We checked in, checked out our equipment, and went through all the testing. We were in the North Stadium as freshmen, and that's not where you wanted to be. Let's just say it wasn't a nice place. The motivation was to get on the varsity so you could get to the south end, where the lockers opened and the hinges worked.

I played freshman football at inside linebacker and then dressed for some varsity games, and even got to go to the bowl game [31–30 Orange Bowl loss to Miami].

During the second half of that season, I sort of got thrown into the fire during practice and I felt I held my own against the big boys. That next spring, I won the job in spring practice. Mike Knox had blown out a knee, so now I was No. 1 on the chart. I was just lucky enough not to lose the job once I had it.

It was a neat deal for me because all the seniors and juniors who were returning starters took me under their wing. Guys like Jimmy Skow, Bret Clark, Mike McCashland, Neil Harris, and Mark Daum were a huge help to me. When you come in as a freshman, it isn't all open arms and kisses, but if you can play and earn your stripes, it's like a fraternity. However, it didn't come without a lot of growing pains, tough practices, and a learning curve.

After about five days of camp heading into the 1984 season, there was a large stench wherever our offensive line went. There were three or four guys who decided after the Orange Bowl loss that they weren't going to shower from the beginning of camp until the first win of the season. We would go to the training table to eat after two-a-day practices, and there would be a huge buffer around their table. I mean, it was so bad that you had trouble eating. They were really ripe. It got so bad that [coach Osborne] had to go tell them they *had* to shower. They actually had stuff growing on them. It was funny, but wherever they went, there was a cloud of stench.

That first game was a neat deal, to run out onto that field all clad in red. During those freshman games, you were lucky if you got four thousand fans there, but now it was time for me to play in front of seventy-five thousand

Marc Munford (No. 41), here returning an interception, was a three-time All–Big Eight linebacker.

fans. You never forget running onto Memorial Stadium's field for the first time.

I was a huge fan of Dick Butkus, and I had a poster of him in my locker. Before each practice and each game, I would sort of pay homage to Butkus. So we went out to play at UCLA in the third game, and the air started to come out of the bladder inside my helmet. When I got to the sideline, I told Glen, our equipment manager, that it needed to be repaired. But we fumbled, UCLA got the ball back, and we had to go right back on the field. I grabbed my helmet and ran back out there, but it was before he got a chance to pump it up again. Well, I went to tackle this guy and [safety] Bret Clark came in and knocked me out with a vicious hit.

The next thing I knew, I was lying on my back counting stars. They were asking me where I was, and I knew I was at a football game, but I really didn't know who was playing. Mike McCashland stood over me and said, "Listen, you sissy, get up! Butkus wouldn't be lying there like that!"

I had noodle legs. I got up and wobbled around, and they got me to the sideline. All I know is I had a trip to California, but I don't remember it. We still laugh about that one when I see the guys.

That defense in 1984 really was a great defense. The year before, we had a great offense and a struggling defense. But now we had the No. 1 defense [203.3 yards per game] and a struggling offense. We gave up only [9.5] points per game and played pretty darned good football for the entire season.

The thrill for me that season was against Missouri, when I got fooled on a bootleg. Well, the quarterback threw back my way, and I jumped up, snatched the football, and ran about 55 yards for a touchdown.

The guys had nicknamed me "the Cruiser." I asked them, "Why 'the Cruiser'?"

They said, "You just sort of cruise around and make plays."

In 1985, I was having another good year when I tore my ACL [anterior cruciate ligament] and MCL [medial cruciate ligament] against Kansas—the week before the Oklahoma game. I got pinned to the ground and it was snap, crackle, and pop.

That was the beginning of one of the most horrible times of my life. About five days after the operation, I had kidney failure. My kidneys just shut down—I wasn't urinating enough and my body got toxic from not expelling the waste. The doctors later told me I was just hours from dying.

It turns out I was allergic to Motrin, which I had been taking for months. After games and practices, it was almost mandatory with all the aches and pains that come with playing football at that level. I probably ate them like Cheerios. They had to put me on dialysis until my body recovered. It wasn't a fun time.

As we were playing at Oklahoma, the television had the game on, but I was fading in and out of a daze in my hospital room.

I spent 23 days in the hospital, and at that point, I wasn't worried about football so much as just thinking about having a normal life. My parents were there for me, and one morning at about 4:00 A.M., as I was about to go through more tests, Dad told me, "I have a good feeling about today."

I said, "I am glad *you* do."

And sure enough, that was the day that the tests showed I was responding to dialysis and my body first showed it was recovering.

By the time they took the cast off of my knee, I had lost about 35 pounds and was down to about 200. My leg had atrophied, and it took a long time for me to regain strength. At that point, my goal was to come back and finish my career with the guys I had come in with, but there was a doubt whether I would play my senior season. The coaches left the decision up to me, but there was a period where there was a question whether I would play or redshirt.

I was one of those guys who, if they told me I couldn't or shouldn't play, was going to go ahead and do it anyway and try to prove them wrong. I know the doctors wanted me to take the year off. My body was shot until the next summer, when I slowly started to gain weight. By fall camp, I practiced once a day to see how my body would respond before I had to make a decision. I was at about 80 percent, and the coaches left it up to me. I decided to go ahead and play, even though I wasn't getting all the mobility I needed out of it at first. But by midseason, I was near 100 percent.

211

The first time I took a chop block against Florida State in the opening game, and then ran down a guy on the sideline, I showed that my speed was back. I then realized I would be OK.

We had a tough loss at Boulder and then the toughest loss I ever experienced was that final game against Oklahoma. We beat them for 58 minutes, but [Oklahoma tight end] Keith Jackson made a couple of circus catches, and then we had a couple of facemask penalties, which led to their 40-yard field goal to beat us [20–17]. I remember just sitting on the turf with my head down for about five minutes, totally dejected.

It was one of those games. I think I had 15 or 16 tackles, a sack, a fumble recovery, and an interception, and it was my last crack at Oklahoma. My final chance, so you can imagine how I felt. We never beat them, and that still is a thorn in my side. During my sophomore and senior years, we played well enough defensively to beat them, but it didn't happen. And as a junior, I was in a daze in a hospital bed. It was almost like they had our number.

But we went out as winners against LSU in the Sugar Bowl [30–15].

Playing football at Nebraska was a great experience for me because if it wasn't for athletics, I probably would have been in the military. I don't know if I would have gone to college as a regular student without an athletic scholarship. But to get an education and play the game I love, and to play it at Nebraska, was special. The fans here are amazingly loyal, and I still enjoy talking football with them. There are no professional teams around this state, so the boys in the red and white are the focal point, and fans don't forget.

After the NFL, I came back to finish school, and my wife and I decided there was no better place to raise a family than in Lincoln, Nebraska.

Marc Munford, who finished his career with 256 tackles, is one of only two three-time All–Big Eight linebackers in Nebraska history. He was named captain and won the Novak Trophy in 1986. He was inducted into the Nebraska Football Hall of Fame in 1997. Munford played five seasons in the NFL and is now an investment banker.

TOM RATHMAN

FULLBACK

1983–1985

MY FIRST MEMORIES OF NEBRASKA FOOTBALL? Had to be Johnny Rodgers. When Johnny wore his white shoes, he'd be on his game and the Cornhuskers wouldn't lose.

I started playing football when I was 12 years old, but they made me play offensive tackle at first. All of the older guys got to play the skilled positions like running back and quarterback, and the younger kids had to play on the line.

Later, at Grand Island Senior High, I played center on the basketball team and was a field-event man in track. I even won the state championship in the high jump, jumping 6'7", and I had a 45-foot triple jump.

In football, we won the state championship in my sophomore year. Ken Fischer, brother of Cletus and Pat Fischer, was our head coach. By the time I was a senior, we had a really good team that started the season 6–0. But I tore the meniscus in my knee, and then we lost to an 0–7 team. I had played my last two seasons at fullback in the wishbone, and I also played a little line-backer, but we had enough good players that I didn't have to go both ways.

I didn't take any recruiting trips, only to Lincoln. I just felt if I would have an opportunity to get a scholarship to *the university*, why would I want to go anywhere else? As a kid, that's what I wanted to do. You grow up in Nebraska, and if you are good enough, you play ball for Nebraska.

To have Ken as my head coach helped because his brother was an assistant coach at Nebraska. It seemed I was in Lincoln every Saturday for all the home games during my senior season, and I couldn't wait to get there as a freshman.

The University of Nebraska speaks for itself. There was tons of tradition, going back to Bob Devaney's arrival. And if you want to talk about a guy you treat with respect, you are talking about coach Osborne. He was a very honest guy, very down to earth, and he possessed a great value system. He obviously knew the game of football, too—all you had to do was check his record.

My first impression of coach Osborne was that you had to be a good person on and off the football field. Coach Osborne is a very religious man and he never swore. Now I can't say I never swear to this day, but I have tried to remember the example he set. He didn't need to swear or raise his voice to get his point across to us—we listened because of who he was and what he stood for.

When I got to my very first practice at Nebraska, I remember that I had planned to go as hard as I could on every snap of the football. I was going to take nothing for granted. Practicing against the varsity, I approached it the same way. I tried to hit them before they hit me. I remember that everybody seemed terrified of Steve Damkroger, our middle linebacker. He was known as a pretty tenacious football player. He weighed about 245, and he was a guy that you always had to look out for.

I played freshman ball and moved up to varsity when the freshman season was finished that first year. I even got a couple of carries in some of those blowout games, but I was No. 3 on the depth the next year and redshirted. Instead of wasting a year playing special teams, it was a wise thing to sit out a year and develop.

In the spring of 1983, it was Mark Schellen and myself for the starting fullback job. He was a senior and I was a sophomore. He started, and then I would come off the bench to play on a team that was being touted as one of the best teams ever to play college football. We had Irving Fryar, Turner Gill, and Mike Rozier, and we rolled through that season. Nobody could stop us, and our defense was very sound. How many points did we score against Minnesota? Eighty-four?

I remember that my first career touchdown came on a reception against UCLA at home. Any time you score a touchdown in front of our crowd in that stadium—well, that's about as good as it gets.

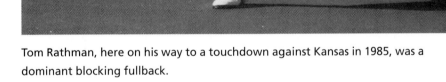

Tom Rathman, here on his way to a touchdown against Kansas in 1985, was a dominant blocking fullback.

We always had great I-backs at Nebraska, and in my three years, I blocked for Mike Rozier and Doug DuBose. Mike had special gifts as a runner—very instinctive, with the ability to make a cut at anytime, and he was good at reading his blocks.

We were getting so much media attention that year, because we were No. 1, we had the leading Heisman candidate, and our receiver was good enough to be taken as the first player in the NFL Draft. The media attention we generated was overwhelming at times.

It was an exciting time, there is no question about it. And I really knew—even going back to my freshman year when I went against our varsity during practice—that I would have a chance to go on and play pro football.

In our system, the fullback wasn't required to catch the football (I think I caught five passes in my whole career), but you had to be a good blocker, and occasionally you ran some traps. My mindset was simple: to hit everybody as hard as I possibly could on every play, even in practice.

In the Orange Bowl for the national championship, I pulled a hamstring in the first quarter when covering a punt, and I didn't play most of the game. We were down that whole game by multiple scores, and just to be able to battle back at the end of the game and have the opportunity to tie it or win it was really an accomplishment. That virtually was a home game for Miami, and they were flying around, playing a level above us.

As far as the two-point conversion play at the end—looking back on it, if we had kicked the extra point, we would have been national champions. But if you took a poll of that team, all of us would have done the same thing that coach Osborne did. We wanted to win that game outright. But that's why coaches get paid the money they do—to make decisions like that. He felt it was in the best interests of the team to go for two, and I would have done the same thing. No doubt about it. If we were the best team ever, like everybody said, it only made sense.

Unfortunately, they got a hand on that pass and we didn't get the conversion.

In my junior year, Doug DuBose replaced Mike at I-back, and he took advantage of it. He had the speed, vision, and instincts to be a great one. Doug was a tough kid, a very tough kid. I started to have some success running the football, too. I knew I could raise my stock for the NFL if I had a good year, and I was ready to take that next step to become a complete fullback.

I had a 100-yard game against Wyoming in the opener, and I don't think that had been done by a fullback since Andra Franklin. Then I had a little problem taking care of the football that season—I didn't always have the "four points of pressure" on the ball that all running backs are taught. I finally figured it out and got over my fumbling problem.

My senior year, I put it all together: I opened the season with a 60-yard touchdown run against Florida State and finished the season with 881 yards on 118 carries [7.4 average]. I had a lot of long runs. But we couldn't beat Oklahoma that year to finish it off right. That was the toughest loss we had.

I have no regrets, other than not winning that national championship. We were winning a lot of games every year, but couldn't win them all.

As a kid growing up, my dream was to play at Nebraska and I did that. Based on our tradition, it was the only place for me.

Tom Rathman, who was named All–Big Eight in 1985, holds the school rushing record for a fullback (881 yards in 1985). He finished his career with 1,425 rushing yards and 12 touchdowns. His 6.48 per-carry average is the best among fullbacks in Nebraska history. He also had four 100-yard rushing games. Rathman was named to Nebraska's All-Century team and inducted into the Nebraska Football Hall of Fame in 1992. He played nine seasons in the NFL, including eight with the San Francisco 49ers. He currently is running backs coach of the Detroit Lions.

STEVE TAYLOR
QUARTERBACK
1985–1988

I DID A VERY UNUSUAL THING IN HIGH SCHOOL, centered around the idea of my football future.

I am originally from Fresno, where I grew up and had my entire family and all my friends, but I moved to San Diego before my junior year when my coach took a new job there.

I lived with him and played at Lincoln High for my final two years. He just said, "With your skills, you could name the school you will go to if you're playing at a big school." He figured it would be better for me, but I didn't know what I was getting myself into. At the time I was thinking, "Southern California, this will be cool!"

Fresno was a small town, but several players from my school had made it into the NFL, like Ickey Woods, Tim McDonald, and Charlie Young.

When I left, I forgot how much everything in Fresno meant to me: my friends and family and the fact that we had an undefeated team all those years. From junior high right through my sophomore year, my class never lost a football game, and I left all of those guys behind. I could have been successful where I was, but I didn't realize that until I got older. I could have had the same success I had, yet taken a different path. I basically was under lock and key for two years, but I was not the type of kid who would have gotten into any trouble anyway.

Obviously, if I knew then what I know today, I would have stayed put in Fresno.

But I did get recruited by just about every school, and I narrowed it down to Washington, Colorado, Minnesota, Nebraska, and Cal-Berkeley. UCLA had told me they might switch me from quarterback to another position, so I never entertained going there.

Colorado was a great place, but they were converting their offense and I wasn't going to be the guy at quarterback. Minnesota was way too cold for me. Lou Holtz was there at the time, and they were great to me. In fact, they promised me some material things, but I thought, if I break my leg here, what will happen to me? I always wondered about that. Coach Holtz introduced me to these people, and then he left the room. And they promised me *a lot* of things.

Washington was great. In hindsight, knowing what I know today, I probably would have gone there. At the time, I was very close to going there, but I talked to Warren Moon and he had some obstacles there because of the perception of black quarterbacks. There was some controversy as far as him being the starter.

Nebraska was awesome to me. I became interested in the Cornhuskers when I watched the 1984 Orange Bowl game. When I visited, coach Osborne just said, "I can promise you two things. First of all, I promise you will play quarterback, and second, you will have a chance to get a good education."

219

I was sold. That's all I wanted to hear.

I knew there would be no controversy about having a black quarterback at Nebraska because coach Osborne just had Turner Gill as a three-year starter. And in the 1984 Orange Bowl, I saw them throw the ball a lot [Gill was 16-of-30 for 172 yards], so I figured I would get to throw often, too.

Of course, as it hit me later, they were behind against Miami for that whole game, so that's why they were throwing it so much. I had never run the option before because we had a passing offense in high school, but I thought I would be a great fit in their offense.

But once I got to Nebraska, I really realized how run-oriented the offense was. Still, I liked running the option. It was a fun offense for me.

We had one of the best recruiting classes in the country. Broderick Thomas, LeRoy Etienne, and a few other guys. And me. We all were either blue-chip recruits or *Parade* All-Americans. I came in early that summer because I couldn't

Steve Taylor, here calling the signals during his 1988 All-American season, was one of college football's best double-threat quarterbacks.

wait to be there. It was awesome to finally be a Husker because that's all I had thought about since signing day. When I checked in and got those red shorts and shirts and all that, I was really fired up to be there.

I was walking out of the dorm one day, and Broderick came walking out at the same time and we started to talk. He looked at me, scoping me out, and said, "You are going to be our quarterback?"

I wondered what he was talking about, but I had on a pair of flip-flops and an Izod shirt. Being from California, I thought I looked cool. But he was from Texas, and he figured I was soft because of the way I dressed. I just said, "Don't let your perceptions of me get to you. I am not from the suburbs."

One day when we went down to the stadium to work out, we went out to play catch, and LeRoy came out and said, "Come on, show me what you got."

So I ran the option against him, threw this move on him, and he was toast. He didn't even touch me.

LeRoy said, "Do it again. Do it again. I'll get you this time."

So I did it again, and he didn't touch me again. Right then, I had all of their respect. They knew I could play. The three of us—LeRoy, Broderick, and me—became really good friends after that.

Broderick and I bonded, and he had a plan for his entire career from day one. I was just excited to be there, and if I could go on to play pro football, that would be great. But Broderick had a plan to become an All-American, become a first-rounder, and have a long career in the NFL. I wasn't a big fan of the NFL, but Broderick was a student of the game. He knew players from all over the country, their strengths and weaknesses, and he knew a lot of players in the NFL. It helped that his uncle was Mike Singletary.

Now I didn't want to room with Broderick because he was always talking a mile a minute, but I was stuck without a roommate because Marvin Sanders, who was supposed to be my roommate, didn't make it. Broderick might be the last person I would want to room with, but we became roommates.

My freshman year was a great year for me. I was very successful on the freshman team, and then I got called up to the varsity and played down the stretch. They were calling me the second coming of Turner, and I felt I was playing well while I was learning.

Like I said, Broderick and I roomed together and we were on the regents' floor of the dorm, but he later got his own room and so did I. Then he talked me into living off campus with him during our sophomore year. I was the responsible one; I got all the furniture and had all the utilities in my name. It was working, but Broderick started eating all of my food and running up all the phone bills. Man, he could talk on the phone! It was typical college roommate type stuff, but finally, I had the long distance service turned off.

I later got my own place, and I think that saved our relationship.

Broderick had a fabulous sophomore year, and he was All–Big Eight like he had planned, and I was second-team All–Big Eight, so we were on our way.

I opened that season with a great game against Florida State. It was going really well until we lost at Colorado [20–10], in which I had a terrible game with a few turnovers and the offense didn't do much. It was one of the toughest losses of my life, and it was the first time I didn't want to read the newspaper the next day.

221

During the last part of the season, I was playing with a hip flexor injury, which I really didn't tell anybody about, and I wasn't able to run like I could. But I finished strong and played well enough in the Sugar Bowl to be named MVP [Taylor completed 11 of 19 passes for 110 yards and a touchdown, and rushed for 63 yards and a touchdown].

The one thing about those three years in which I was starting at Nebraska, we always played very tough teams before the Big Eight season. We played Florida State, Arizona State, UCLA, and Texas A&M. We never took the easy route that a lot of other top programs took before the conference kicked in.

In 1987, we played UCLA at home and we were ranked No. 2 and they were No. 3. We had a great game offensively [a 42–33 Nebraska win], and I threw five touchdown passes that day. We were 9–0 when we played Oklahoma at home in another Game of the Century. We were No. 1; they were No. 2.

That game was a huge learning experience for us because after we beat Missouri [42–7], Oklahoma struggled with Missouri. So we were saying things in the media. We were talking about how we could beat Oklahoma, and some guys were saying things like, "We will really put the hurt on them." Well, they were fired up that day, and it turned out they had all of those quotes posted everywhere to motivate them. We should have kept our mouths shut.

Their defense was the toughest defense I ever saw: Tony Casillas, Ricky Dixon, and Brian Bosworth. And they had Barry Switzer, who was a master of preparing to play Nebraska. So we didn't play well at all [a 17–7 Nebraska loss].

The next year, we had a great team, but when we went out to California to play UCLA in the third game, some of our guys weren't focused. I learned much later that some of our guys who were projected to be high-round NFL picks had rented limos and were out clubbing the night before the game.

It seemed we were always one or two plays from competing for the national championship, and that was an example of it. We never lost again after that UCLA game [a 41–28 loss], but we could have played for a national championship if guys had been focused for that game.

The Orange Bowl game against Miami was the first time that we played when no matter what we did they were just much better. Coach Osborne had put some things in during practice, like designated scramble packages, and I wondered why we were doing it. But he knew we would have a hard job protecting me, and he was right. They were that fast and that quick. As

I was getting the snap, they had guys in the backfield [in a 23–3 loss to Miami]. We couldn't run it or throw it in that game.

And Miami had what I always wanted—a pro-style offense.

I think that is the one thing that kept me out of the NFL. At Nebraska, as a quarterback, I read the nose guard. In the pros, quarterbacks read the free safety. I could throw the football, but the NFL had preconceived notions because of the offense I was in during college. I always knew I could go to Canada and play, though.

Still, I want to say that I have absolutely no regrets. When I came here, people talked about how great coach Devaney was. They would say, "Coach Osborne is good, but he's no Devaney."

Now that I am much older, I am an Osborne guy. I loved Devaney, too, but there can never be another Tom Osborne.

I am still a supporter of the university, where I got my degree in speech communications and where I met my wife, Stephanie, during my junior year. And we have three lovely girls—Sydney, Skylar, and Sammie.

I want to take this opportunity to thank my Lincoln parents in the Lincoln Parent Program, Dan and Susan Semrad. We really bonded, and their two boys, Scott and Jeff, are like brothers to me to this day. That is one program that I wish still existed, but the NCAA stepped in and disallowed it, contending that it gave Nebraska an unfair advantage. But in reality, all the Lincoln parents had rules to abide by and didn't do anything against NCAA rules.

The people in Nebraska were so good to me and playing at Nebraska was a great experience, given all the tradition we have and all the people I met over the years. I still fly my school flag on game days and I will always consider myself a loyal Cornhusker.

Steve Taylor completed 184 of 404 passes for 2,815 yards and 30 touchdowns in his career—sixth-best in Nebraska history. His five touchdown passes against UCLA is a school record (tied with Eric Crouch, versus Iowa in 2000). He was named an All-American in 1987 and All–Big Eight in 1987–88. He played eight seasons in the Canadian Football League and was inducted into the Nebraska Football Hall of Fame in 1999.

NEIL SMITH
DEFENSIVE TACKLE
1985–1987

I WAS BORN AND RAISED ON THE BAYOU, in New Orleans, Louisiana, and I will never forget the day I was out raking the front yard when I was about six years old. A guy pulled up to the curb in front of our house in one of those little cars and said, "My name is coach Earl, and we are opening up a new park and would like you to come play some baseball."

He then went and talked to my mom, and from that point, I started playing sports right there in McQue Park. Coach Earl helped me learn to throw and catch and do all the little basic things you learn when you start playing sports. I learned to play all the sports, but I never was that big—I was tall and rangy. I wasn't one of those super jocks by any means.

When I got to McDonogh No. 35 High School—it was in midtown New Orleans—I was just an average football player. At first I was at middle linebacker, but we didn't have a defensive end, so they moved me there before my junior year. I never lifted weights in high school, but I grew about three inches to 6'4" in my senior year and I weighed only 215 pounds.

Like I said, I wasn't a blue-chipper at all, but I ran around and made some plays. Colleges were looking at our quarterback, L. J. Tapp, and that is how I got discovered. I had no scholarship offers whatsoever, not even from Tulane or LSU—the schools right in my own backyard.

But Nebraska was looking at film of L.J., and they kept noticing me. Back then, high schools didn't break down film by position, so if you watched it, you had to see the whole game. [Nebraska assistant coach] Jack Pierce called me and said, "You keep showing up in the picture when we are looking at L.J., and we like we what see."

He told me they had only one scholarship remaining, but they had offered it to this blue-chip offensive lineman who was deciding between Nebraska and Oklahoma. But they wanted me for the walk-on program. Mom and I flew to Lincoln, and I had never been on an airplane in my life, but we enjoyed the trip. It was everything we expected and more, and they made it known that getting an education was a priority.

Mom worked two jobs to raise three kids, and she couldn't afford to pay my way, so it wasn't looking good for me if I didn't receive financial aid. I mean, I had grown up in the housing projects until our house was broken into and we moved. We had about a month after the visit until we found out, and Mom prayed on it that I would get that final scholarship. She always believed that scholarship would be mine.

When it was pending, the local media got wind of it and wrote some stories about me maybe going to Nebraska. I thought for sure that some other schools would step in and offer me scholarships, too, but it never happened.

A few days before signing day, by the grace of God, that offensive lineman—and I can't even remember his name now—decided to go to Oklahoma.

So I got the very last scholarship to Nebraska that year, and I have no idea what would have happened to me if I hadn't.

When I flew out there to start my freshman year, I cried the whole way out there. I felt like I was going out there to bury somebody; I was so scared. I was leaving my mom and my family behind, and I knew this was going to change my life, but at the same time, I was excited about it.

I remember seeing all that flat land and those cornfields, and thought to myself, "Well, now I can see why they call them the Cornhuskers."

But I made a decision that I was going to make something out of myself, and I couldn't turn around and go back home because there were people there who thought I would fail at Nebraska. I never wanted to prove them right.

That first week, I was scared and homesick because I didn't know what was going to happen. I knew it would be the challenge of my life, but I knew going through it would make me a better man in the long run.

There were times I wanted to give up and go back home, but Mom would always give me the wisdom to stay there and do what was needed.

Neil Smith (No. 99) closes in on a ball-carrier at the line of scrimmage.

"Don't you do it," she would say. "Don't let the devil step in and make you quit. He wants you to quit!"

She really pushed me to stay out there, and it motivated me.

It took about two months, but I adjusted, and I knew I would be OK. I know I still called home whenever I had the opportunity, and Mom always gave the greatest advice a mother can give her son: "Just do your best. You don't have to prove anything to anybody else. Just do your best for yourself."

One of the first guys I met when I got to Nebraska was Mark Behning, who was getting off the elevator when I was getting on. I looked up, and it seemed like he was about 6'10". He was so huge, and he was an offensive tackle that I had to go against right away. He did me in and manhandled me during practice, but I knew I had to just hang in there against those varsity guys and work hard, and things would turn out OK.

Still, physically, it was hard on me. Academically, it was hard on me. I remember walking into coach Osborne's office one time and being very discouraged with it all.

He looked at me and said, "People on the outside think this is easy, but it isn't. There is plenty of work that comes along with that scholarship. You just have to do the work, be patient, and things will turn out right for you."

As usual, he was right.

I had a good year during my freshman season, even though I was undersized to play inside at tackle, but I knew I had the speed, quickness, and agility to get the job done. I gained about 10–15 pounds each year at Nebraska until I grew into the position.

In my sophomore year, I think I would have played more, but I had a really bad hip injury that I never told too many people about. I had a bone spur growing in the muscle, and it almost ended my career. I couldn't even lift my leg up to get into the car at times, and it took a long time to heal.

By the spring of 1986, I was backing up Chris Spachman and Jim Show at each tackle spot, but I played in every game that year. I really felt like I should have started, but I held that anger in the whole time.

I knew what the system was at Nebraska, and it was for the seniors to play even if you were younger and you felt you were better than them.

Charlie McBride would always tell me, "Your time will come. Your time will come."

Charlie always pushed me very hard in practice and he would jump on me verbally, but it was only because he wanted me to become a great player. One time during practice, he brought tears to my eyes when he pointed to me and said—right in front of all the other D-linemen—"Now this kid right here will be one of the best players I ever coached. He will make more money [in the NFL] than any of you other suckers."

When it was time for my senior year, I was so hungry inside that I knew nothing would stop me. I knew that I would become an All-American and I had a year to make myself into the best I could be on the field. I wanted to have my painting done and have it placed on that wall [Nebraska's All-American paintings], and I was going to do whatever it took to get it done.

It was my time to show everybody that I had persevered and was ready to become a great player. That was going to be my year. I was on a mission and had a very good year, even though we didn't win a national championship.

My one regret is that we never beat Oklahoma in my four years. It seemed they always made one more play than we did, and I heard about it over the years in the NFL from the Oklahoma players I knew.

Miracles do happen, and when I look back on my career, I believe it was a miracle that by the grace of God I was able to play football at one of the greatest universities in the land. I started out with low self-esteem and ended up an All-American and first-round NFL pick.

Maybe if I went to a place like Oklahoma or Miami, I could have been part of national championship teams, but I wouldn't be the man I am now. I love middle America and college towns and the suburbs—it was good for me to get away from city life.

Coach Osborne? I love him because—although most people look at him as a hell of a coach—he was more of a teacher and a father figure to me. He dealt with all types of kids from different backgrounds, and he was all of those things to all of them, too. On the football field, his record speaks for itself. Off of it, he really cared.

After my senior year, when it was obvious I was headed to the NFL, he called me into his office.

"I'll make a deal with you," he told me. "If you ever want to come back and finish school, the door here is always open. If you do graduate some day, I will put your name on a plaque and put it right here on my desk."

I am 17 hours away from my degree and I own a restaurant here in Kansas City, but I haven't given up on that goal. I will finish school some day, and I hope he puts my name on a plaque for his desk—especially if it's in his congressional office or governor's office or wherever he will be at the time.

I just thank God he had that last scholarship for me.

Neil Smith finished his career with 14.5 sacks and was named an All-American in 1987. He was a first-round pick of the Kansas City Chiefs and played 13 seasons in the NFL, including nine with the Chiefs. He was inducted into the Nebraska Football Hall of Fame in 1998.

TURNER GILL
QUARTERBACK
1981–1983

IGREW UP LOVING SPORTS, THERE WAS NO DOUBT ABOUT THAT. But mainly, baseball was the sport I loved the most and played most of the time, from Little League all the way through high school at Arlington Heights High in Fort Worth, Texas.

I was a shortstop and fortunately, I was good enough to get drafted by the Chicago White Sox in the second round. Team owner Bill Veeck even came to my house to try to talk me into signing.

In football, we ran the old Houston Veer offense that Bill Yeoman had designed. I had been a receiver and cornerback until my senior year, when our quarterback graduated and I replaced him. I had an unbelievable year and suddenly, people were taking notice of my football prospects. I went from believing my future was in baseball to having all of the football schools interested in me.

I knew right away that I didn't want to stay in Texas, that I wanted to play quarterback and also baseball in college. But as you can imagine, the two-sport issue was a big issue with a lot of coaches.

One of the kids on my team had a father, Darrell Cooper, who had played football at Nebraska, and he sent one of my tapes to Nebraska. And that became my first visit during recruiting. When I got to Lincoln, it was cold and snowing, one of those typical winter days, but that did not really bother me. I knew the weather wasn't an issue when it came time to choose a school.

Paul Letcher showed me around one day and Andra Franklin the next, and I really liked the place. It was easy to see right away that people in Nebraska really loved their football.

My high school coach had suggested I visit at least one Texas college, but I still knew I was leaving the state in the end because being away from home would help me grow as a person. I was only interested in the University of Texas because of their baseball program anyway.

When I visited Oklahoma, J. C. Watts showed me around, and that was a good trip. I have to say that when I visited there, I thought I would go there.

But about 10 days before signing day, I had a few questions for the Oklahoma coaches. I called them on the phone, but I couldn't reach them and no one got back to me. When I called Nebraska, however, [assistant coach] Lance Van Zandt was always there for me. That really had an effect on me, and it turned me off of Oklahoma.

Still, the biggest reason for my decision to go to Nebraska was coach Osborne. When I talked to him, it was obvious to me that he spoke from the heart. People said you could count on his word and right away, I could tell I did trust him. In talking to coach Osborne, I realized that they had never had an established, starting black quarterback there before. That also was a draw for me, as an opportunity to become the first to do that. I really believed someday they would have a black quarterback, so why couldn't it be me?

Coach Osborne said he would give me the opportunity to play quarterback and not move me around, and that's all I ever wanted. And he said I could play baseball at Nebraska, too.

Still, the White Sox tried to sign me, but they didn't quite come to the amount I had in mind. They offered me $80,000, but my figure to sign with them was $100,000. I think back on that now—if they had thrown in that extra $20,000—my whole life would have been much different.

Another thing was that I really wanted to experience the college environment. I had watched college football on TV for so long, I wanted to be a part of it. I wanted to play football on TV.

After my visit to Lincoln, coach Osborne had a function to attend in the Dallas-Fort Worth area, and his wife, Nancy, was attending with him. So when he came over to visit me at the house, he brought her with him, and that spoke to me a lot. Family was very important to me, and that left a big impression on me that he would bring her with him.

When I talked to him, I got the feeling he cared about me. I just knew it. That's really why I ended up at Nebraska.

When I got there, I roomed with Irving Fryar, and I thought it was kind of neat for the quarterback to be rooming with a highly touted receiver like him. We talked about all the plays we would make together in the future, things like that.

Coach Osborne asked me if I wanted to redshirt or play varsity, and I told him I wanted to play on the freshman team to get some experience. My goal was to become the starting quarterback as a sophomore and to play the next three seasons. I still had baseball on my mind, though, thinking it still might be in my future.

That next spring, I can't remember if it was before spring ball or after it, I came down with a pretty strong case of homesickness. One day I just got in the car and took off for home. There really wasn't anything specific that made me do it, it was just a little bit of everything. Everything seemed overwhelming to me.

When I got home, Mom and Dad said right away, "Hey, get back up there. When you finish the semester, then we will talk about you either leaving for good or staying. But not now."

So I went back to Lincoln, and things were fine for me after that.

Going into the next season, 1981, the first thing that comes to my mind is that coach Osborne wanted me to go to his office. He told me, "You are the third-team quarterback."

Nate Mason and Mark Mauer were one and two at that point, but I thought I should have been one of the top guys, at least the backup.

He said, "Well, that can always change, but for right now, these two guys are best."

I really think he wanted to give the upperclassmen the first opportunity, if they were playing well.

In the second game against Florida State, coach Osborne put me in the game and we made a first down right away. On the next play, I ran the option and fumbled, and a Florida State player recovered it and they soon scored. That was my chance, and I figured I wouldn't get back on the field. I didn't for the remainder of that game. We won, but I was extremely disappointed.

The next week, at Penn State, I didn't play at all, and we lost to fall to 1–2. Unfortunately, Nate Mason got hurt, so it was between Mark Mauer and myself after that. The next week, Mark started and we were tied 3–3 with

231

Auburn at the half, and as we ran to the locker room, Nebraska fans booed us. (It was the first and last time I ever heard booing at Memorial Stadium.) Coach Osborne walked over to me in the locker room and told me I would be the guy in the second half.

We won that game 17–3, and I became the number one quarterback.

The next week, I had my first start, against Colorado, and it was like a dream for me. Everyone played great, and it was a great situation for me. It was one of those days I'll never forget [a 59–0 Nebraska win]. But the game that really gave me some confidence was at Missouri, because we were playing on the road against a quality opponent [ranked No. 19]. We won it [6–0] on a trap play at the end of the game, and I came away from that game with a big boost mentally.

A few weeks later, however, my whole outlook changed. During the Iowa State game, my right calf started to hurt, and it got worse as the game went along. We won [31–7], and after the game, it just got worse and worse. At about midnight on the day of the game, I had to have emergency surgery because I had damaged the peroneal nerve.

When the coaches went back to look at the tape, they couldn't see a time I really took a blow that would have caused the damage, so we never really knew what caused it. All I know is that it was very serious, and I didn't know if I would ever walk again. That's how serious it was. You think the doctors will heal you in a situation like that, and then they tell you, "All you can do is pray."

I know I followed their orders.

It was a very scary time, and I realized I would be out for a while. I had to miss the Oklahoma game and the Orange Bowl [against Clemson]. Things go through your mind—maybe your athletic career is finished, the leg might never be normal again. It took about five months to heal, and right around March I got some movement in my toes and ankle.

By the fall of 1982, I was 100 percent again.

We knew we would be a great football team that year because we were very, very talented, but that Penn State game [27–24 loss] was definitely our heartbreaker. I just remember what a great football environment that was at State College, on national television, Joe Paterno versus Tom Osborne, a packed stadium.

At the end, I thought we had the game won, but they ended up pulling it off. They had a third-and-long and made that great catch on the sideline [on

Turner Gill, here against Iowa in 1982, rushed for more than one thousand yards and passed for more than three thousand yards in his career.

what would turn into one of the most controversial official's calls in the history of Nebraska football]. Later, I met the receiver who caught that pass at some function, and he just said, "Turner, I am sorry it happened."

I am not sure even he thought he made a legal catch, but what could you do? We played the game, and they came away the winner. As it turned out, it was our only loss. We were just one game away, just 17 seconds away from being undefeated.

That next spring, I hit .285 for the baseball team and got drafted again, this time by the Mets. Coach Osborne asked me if I would be back because he was thinking about accepting an invitation to the Kickoff Classic to begin the season. He certainly didn't want to play in that game with a first-time starter at quarterback. I still had that love for baseball, but I thought, "Hey, if they want me now, they'll want me a year from now."

How many chances do you have to get to play football at Nebraska and be on the No. 1 team, which I figured we would be? I didn't want to miss out on any of it.

In that Kickoff Classic, it was a dream come true. We beat Penn State 44–6, and we were a different team than we had been the previous season. I could sense right away that our team would be special that season. It wasn't a cockiness, just an extreme confidence. We just believed we were going to win every game, and we had a great togetherness.

And it was fun, which is what football should be all about. We were all really close on that team.

We scored 84 points against Minnesota, and I had never seen a game like that even in high school. It was an unbelievable game, and I really felt bad for Minnesota's players.

As we rolled through the season, the second team got a lot of playing time, but they scored as much as we did. The old saying going around Nebraska was, "Maybe they should put the first team back in the game, because the second team is running up the score."

In that Oklahoma State game, we had way too many turnovers [a 14–10 win, Nebraska's closest victory of 1983], but that was the only glitch. Our team scored more than 60 points five times and more than 50 seven times. I walked into the huddle, and I just felt that we were going to score on every play, whether we called a pass or a run. But when we got in trouble, our signature play was either the "41 pitch" or "49 pitch" to Mike Rozier. On his way to the Heisman, he had a great season. Look at the talent: Irving [Fryar],

Mike [Rozier], and all the great linemen we had up front, like Dean Steinkuhler, Mark Traynowicz, and Henry Grimminger.

(When I compare those two teams, I think we were a little better defensively in 1982, but a little better offensively in 1983. So which team was better? I don't know, but I do know they should rank among the greatest teams in Nebraska history.)

Going into the Orange Bowl, we weren't any less confident than before any other game. I knew it was my last time to put on a Nebraska uniform, and it was what we all dreamed about. It wasn't about Miami—or playing them in Miami—it was about doing our thing and winning the national championship.

Mike [Rozier] got hurt early in the game, and we didn't get off to a good start, but Jeff Smith came in to play a great game. Once we got behind 31–17 in the fourth quarter, the thing I am most proud of is how we pulled together and responded. We played together with heart and never quit.

When it was 31–24, I got in the huddle—and this is what the guys told me later—I said, "We are going to take it down there and score; and when we do score, don't celebrate because we will be going for two points to win the game."

Coach Osborne and I had never talked about it; I just figured that's what we were going to do. When we did score [on Smith's 24-yard run], I looked toward the sideline hoping to see those two fingers that meant we would be going for two points. I saw them, and right away I figured what play we would run for the two-point conversion, because we had worked on it: "51 I-back flat," and that was the call. Remember, we didn't have any timeouts left.

235

The play called for Irving to be in the slot and to head inside to become a decoy as [I-back] Jeff Smith went out into the flat. When I took the snap and rolled right, I saw that Jeff had a half a step on his guy, and I had to make a quick decision. It was on the run, but I threw it inches behind him, and a Miami guy got his fingers on it. (When we went back to look at the tape, the guy had come off of Irving to tip the ball).

That was it [a 31–30 Nebraska loss].

It was painful. I mean, it hurt. I felt like I had let the team down, because I didn't make a good enough throw. We had come all that way, won all of those games, and walking off of that field that night, all I felt was dejection. We had set a goal and we didn't finish it. And we played our hearts out. I had to go to the East–West Shrine game in California, but I don't think I slept for a day or two.

It took a week or two to get over it. I am the type of guy to look at something, diagnose it, and keep moving forward. And I tried to learn from it. I had so many things going on after that game that kept me busy, so I tried not to sit around and think about that game, but people kept bringing it up.

Twenty years later, it is amazing how that game has taken on a life of its own. I still feel that I had a part of something special in that Orange Bowl, even though we lost. It's not a haunting thing to me at all. It was exciting. It was an opportunity for us. And it was just a game. That's how I look at it.

When we finally won the national championship [the 1995 Orange Bowl], people asked me if it meant less to me because I was a coach and not a player, and I always answered, "No. Why should it? I had as much joy that night as I would have had if I was a player."

I have to really thank coach Osborne—and not for just being my football coach. He taught me so much about life and the spiritual part of myself. He was the main reason I chose the University of Nebraska in the first place, and he was the one who helped me grow into the person I am. I knew he would make me a better person, not necessarily a better quarterback or a better football player. And I was right.

We have so much tradition, loyalty, and integrity at Nebraska, and that's what this football program has been about all these years. I thank God for putting Nebraska there for me.

Turner Gill is Nebraska's only three-time all-conference quarterback, earning All–Big Eight honors from 1981 to 1983. He also was a team captain in 1983. He ranks fifth on the school's career passing list with 3,317 yards and 34 touchdown passes. He was inducted into the Nebraska Football Hall of Fame in 1989. He played two seasons in the Canadian Football League and has been an assistant coach at Nebraska since 1992, coaching under Tom Osborne, Frank Solich, and now Bill Callahan.

The
NINETIES

WILL SHIELDS
GUARD
1989–1992

My father was in the U.S. Army, so we moved around to wherever he was stationed when I was a boy. I was born in Fort Riley, Kansas, and then we moved to Texas and then on to Lawton, Oklahoma. I played football and track at Lawton High, and I also loved being part of the arts. It was my second passion. I was into building the sets and working in sound production for plays, but I wasn't the guy who wanted to be up on stage.

My stage was a football field, and football was my love. I played both ways on the line, and I weighed about 270 pounds as a senior, but I didn't have a whole lot of options. I was probably down the list when it came to recruiting. Oklahoma, Tulsa, Arkansas, Oklahoma State, and Nebraska recruited me, but once I had a problem passing the ACT, some of those schools fell by the wayside, too.

An assistant coach at Oklahoma then let me in on something that I didn't know: he said I could take the composite of three tests to get into college. And he told me, "I am not telling this to you just to get you into Oklahoma."

But it helped.

I wanted to get a chance to play for a national championship, and I knew about the production of offensive linemen from Nebraska. Barry Switzer was still at Oklahoma, and there was word out that they were about to go on NCAA probation. [Oklahoma quarterback] Charles Thompson was from our high school, so I knew all about Oklahoma's problems at the time. Nobody knew what was going to happen, or when, but everybody knew something was going to happen. I never watched much college football growing up, so I had no emotional ties that affected my decision. I watched only pro football, and I used to love the Dallas Cowboys. Dallas had so many fans in that region of the country, and I certainly was one of them.

I had gone to a camp at Nebraska, and like I said, the history of offensive linemen at Nebraska really drew me there. That tradition was its biggest selling point to me, but nobody from the state of Oklahoma ever went to Nebraska before.

Arkansas wanted me to be a defensive end, so they were out of the mix. I felt that the coaches at Nebraska, like coach [Milt] Tenopir, were honest with me when they were recruiting me. Coach Osborne was so calm, cool, and collected when I met with him. He had this demeanor about him, and I wondered, does he ever get angry?

I decided to go to Nebraska, becoming the first football player ever from the state of Oklahoma to do that.

The first people I met there were the academic support group, which didn't exist at other schools. I knew what my deficiencies were. Right away, I got a feel for the love that everybody in Lincoln has for the Nebraska program.

The first week I was there, it was my birthday, and the people on my floor who had never met me before threw me a birthday party with a cake and everything. It was like having an adopted family. Here I was, an athlete in a dorm with nonathletes, and they welcomed me like they had always known me. That made me feel right at home from the beginning.

In that first fall camp, I started off on the scout team, but I had one huge advantage. We ran the same offense in high school, and I knew the terminology. It was awesome for me, and it became a good joke between me and coach Tenopir.

He would say, "This kid is brilliant. He's been here a few days and he knows this offense like the back of his hand." I was making line calls right from the beginning.

On the first day of practice, we were running counter plays where the guard pulls and is supposed to cut the end during a game. I always practiced the way I played, so I came around the end and cut Mike Croel, who was a starter. Man, the coaches went crazy. They were screaming, "We don't cut our players here! You can't do that here!"

Three or four days later, they moved me from the freshman locker room to the varsity locker room, and I practiced with the varsity for that whole year. I played in some freshman games, but it wasn't even challenging for me. It was like I was back in high school. There was a decision whether to red-shirt me or not, and then one senior in front of me had a knee injury and another had an ankle problem. So, luckily, I fell into a position where I could play right away. I played in almost every game as a freshman.

The toughest part of being a freshman was being away from home. In high school, it always seemed like somebody was telling you what to do. Then in college, you suddenly had freedom, and my grades suffered because of it because I didn't know what true studying was. I didn't know how to get the work done on time. It was a learning process, and I had to go on academic probation that first year. One thing I had to learn, which I was not good at, was how to budget my time. As a sophomore, I practically lived at the study table, but I never had a problem with grades again.

After I learned I was not going to be redshirted, I knew what to expect on the field. So I knew if I wanted a chance to go pro, I wanted to make sure I was going to graduate on time. From that point on, I just buckled down and got the work done. I stayed in Lincoln every summer, went to school, and worked at the post office.

Now that was a great job for me. I worked back in the mail room, and it was the coolest experience I ever had. There were actually doctors and lawyers and other businessmen who quit their other professions to work at the post office. They liked the job because they could work 8 to 10 hours each day and go home. There wasn't the pressure of being a doctor, where they had to make sure everybody was healthy, or the pressure of a big case if they were a lawyer. I have to say that I loved working there and meeting people.

The next spring I was a starter. I had such an advantage over the other guys my age because I had been running the same offense for three years. I just thought I was an average player on a good team. I never thought of myself as being a great, great player, but looking back, there was a reason for that. Reflecting back, our standards were so high at Nebraska that I didn't have an accurate feel for how good I was. It seemed that everybody next to you and the defensive players you went against became NFL players, so we were practicing against the best every day.

In the third game of my junior season, we were playing Washington, and I was going to be facing the great Steve Emtman. I kept hearing how he was

Will Shields (No. 75), here blocking against Colorado, is Nebraska's only three-time all-conference guard.

unblockable, almost unstoppable. I bought into the great hype, and I was mentally whipped just listening to it. I thought, "Well, if nobody can block him, I guess I can't."

Then I hit him once and he went to the sideline. By the time I figured out I could block him, it was late in the game. It was a big learning experience for me. I learned that regardless of what you do, you have to play your own game at your own pace and not spend too much time worrying about the guy across from you.

Against Kansas, I tore up my knee right after halftime. It was on a field goal, and the other guard got driven over the top onto me. I heard a large pop. I had it taped up and finished the game, but after I looked at the film, I realized I should have taken myself out. I just thought I could still play hurt because that was the thing tough guys did.

In my four years, we lost four bowl games. I think that shows where the program was—that we were not yet ready to win a bowl game. We probably didn't have the right components, the right leadership, or the right discipline to get it done. It seemed we shut it down and enjoyed the week or two weeks leading up the bowl games like it was vacation. We were not in the running for a national title, and after you lose a game in college football, you are out of the hunt.

Coach Osborne had built it to the point where he understood how to get to that point, but we couldn't get over the hump. When I look at the 1994–1995 teams that won national championships, I think, "Man, we had more talented athletes, because those are the guys we used to beat up on."

But those guys matured into a team, and our teams may have been a bunch of individuals.

The great thing about Nebraska is that each player had his own uniqueness about him. We had guys from all over the country. The program sets the standard for what you want to be and you need to live up to it. The tradition kept itself up before I got there, and hopefully, it will continue as the years go on.

To be a Husker is something they can't ever take away from you once you have been a part of it. And I am proud I was a part of it.

Will Shields was a three-time All–Big Eight guard and an All-American in 1992. He was inducted into the Nebraska Football Hall of Fame in 1993. He was a third-round pick of the Kansas City Chiefs, with whom he has played the past 11 seasons. He and his wife Senia founded the Will to Succeed Foundation (Willtosucceed.org), which supports battered and abused women and children. Shields was named the winner of the NFL's Walter Payton Man of the Year Award in 2003 for his off-the-field contributions.

MIKE MINTER
SAFETY
1993–1996

WATCHING FOOTBALL ON TELEVISION SHAPED MY FEELINGS and actually determined my future. I was always a Dallas Cowboys fan from the time I was a little boy because I watched only the NFL at the time. When I started watching college football later, one of the first bowls I watched was the [1984] Orange Bowl game between Nebraska and Miami. From that point on, I wanted to play for the Cornhuskers, even though I was from Lawton, Oklahoma. I can still picture that game, with those white helmets and the red *N* and Mike Rozier, Turner Gill, and Irving Fryar playing.

I know this sounds simple, but from the third grade on, I knew where I wanted to go to play football and I was determined to get there.

I was a running back and free safety at Lawton High. I led the state in rushing, and most of the schools in that region recruited me. When the Nebraska coaches called me, I told them that I was very interested, so come on down to Oklahoma to see me. Milt Tenopir and Tom Osborne came down to the house.

I had been watching coach Osborne on television since I was a little kid, and he already was a giant in my head. When I got home that day, he was already in my house, but he was sitting down. When he stood up, he was about 6'4", and he really looked huge in my little house. He got straight to the point and I liked that. He asked me, "Do you want to verbally commit to us?"

"Yeah, I am coming," I said, having never even talked to any other school.

A week after I committed, I took a trip to Lincoln for the first time. It was about 12 degrees, and I didn't pack a coat. I really didn't know anything about the school, and I thought, "Man, I didn't sign up for this weather." But I overlooked it, and on signing day, I never wavered one bit.

It must have been the easiest recruiting job ever for coach Osborne.

I was always asked, "You're from Oklahoma and you went to Nebraska? How did that happen?"

Man, that's the power of television.

Will Shields was the first from my state to play at Nebraska, and I became the second.

When I got to campus, the first few days were interesting to say the least. When they are recruiting you, they tell you about the two starters at your position, but they don't mention all the other names who are competing for the position. Let me tell you, there were a lot of guys playing safety around there.

I could have played running back, but I looked over there and I saw Derek Brown, who was already All–Big Eight, and I saw Calvin Jones as his backup, and I said, "Coach, I think I'll go to defense."

If I didn't, I knew I wasn't going to see the field any time soon. I loved to hit anyway, so it was no problem for me. Most kids that age want to be in the limelight, and let's face it, the I-back position at Nebraska is the limelight, but I didn't care about that. I like to think that I was mature enough to think toward the future.

I redshirted that year, and it was frustrating at times. Sometimes I thought about going back home, but I remember Will came up to me once and said, "Look, the coaches like what you are doing, so just keep doing it and don't get frustrated."

What helped was that we created our own game situations in practice, like, "Who can get an interception against the number one offense?" That made it fun. Plus, I started to get involved in school activities. I knew this was the place I needed to be if I wanted to go on to play professional football, and if I wanted to get my degree. Those were my two goals at the time.

Toward that second goal, I stayed in summer school during every off-season.

I was alternating with Toby Wright at the position heading into the 1993 season, and on the day they gave out black shirts, I went to my locker and opened it, and there it was. As a redshirt freshman, I was a Blackshirt! What a thrill. I was so pumped up that day.

Before that first game, coming out of the tunnel before we played North Texas, I was just numb. There is so much going on, your body is just numb. Then you have to calm down and play the game.

I can still remember my first tackle. This running back from North Texas cut back as I was coming up through the hole, and he cut back right into me and I hit him. I got a stinger on the play, and there was a picture of that play in the newspaper the next day. Then it appeared in my hometown paper.

Right before the Orange Bowl that season, my knee was messed up. It was a week or two before the game, and I had sprained my MCL. All the Black-shirts went out to the beach to get their annual picture taken, and here I was in that picture with my knee all wrapped up. I played on kickoffs, but never got in on defense, but I remember that game like it was yesterday. On Florida State's last drive, they were hitting Warrick Dunn out of the backfield one play after another. Then they threw a pass down the middle of the field and Toby Wright got called for pass interference. After they scored to take the lead, Tommie [Frazier] marched us down the field, and when we kicked the final field goal, I started running onto the field because I thought we had made it.

Of course, we didn't, and we didn't win the game or the national championship, either.

That game hurt so much. We knew we were coming back next year. We just knew it. We knew how to get there, and we knew what it took. Now we just had to finish business. We had shirts made up that read: "Unfinished Business." Then when we worked out in the off-season, the stadium clock read: "1:16"—the time remaining when Florida State started their drive.

When we dominated West Virginia [31–0] in the opener in the Meadowlands, I thought, "We are really going to be good. Really good."

Then on the second play of the second half at Texas Tech in the next game, I tore my ACL when I went to tackle this guy. My foot got stuck on their turf, and it popped. That was a prime-time night game on ESPN, and I spent it lying on their turf in agony.

That injury forced me to become a cheerleader for the rest of the year. But we kept rolling, even though Tommie Frazier was out with blood clots. It was the toughest thing I ever went through in my life: to see the guys having so much fun, and to see them competing and winning every week. I couldn't be out there to enjoy it with them, and that was killing me. It was a tough pill to swallow, and I didn't get over it until the end of the season.

Mike Minter (No. 10) chases an Iowa State running back.

246

When we went back to the Orange Bowl to play Miami, they had that mystique of the Orange Bowl behind them and nobody picked us to win that game, even though we were undefeated and ranked No. 1. Brook Berringer played well and then cooled off, and then Tommie came in to give us a spark. By the end of the fourth quarter, we were just killing them with the fullback—they couldn't stop Cory Schlesinger.

It was the most exciting game I had ever seen. When we won [24–17] that night, I looked over at coach Osborne, and it was as if one thousand pounds came right off his shoulders. It was in that very stadium that he had missed that two-point conversion against Miami all those years earlier when I was watching on television. I felt so good for him.

After that game, I just grabbed everybody and told them, "You got to play in this championship game and I didn't, so get ready, because I want to do it all over again next year!"

I had rehabbed so hard that I was in the best shape of my life coming back. The trainers, Brian Bailey and Doak Ostergard, helped me so much. It was tough, it was rough, but it also was fun at times. I came back the next season stronger than ever, and I was ready to roll by spring practice.

Then right before the season started, my knee started hurting. I just figured I had to work harder, but the doctors said it was fatigue. Right after the Arizona State game [a 77–28 Nebraska win], in which I had a terrible game, the leg felt like it was dead to me. I was waking up the next morning, and my wife brought me the sports page. [Defensive coordinator] Charlie McBride was quoted as saying something like, "Mike is finished. His knee is messed up."

Was I fired up by that? Yeah, you could say so. From that point on, I didn't limp. I just played through the pain until it got to the point where it felt better. I still have that article. I guess that was the fire I needed. A couple of years later, I told coach McBride, "I don't know if you said that on purpose to fire me up or not, but it worked."

That was a great year for me. I was leading the team in tackles at one point [and finished second to Terrell Farley], and we just dominated every team. We trailed one time all year—7–0 to Washington State. That was the closest game we had, and we won that game by 14 points [35–21].

I remember how cocky Florida was before we played them in the Fiesta Bowl. Everybody in the media was talking about how fast Florida was. We thought, "Not only do they not know how fast we are, they have no idea how physical we are."

We were confident that not only would we win, but we thought we would blow these guys out. I remember coach Osborne had this one play—that screen pass to Lawrence Phillips—scripted. They had worked on it all week, and then it worked perfectly. It seemed Lawrence was in the end zone all night. So was Tommie. Our offense just shredded them. After the game [a 62–24 Nebraska win], I remember taking all those pictures and grinning from ear to ear. Then we had the parade the next week, and I woke up and sort of asked, "Is that it? That's it?"

You come down so fast from the euphoria that you feel that you need to do it all over again.

I thought we would do it again the next season, but I knew the critical part would be the quarterback position. Tommie was gone, and Scott Frost was stepping in. Scott was a great athlete, don't get me wrong, but he wasn't making decisions quick enough when he first started to play. When I looked at the schedule before the season, the Arizona State game on the road was the one that scared me.

Then I was watching ESPN that week, and I heard Beano Cook say, "I think Arizona State will upset Nebraska."

He was right. We just couldn't score that night; we couldn't do anything [a 19–0 Nebraska loss].

It was the first year of the Big 12, and we had a chance to make up for it as long as we won the Big 12 Championship Game against Texas. It came down to that play where they had fourth-and-inches, and I have thought about that play a lot over the years.

Texas came out with a full backfield and a power–I formation, with double tight ends. We knew they were going to run it, but then they ran that option pass. Ralph Brown was the cornerback who was responsible for the tight end, but Ralph was a true freshman. When we looked at the film later, he was lined up over the guard when the ball was snapped. He thought it was going to be a quarterback sneak. I was responsible for the quarterback. As the quarterback faked it and rolled out, I saw it all the way, and I was coming right at him. As he rolled out, I thought, "It's me and him for the first down, and he is not getting the first down!"

Then he planted as I was about to hit him, and I thought to myself, "Who is he throwing it to?"

He raised up and threw it, and I turned around and saw it was Ralph's guy—he was wide open.

That was the toughest loss of my career, along with the Super Bowl, and it took me a month to get over that game.

Being at Nebraska was the best five years of my life. It is, without question, the best decision I ever made. It is where I met my wife, and now we have four beautiful kids. It is where I found God and was saved. And it is where I got my degree.

Nebraska means everything to me. I bleed those colors. I talk about it every day to anyone who will listen, and it will always be in my heart. In fact, all four of my kids are going to go to school there someday. And maybe someday, we will return there as a family.

Mike Minter was named All–Big 12 in 1996. His 84-yard interception return against Michigan State in 1996 is the eighth longest in school history. He was recently voted to the Nebraska All-Century Team. He has played for the Carolina Panthers since 1997.

RUSS HOCHSTEIN
OFFENSIVE GUARD
1997–2000

As a young boy, I dreamed of playing football at Nebraska and I dreamed of playing in a Super Bowl.

So can you imagine how I feel now, having had both of them come true? I am a very lucky person and I realize that not a lot of people have been in my shoes. I played on a national championship team with Nebraska and on a Super Bowl–winning team with the New England Patriots. Not bad for a kid from tiny Hartington, Nebraska.

Hartington is in the northeast corner of the state, a town of about 1,650 people, about 22 miles south of the South Dakota border and west of Sioux City. But it's still Nebraska, which means all the people around there were Cornhusker fans. That's all you see—Big Red fans—and I knew if I ever had a chance to go there, I would. It was my dream to play for the Cornhuskers.

At Hartington Cedar Catholic, I started as a freshman at center. Then they moved me to guard as a junior and to tackle as a senior. I also played linebacker on defense. I wasn't heavily recruited though, because I came from such a small school. I went to the University of Nebraska football camps, and I think that is where I got noticed. I didn't really care who else recruited me, I just wanted to play for one team, and that was all that mattered to me.

At the camps, some of the Nebraska coaches told me, "Don't be surprised if we get in touch with you later."

So when [assistant coach] Dan Young recruited me, I was pretty excited abut my chances. Then coach Osborne called me. I remember I was so nervous talking to him on the phone. But he couldn't come to my house because something came up and he had to cancel his scheduled visit. It wasn't a big deal to me because when they offered me a scholarship, I knew I was going there. He didn't need to come to see me to convince me. It was the only offer I had at the time, but after that, some schools like Iowa State and Kansas State called—not that it would have mattered. I was headed to Nebraska no matter what.

I remember walking into the weight room during the summer before my freshman year, and I was humbled right away. I couldn't even bench press 300 pounds, and there were Jason Peter and Grant Wistrom pumping iron. They were huge and intimidating. One of the weight coaches came up to me and said, "Don't worry about it, Russ. It doesn't matter how much weight you are lifting now because by the time you are ready to leave, you will be doing a lot more."

The campus was overwhelming to me, too. I graduated with 30 people in my high school class, and some classes at Nebraska had 200 or 300 people. The professors were speaking 80 mph, and I was always playing catch-up.

When they brought me in, I told them I would play anywhere they wanted me to play. They brought me in as a center, but I grew bigger and they had a lack of depth at guard, so I moved to guard right after my freshman year, when I redshirted.

Coach [Milt] Tenopir looked at my weight, which was about 235, and said, "Coach Osborne would like you to redshirt, put on some weight, and get stronger." I said, "No problem."

I actually loved that redshirt year, and when I look back on it, I know it was the best thing for me in the long run. I just had to go out every day, eat the right things, lift weights, go to practice, and try to improve on the field. Sounds simple, doesn't it? In that first year, I think I put on 20 pounds just by lifting and eating.

It is hard being on the practice squad, though, because I was going against guys like Jared Tomich, Jason Peter, Grant Wistrom, and Mike Rucker. I just thought, "Man, these guys are really fast."

It was more humbling than anything else, but their duty was to tear you up. Their whole objective was to beat you, and most of the time they accomplished their objective. When I graduated from high school, I thought I was a decent athlete, but I would try to block Terrell Farley when he was coming

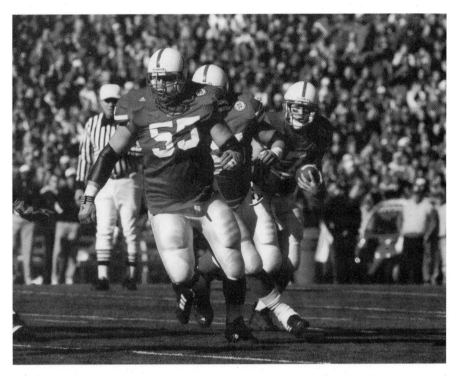

Russ Hochstein (No. 55), here leading the way on a sweep, went from being lightly recruited to developing into an All-American guard.

around the end, and he would blow by me like I was standing still. And Jared Tomich would put that club move on me. Let's just say I was knocked on my can a few times. But you remember it, learn from it, and take your licks. I knew if I worked hard and learned, I would eventually get my chance.

I played both center and guard in 1997, and I worked my way up to three-deep. I would get three or four minutes of mop-up when we were beating somebody pretty bad, like against Oklahoma when we won 69–7, which was coach Osborne's 250th win.

Every year we would list our goals and, at the top, it was to win the national championship. So I was very proud to be part of that team in 1997, which rolled right through the schedule. My buddy and Patriots teammate Tom Brady and I always argue about who was best that year—us or Michigan? They were undefeated, too, and we split the championship, but I still think we would have beaten Michigan if we played them.

When coach Osborne retired, it was obvious that nobody wanted him to go, but I was just in my second year, so I didn't have the history with him that the upperclassmen had. I know we all wanted him to stay, but we realized he couldn't coach forever. He was leaving the program in good hands with coach [Frank] Solich, and everything would stay intact. He just said it was time to leave, and we all respected that. In fact, as I am writing this, I am looking at a letter he wrote me, congratulating me on our Super Bowl victory. He really is a great, great man.

I also enjoyed playing under coach Solich, who was a tremendous competitor. One time I got in a fight in practice, and he got right in my face and got that finger in my chest. He was a little guy, but you could tell he must have been very tough and aggressive when he played for Nebraska.

I remember we were playing Southern Miss in 1999, and I had a really bad series in the first half. Adam Julch, a tackle who was next to me, just looked at me and said, "Man, you had better get your act together, because Coach is going to let you have it at halftime." Sure enough, he did let me have it at halftime, but I played much better in the second half.

Of the toughest losses I have ever experienced, that 1999 game at Texas [24–20] was the worst. It was as hard as anything I had ever experienced on the football field. It was a nip-and-tuck game when Correll Buckhalter got hit hard on the goal line and fumbled. But we came back and won every game after that and beat Tennessee in the Fiesta Bowl to finish 12–1. I think that team was good enough to win the national championship.

As a senior, I was voted captain, which was a great, great honor for me. Those are your peers voting—the guys you sweated with and worked out with.

To sum this all up, I feel very blessed to have played at Nebraska. I had dreamed about it, and when it became reality, it was even better than I ever had imagined.

Russ Hochstein was named two-time All–Big 12 and an All-American in 2000. He also was the 2000 winner of the Cletus Fischer Native Son Award, named after Nebraska's long-time assistant coach. Hochstein was a fifth-round pick of the Tampa Bay Buccaneers. He has played with the New England Patriots since 2002.

AHMAN GREEN

RUNNING BACK

1995–1997

WHEN I WAS A KID GROWING UP IN LOS ANGELES, the only sport I didn't play was soccer. I was born in Nebraska, but Mom and I moved to Glendale when I was about four. In California, I would ride my bike from one town to another to play Little League football. I really had a blast out there and enjoyed living there.

When it came to playing football in California, everything was about speed. Who was the quickest? Who was the fastest? And it seemed to me that everybody was fast out there. The linemen were fast and the running backs were faster. If you were the fastest, you got picked up to play, so I always tried to outrun everybody. I had that mentality of "speed, speed, speed." That is probably why I was a Miami Hurricanes' fan back then, because I loved their speed and how fast they played on both sides of the ball.

Everybody there called me "Batman" because I loved the old TV series with Adam West. Then they made the movie with Michael Keaton, and everybody loved my nickname. When I was younger, I was kind of a techie—I loved computers and video games and I took a lot of math classes and learned how to type.

When it came to football, you can say I was "old school."

Mom had been remarried, and my stepdad, Edward Scott, had played on the offensive line when he was younger. He knew the game of football. He would tell me war stories of the trenches, and how to work hard, be tough, and play football the old-school way. He also taught me how to play hard until the whistle blew.

In June of 1991, we moved back to Omaha, and it was tough on me at first because I had left all of my friends that I had from elementary school and junior high. I had a lot of relatives in Nebraska, but I didn't know them very well.

I remember on my first day of tryouts for midget football, nobody knew me. Anyway, on our first day, we were hitting and doing all the old-school drills. We would lie on our backs and the coaches would drop the ball in your belly, and you would get up and try to beat the defensive guy. When I had the ball, I never got tackled. And when I was on defense, I was just laying people out. So they were suddenly calling me the "California Kid," and I was making new friends.

My oldest brother took me to the Nebraska high school all-star game that summer, and we were trying to decide if I was going to play varsity that next year. I saw the size of these guys at this high school all-star game and asked my brother, "Are these the size of the kids I would be playing against on the varsity?"

He said yes and I told him, "I am not quite that big yet. I think I'll wait."

The thing I remember about that game is Tony Veland was playing quarterback, and he was running up and down the field. He later played at Nebraska and then won a Super Bowl ring with the Broncos.

As a freshman and sophomore, I played at Omaha North and then transferred to Omaha Central for my final two years. My mom had graduated from there, and they had a better curriculum. Before my junior year ended, all the recruiting letters started coming in. My first letter was for a track scholarship to North Carolina.

I played running back and linebacker, and rushed for more than one thousand yards in three straight seasons, so everybody was recruiting me by the time I was a senior. I have to say that the recruiting process was fun for me. I had compiled this huge chart of every school before my junior year ended. I included what state they were in, the weather and climate, the offense and defense they ran, the coaching staff, and what the curriculum was. I even had some Ivy League schools on the list.

On the first day that coaches were allowed to make phone calls during recruiting, within minutes, Tom Osborne was the first one to call me. Then Lou Holtz, who was at Notre Dame, called and then the phone started ringing off the hook.

I had planned to visit Penn State, Nebraska, Notre Dame, Michigan, and Arizona. But Penn State wanted me to commit before I went there on my visit, so I dropped them off the list.

My first trip was to Arizona, and it really appealed to me. That's back when they had Teddy Bruschi and that great "Desert Swarm" defense—they were ranked really high at the time. [Arizona coach] Dick Tomey sat down with me one on one and asked me, "What do you want?"

I had certain criteria that I wanted in a school, and one of them was a chance to win a national title. I told coach Tomey that I would play anywhere he wanted me to play. I remember saying, "Whatever y'all want me to play, I'll play it." I knew I could play at linebacker, safety, or cornerback, or I could catch passes. But of course, I loved running back.

I just knew what I wanted to do—I wanted to contribute right away, play my three or four years, win a national championship, and go to the NFL.

Notre Dame was not what I expected during my visit. They played that "tradition" angle too much for my tastes. It was all about Touchdown Jesus and Irish this and Irish that. By the end of the second day, it was overkill for me, and I was ready to leave town.

I admit that I wasn't overcome by "Big Red Country" yet because I had spent so much time in California. I had been to the football camps at Nebraska and already met coach [Frank] Solich and coach Osborne. I had taken my visit there, and liked it, but noticed they had a lot of running backs there—Lawrence Phillips, James Sims, and Clinton Childs.

My final decision came down to Arizona and Nebraska, and I made up my mind on the night that Nebraska played Miami in the 1995 Orange Bowl for the national championship—but not for the reason you may think.

I was at a friend's house watching the game when my mom called me. Right before halftime, my stepfather had suffered a mild heart attack, so I rushed to the hospital to meet her. Fortunately, it wasn't life-threatening. He had to change his eating habits, but he came out OK. It was a bad scare for us, and I made my decision right there that night. I never knew when my family was going to need me. I also knew it was easy to get to Lincoln—you just had to drive right down the road—so that was where my future was.

I remember that coach Osborne asked me if I wanted to redshirt or play as a true freshman, and I told him right away, "I want to play right now. I want to be here for three or four years, get my degree, and go to the NFL. No redshirt."

255

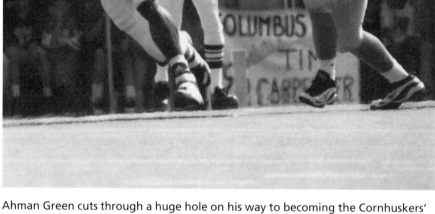

Ahman Green cuts through a huge hole on his way to becoming the Cornhuskers' second all-time leader rusher.

He just said, "OK, you don't have to redshirt."

In my first few practices that freshman season, I got tested right away. There were bigger, faster guys, and I was getting my share of hits. In the first scrimmage, Lawrence Phillips went 50 yards to score a touchdown on our defense, and then Damon Benning went in. When I got my chance, Christian Peter hit me and then started talking stuff: "Hey, high school All-American—this isn't high school anymore!"

Christian was a huge dude, but I was prepared for that type of intimidation, and it never scared me. I knew I could play. Then I started to run even better during that scrimmage because it motivated me. Christian later came up to me and gave me my props—he told me he liked the way I ran, and from then on, I knew I could play college ball.

In that first year in 1995, I was nervous. I admit it. It took a while for that to wear off. I just felt more at ease coming off the bench, but I got my first start against Missouri and rushed for 96 yards. I was named the Big 12 Freshman of the Year, and I knew I was on my way.

The next year, Lawrence was gone, so I knew it was my time. I was ready for it. The season started off great for me and then I got hurt in the Kansas State game with a toe injury. I think I tried to come back too early, and I was sore. I had a stress fracture in my second toe for compensating for my initial injury. I missed the Big 12 Championship Game, which we lost to Texas, but I did play in the bowl game against Virginia Tech.

At times, I did feel like I was in the zone that people talk about. In one game in 1997, I had 189 yards against Kansas State and scored four touchdowns—and I was playing hurt. The week before, I had banged up my right shoulder against Washington, and I was favoring it. But it was one of those games where you play through the pain and just keep going.

That was sort of like a dream season for me. Once Tommie Frazier was gone, however, people said we wouldn't be able to win a national championship without him. My thing was that once Tommie left, I still felt we were going to win. It's a team game, no matter who the quarterback is. Scott Frost had played the year before, and I was confident that we could win them all and do it again.

257

We did just that, beating Texas A&M in the Big 12 Championship Game and then Tennessee in the Orange Bowl for the school's third national championship in four years. We were so close to having four in a row. If not for that loss to Texas the year before we would have had a chance at it. Those times were very special because we just kicked butt and took names. We weren't afraid to play anybody, and everybody had each other's back. We had a great coach, one of the greatest ever, and he had a great coaching staff.

When we were headed to one of those college football awards shows, coach Osborne told a group of us—me, Aaron Taylor, Grant Wistrom, and Jason Peter—that he was retiring from coaching. I just thought, "Wow," but it really didn't surprise me. In fact, I saw it coming. He had dealt with all the stuff off the field that Lawrence Phillips and Christian Peter had gone through, and I think it took its toll on him. I think the media's criticism of how he handled it really got to him.

Then I realized just how lucky I was to get to play for him—a football coach with his smarts, knowledge, and psychology. Let me put it this way, they didn't call him "Doctor Tom" for nothing. He was a great, great coach.

When it came time for my next decision, I knew I was ready. I made another one of my lists of the positives and negatives to it. I had accomplished what I set out to do. National championships? We won two. Graduating? I was close enough to come back to do that, which I did, getting my degree in geography. I wanted to lead my team in rushing. Did that.

Nebraska had become my weigh station. I went there to become a man, and it was time to move on to the next level. I wanted to play in the NFL since I was a little kid, and now I knew it was my time to go.

When I look back at my time at Nebraska, and I look at today's teams, it is all about teamwork and heart. We played together as a team, and we always played with great heart. And to me, that's what Nebraska football is all about.

Ahman Green is Nebraska's second all-time leading rusher with 3,880 yards (behind Mike Rozier). He finished his three-year career with 42 touchdowns (third best), four 200-yard rushing games, and 20 100-yard games. His 1,877 rushing yards in 1997 was the best ever by a junior and the second-best season in school history. He was named All–Big Eight in 1995 and All–Big 12 in 1997. Green played two seasons with the Seattle Seahawks and has been with the Green Bay Packers since 2000.

TREV ALBERTS
LINEBACKER
1990–1993

I'LL NEVER FORGET THE DAY IOWA COACH HAYDEN FRY walked into my house to recruit me. I couldn't believe he was actually in my house. My parents were so excited that they called the neighbors. He was an icon in the state of Iowa, and I was from Cedar Falls, so it was natural for people around there to worship him. And we were huge Iowa fans. We even went all the way to Atlanta one year to see the Hawkeyes play North Carolina State in the Peach Bowl. I could name every Iowa player, and I remember my whole family being distraught when Chuck Long came in second to Bo Jackson in the [1985] Heisman Trophy race.

Nobody at my high school—NU High—had ever received a scholarship for football before. It was a tiny lab school, and I graduated with 60 kids, seven of whom were foreign exchange students. So it was pretty exciting for me just to be recruited. I had told the local newspaper that if Iowa ever offered me a scholarship, I would go there in a heartbeat. It was a dream for me and my older brother, Troy, that I would play football for the Hawkeyes. He even had paid for me to go to Iowa's football camp. Well, I did get that offer, and I verbally committed to play for Iowa.

So you may ask, how did I end up as a Nebraska Cornhusker?

You could say that the good doctor—otherwise known as Tom Osborne—was the main reason I ended up in Lincoln.

But it all started when my school principal, Dr. Moore, sent an article about me to [recruiting coordinator] Dave Gillespie at Nebraska. John Melton then recruited me, and he mentioned that coach Osborne was visiting some people, and Dad said, "Well, you know, he's never come here to Cedar Falls. If he really thought highly of Trev, wouldn't he make a trip here to see him?"

Coach Osborne then came to Cedar Falls to see me. After seeing him, my parents and I decided, "Let's go to Lincoln to see the place. It's only 300 miles away and it will be fun."

So we loaded up the family Cadillac and headed to Lincoln. I'll never forget getting off the interstate and seeing Cornhusker Highway, and then we stayed at the Cornhusker Hotel. It was clear to me right away that football was very important in Nebraska. But once I got there, they didn't talk about football to me. They talked about all the other aspects—academics, your spiritual life, how you would develop socially.

I remember that I was so skinny, about 6'4" and 205 pounds, that [Nebraska strength coach] Boyd Epley asked me, "Trev, what do you play . . . quarterback? Punter?"

And I was not that talented, either. I had some athletic ability. I mean, I was fast and I could jump high, but I wasn't big and strong. Our high school didn't even have a weight room, but I had piddled around with some weights at the YMCA. I was one of those guys that the Nebraska program has made a living on—I was one of those guys who would have to outwork people to make it.

I remember they had something like 26 outside linebackers on the roster, and some of them were walk-ons. I had asked coach Osborne about that, and he responded, "Trev, all you have to do is be one of the top two."

"Well, that makes sense," I figured.

When we started the drive home that day, not much was said in the car. Finally, after about 70 miles, Dad said, "Trev, we would really like to see you go to Iowa, but we would understand very much if you decided to go to Nebraska." That's how impressive it was to all of us.

It really was a gut-wrenching time for me. On one hand, my family loved Iowa; I loved Iowa. On the other, I loved my visit to Nebraska and I believed in coach Osborne. The fact is, I loved a challenge, and I had people around my town telling me that I wouldn't play at Nebraska. They would say things like, "They are out of your league."

That is one thing about our family—we are so stinking competitive. When somebody told me what I couldn't do, I thought I would show them what I would do. In my heart, I felt Nebraska would be the perfect place for me. So when I got home, I called coach Osborne and told him I was coming.

Now, as I said, I had verbally committed to Iowa, and that goes against anything my family would ever do. When you tell somebody something, you are as good as your word. But I had to pick up the phone and call [Iowa assistant] Dan McCarney. I was scared to death, but I had to. He was shocked. I think he said, "You've got to be kidding me."

But he was a class guy about it. He still sent Christmas cards to us every year.

Turning down Iowa absolutely destroyed my brother. It had been our dream for me to go play for the Hawkeyes, so it took a few months for him to get over it. He actually didn't speak to me for a while.

I got to Nebraska, and after a few days, I figured I would never make it. I mean, my high school didn't even have a tackling dummy, so I was way behind. Kevin Steele was the inside linebackers coach at the time, and when we had those "take-on" drills, I gave some guy a forearm shiver instead of doing it right. I can still hear coach Steele. "Whoa, whoa, whoa!" he yelled. "What is this?"

Everybody was laughing at me. Then I saw these 6'8", 300-pound linemen I would be going against. I called Dad that night and told him, "There's absolutely no way I can play here. These guys are huge!"

After a few days, they read a list of names, including mine, and said, "Coach Osborne wants to see you six guys."

I thought, "Well, that's it. I am done. It took him three days to figure out that I can't play at this level."

I went to see him, and he said that I needed to take a year, put on some weight, work hard, and be a redshirt. He said I would get to contribute "next year." I was all excited. I called Dad and said, "Guess what? I get to redshirt."

Dad said, "What do you mean? What's a redshirt? You mean you have to wear a red shirt?"

Then I got moved to outside linebacker. I believe coach Steele felt I wasn't tough enough to play inside, so I got moved. It was motivation for me, too. When I moved, Tony Samuel became my position coach, and I have to give him a tremendous amount of credit because he really shaped and developed me.

I roomed with Troy Branch, who was from Camden, New Jersey, and he would tell me stories of gunshots flying over his head, sirens going off all the time, and tales from what it was like to live in the city. And I roomed with Travis Hill, who also was a high school All-American. I walked into my room that first day, and Troy had all of his No. 54 jerseys hanging on the wall already.

Troy was about 6'2" and 240, and he had this big goatee. He stood up and said, "I am Troy Branch and I intend on being a Blackshirt next year."

"That's great Troy," I said. "I am Trev and I intend to be on the team." At that point, that was my goal.

But I wouldn't be the person I am today if I had not roomed with those guys. When we went to eat at the training table, at times, I would go sit with those guys. People would ask me, "What, are you trying to be black?"

Well, no, it wasn't about that. I never saw it that way. I learned a lot from everybody on the team, and I hope they learned something from me, too. We never had any racial problems at Nebraska, but it was just natural that all the African Americans sat on one side of training table, and all the white guys on another. I figure it is that way in most programs. But I liked to sit over here one day and over there another.

262

That first year I was really getting beat up on the scout team, and I really wanted to quit. One time I was sitting in study hall with Gerald Armstrong, who was a walk-on tight end. I was venting about everything going wrong for me, and how this was so difficult, and all of a sudden, Gerald said, "Man, I don't feel sorry for you one bit. You scholarship guys don't have a clue!"

Gerald told me his story of how he grew up on a farm, and his parents had no money—just enough money to send him to school for one year. If he didn't get a scholarship after that, he would have to come home. Now try playing with that burden. But that made Nebraska football so special—those kids from Nebraska grew up with it in their blood. And no kids in the country are tougher than they are.

One night around that time, I was out in Memorial Stadium, just walking around and feeling overwhelmed by it all. I was standing right on the big N, and I looked up at the stars, and it was totally dark and dead silent. I just told myself, "Screw this. I am now making a total commitment to myself. I might flunk out of school, or I might not, but I will get this done. If I fail at this, it won't be for a lack of trying."

Right then, I decided I was laying everything on the line.

The coaches had a depth chart behind this big curtain in one of the meeting rooms, and I can now admit that I used to sneak up there all the time, pull back the curtain, and see where I was on the depth chart. Then I would call home: "Dad, I am fourth team!" . . . "Dad, I am up to third team!"

I did that all the time.

That next year, 1990, I had 26 tackles and five sacks while backing up Kenny Walker in pass-rushing situations, and I was named Big Eight Defensive Newcomer of the Year. That next year, the position at right outside linebacker was wide open after Mike Croel went to the NFL. I knew if I didn't win the job, I might have to sit on the bench until my senior year. David White was ahead of me.

In spring ball, I remember being so disciplined. I was thinking on Friday or Saturday nights that David might be out partying, so I was working. I wanted to give myself every opportunity to win the job, but I was having a problem with my right shoulder that year. It kept going numb. I went to the trainer, George Sullivan, and he said, "Trev, this isn't high school anymore—you will have a little pain."

Later I had surgery, and when I woke up, Mom and Dad were there. Dad said, "Trev, we're sorry, but it was worse than they thought. You are out of spring ball." Dad always had a way with words.

263

Right before the 1991 season started, coach Samuel announced in a meeting, "OK, we are going to start Travis [Hill] on the left and David [White] on the right."

I went up to coach Osborne's office and told him I wanted to transfer.

He said, "What do you mean? You are on the second team and you are only a sophomore."

I just said, "I love it here, but I only have four years to play, and I am thinking about transferring to Division I-AA so I can play right away." Fortunately, he talked me out of it.

I played in more than half the games in 1991 and had [53] tackles, but I wasn't a Blackshirt, and I couldn't stand not being a Blackshirt. I would go out to practice and have to wear a lousy yellow shirt. That was so important to me—to be a Blackshirt—but I wasn't. The next spring, I thought I had outplayed David White, but I knew he was going to be a senior and the returning starter. I worked and worked and worked, but still figured I wouldn't replace him because he was the returning starter.

Then in a meeting, coach Samuel announced, "OK, we are going to start Travis on the left and Trev on the right."

Those were magical words to me. I know it took an inordinate amount of courage for coach Samuel to name me the starter, but David never complained. He never moaned and he never treated me differently. I really respected him for handling it that way.

We had always played a true 5-2 defense, where the outside linebackers would line up on the line of scrimmage. But halfway through that season, we played Colorado, and we played nickel [coverage] the whole day because they were throwing the ball some. Travis and I just dominated them. We were making tackles in the backfield all day, and so was Ed Stewart. I think after that game the coaches just said, "Hey, we've got a lot of speed. Why don't we just play nickel for the rest of the year?"

So we did.

After that season, heading into my senior season, we had changed to a 4–3, and they told us, "Now you guys will be rush ends."

I am thinking to myself, "Hey, I just had a great year [73 tackles, 11 for losses], and now they want to change things."

But coach Samuel convinced me things would be OK. He just said, "No, chief, this will be good for you. You are going to like it. You are going to line up wider than the widest and just go make plays." And he was right.

Heading into that season, I was on the initial Butkus Award watch list, one of about 50 guys, and I told Mom and Dad right away that I was going to win it. I figured I would do whatever it took. I would get up early in the morning three days a week and run about three miles. I was doing extra work all the time. I was eating right, and I had put on about 10 pounds of lean muscle each year. I was up to 235.

We were about to play North Texas in the first game, and I looked at the scouting report and saw that the guy across from me was 6'4" and 230. I called Dad and told him, "I might win the Butkus in this game alone."

In that game, we won 76–14, but I had only one tackle and no sacks. North Texas was smart. They ran to the line of scrimmage and came out in an unbalanced line, so we didn't adjust right away. Our signal for the unbalanced line was to get both hands straight up to signal it to make the calls. All day long I would see them come to the line of scrimmage in that unbalanced line, and I would throw my hands over my head.

Trev Alberts, here making a tackle in the backfield, was the Big Eight Defensive Player of the Year in 1993.

So we got done with this game, and Dad said to me, "Son, if you play like that, you not only won't win the Butkus, you won't even be starting. You need to spend less time getting the fans involved and more on just playing football."

It took until Wednesday after the game to figure out what he meant by that. He had confused our signals for the unbalanced line with trying to wave our arms to get the crowd involved. After I figured it out, I told Dad, "Don't try to talk football with me again." But I always called my parents, probably after every practice. They missed only one game in my whole career and that was the game in Tokyo.

I had a great season, and when we played Kansas State, I needed one sack to get the Nebraska career record. I was going against Barrett Brooks, who was a great left tackle, and by the end of the third quarter, I was dead tired. I didn't have a sack, and as we walked down to the other end of the field, he started yapping at me, telling me how bad I was.

I walked up to him and said, "Barrett, let me tell you something, you are the best offensive tackle I have ever played against."

"Really, are you serious?" he asked.

Two plays later, I got my sack. I figured I had softened him up some. Then I walked by him and said, "Well . . . almost the best."

In the Oklahoma game, the field was icy, and I slipped on a play and dislocated my elbow. I remember being in the locker room getting worked on, and my arm was in a sling when this scout for the Green Bay Packers walked in—I don't know how he got in there—and asked me, "Are you playing again?"

"What? Playing again?" I said. "My elbow is dislocated!"

Here we were, undefeated, I was having a great year, and we were about to play Florida State in the Orange Bowl for the national championship, and my elbow was in a cast. I went from event to event after the season—and I did win the Butkus Award—with this big ol' cast on my arm.

I knew the NFL was around the corner, and I even had agents telling me not to play in the Orange Bowl. They said I would lower my draft status if I didn't play well. When they finally took this cast off, I had atrophy and I had lost weight. I was out of shape, too. I couldn't move my elbow and I wondered how in the world would I play in this game. Then I thought, "Man, coach Osborne has done so much for me. He has never won a national championship. How could I live with myself if I didn't try to play in this game?"

We got down to Miami and I took some dumbbells and just ripped it all apart, but the doctors told me, "Don't worry Trev, it's just scar tissue."

I got in two practices in half-pads, and they made this big brace for me. We were out on the field warming up before the Orange Bowl, and the game officials came up to me and said, "You can't play with that on your arm." Then there was a big argument between the training staff and the officials, and coach Osborne got involved. Finally, they put some padding around the brace, and the officials allowed me to play.

Florida State had a great team, and they were 17-point favorites. We were in the locker room before the game, and the Orange Bowl had placed these commemorative jockstraps in our locker. Ours read: "1993 National Championship Game." But one of the equipment managers brought me one from Florida State's locker room and it read: "1993 National Champions."

I didn't say anything about it until we gathered as a team before we went out. I held it up and said, "Let me show you Florida State's jockstrap." I didn't say anything else. You should have heard the place. Guys were ready to play right then and there.

I think that game was my crowning achievement. I got three sacks on Charlie Ward, and it was gratifying to come back like that, but it was so devastating to lose that game [18–16]. We all felt that we cost coach Osborne the national championship, but the fact is, we got homered so badly by the officials. One call after another. This is not sour grapes, but we absolutely had atrocious officiating go against us.

267

At the end of the game, coach Osborne told us, "Gentleman, don't ever hold your head down. You may not be national champions, but you played with heart and you played a great game."

To come so close, and yet be so far from a national championship—that was so difficult. But I think it was the turning point for the program.

The next year, I was on that Orange Bowl sideline when Nebraska beat Miami to get coach Osborne his first national championship, and I walked into the locker room to congratulate him. Here he was, he had just won a national championship, and when we hugged, he told me, "Trev, I really feel bad that we couldn't win one for your class." That's how much he truly cared about his players. I think he cared almost too much at times.

Coach Osborne had made a promise to me and my family about education and the chance to play and develop, and he had delivered everything he promised. My mom and dad established my moral compass when I was growing up, but coach Osborne reaffirmed it and took it to another level. He taught me about perseverance and loyalty and dedication. I absolutely love that man.

To this day, I have a yearning for the state of Nebraska and for those people, and it is something I will never lose. Who knows? If I had gone to Iowa, it may have turned out exactly the same, but I doubt it. If I could have, I would have played at Nebraska for 10 years for nothing. Coach Osborne and the state of Nebraska will always be very, very special to me.

Trev Alberts, who won the 1993 Butkus Award, finished his career with 248 tackles, including 45 for losses. His 29.5 career sacks is a school record. He was a team captain and also was named an All-American and the Big Eight Defensive Player of the Year in 1993. As a student, he was a three-time Academic All–Big Eight and an Academic All-American as a senior. He was a winner of the NCAA's Top Eight Award and was inducted into the Nebraska Football Hall of Fame in 1994. Alberts was drafted in the first round by the Indianapolis Colts, with whom he played three seasons. He currently works as a college football analyst for ESPN.

TOMMIE FRAZIER

QUARTERBACK

1992–1995

I WAS MOTIVATED FROM THE BEGINNING of my college football career because of all the schools that turned their backs on me and told me I couldn't play quarterback. Being from Florida, everyone realizes that Florida, Florida State, and Miami have been college football powers for years. Here I was, a quarterback who wanted to stay a quarterback in college, and Florida State wanted me at defensive back, Florida wanted me to play running back, and Miami wanted me as an athlete.

My goal was to show them all that they were making a big mistake by not taking me as a quarterback.

As a young kid growing up in Palmetto, Florida—on the coast of the Gulf of Mexico just south of Tampa—I stayed very busy by playing every sport possible. I even played soccer, although it wasn't my best sport by any means. It was my least favorite sport, too.

I had four brothers and one sister, so we were always doing something. I played quarterback from the start when I played football, but I took my freshman year off to get acclimated to high school at Bradenton Manatee. I started on the junior varsity as a sophomore, and then moved up to the varsity for the end of the season when we won the Florida state championship.

We had lost most of our starters going into my junior year, and we weren't picked to win much, but we went all the way to the state semifinals. Then we were favored to win it all when I was a senior, but lost in the first round of the playoffs. That was very tough on me because I knew we had a very good football team, but we just played a terrible game—too many turnovers and penalties.

When it came time to be recruited, I took unofficial visits to the Florida schools, mainly because I had friends who played at each school and I could get there whenever I wanted. But as I said earlier, I had pretty much eliminated them because I wouldn't be behind center anymore. We had run the option in high school, but we still had a lot of passing in the offense. But they still didn't want me as a quarterback.

So I focused on the schools that wanted me to play where I wanted to play, and I visited Clemson, Colorado, Notre Dame, Nebraska, and Syracuse.

I didn't really like the atmosphere at Notre Dame, but coach [Lou] Holtz was a very energetic guy. It was hard for him to sit still for a few minutes. It just seemed like there was nothing to do there but play football, and there's much more to life than that.

I loved Clemson. [Quarterbacks coach] Rick Stockstill did a great job recruiting me. I enjoyed Syracuse, too, but they pretty much told me I would redshirt because Marvin Graves was coming back at quarterback. I didn't understand how they could tell me that before I even got there.

Colorado originally wanted me as a quarterback, but after they got a guy named Koy Detmer, they changed their minds. Looking back, I really think they had the inside track on me until they made that phone call to tell me that. There was a good chance I would have gone to Colorado, because I loved the atmosphere there.

I visited Lincoln on the final weekend of January, and it was in the sixties—I didn't even need a jacket. Everybody said, "Don't worry Tommie, it doesn't get any colder than this."

I just said, "Yeah, right," but I knew better.

The first time I had met coach Osborne was the day after the [1992] Orange Bowl [a 22–0 loss to Miami]. He came over to my house and was very quiet, but he did something that none of the other coaches did. He never once talked about football. Mostly, he talked about academics, and that's what sold my parents on Nebraska and coach Osborne.

In the end, it really was a toss-up between Clemson and Nebraska. The night before signing day, I didn't know where I was going. When I headed to school that day, I didn't know where I was going. When I got to school that day, everybody asked me where I was going. I didn't know. I made my decision about 40 minutes before I was going to sign. I was just sitting at my desk in class and it just came to me.

The factors? First of all, Nebraska ran the same style of offense I was used to. And then coach Osborne put me over the top. I knew he was going to be there for the rest of my career, where Clemson coach Ken Hatfield could have been fired with one bad season.

After I signed with Nebraska, I wondered: did I do the right thing? There I was, leaving home and going fifteen hundred miles away. And early on, there were times I thought about leaving and transferring. The simple fact was that I was improving, yet I was still number three on the depth chart. I didn't want to waste a year at number three or even number two, and I did not want to redshirt. I went to see coach Osborne and said, "If I am not going to play, let me redshirt." It was frustrating for me not to be playing.

"Just be patient," he told me. "There are things we are evaluating"

I said, "I came here to play football and help the team win, and I am not doing that by sitting on the sideline."

I started against Missouri, we won 34–24, and I started for the rest of the season. We were in a rebuilding year and had a lot of young players. I just figured, the job is mine now, and only I could lose it, but I was still wet behind the ears as a quarterback.

That next game, against Colorado, meant the most to me because Koy Detmer started for them. It was really personal for me, and I wanted to show them what they missed. I proved coach McCartney wrong that day and we won [52–7]. I have never spoken to him since that phone call when he told me I wouldn't be playing quarterback. Why would I? He pretty much had told me I was not good enough to play in his system. I talked to some of the coaches on their staff later, and they pretty much admitted, "We signed the wrong guy."

The loss at Ames to Iowa State [19–10] was the game that really hurt. We just didn't show up that day. We had come off two big wins over Colorado and Kansas, and we just overlooked them. They had won one or two games that year, and we took them lightly.

We got to 9–2 and were headed to the Orange Bowl to play Florida State. The speed of their defense was the biggest change for me. They were faster than any team we had ever played, and that was a big learning experience for me. I knew we had to get stronger and had to get faster to compete with them. And we weren't ready to beat them [a 27–14 Nebraska loss].

Tommie Frazier in a 1995 game against Missouri.

When it came to the 1993 team, nobody expected us to be that good. I was a sophomore and people just figured we would slip up and lose somewhere down the line, but we took them one game at a time and never lost. When we won 14–13 at UCLA, that was the coming-out party for Lawrence Phillips. He was a true freshman, but people could just see his talent when he took over.

By the time we got to the Orange Bowl for the rematch with Florida State, we were 11–0, and all we had to do was win the game to win the national title. I can honestly say we truly beat those guys. I have never been the type of person to blame a loss on anyone else, but there were a couple of very questionable calls that went against us. I know that William Floyd fumbled the ball before he crossed the goal line, but they still gave them a touchdown. It was the hardest pill to swallow that night. It wasn't like they beat us in all facets of the game. The fact is, it was taken from us.

The one step we had made from one year to the next was that we were ready to play with them. The year before, I think we were intimidated by Florida State's players. Everybody saw them on TV and saw how good they were and how fast they were, and we just didn't concentrate on us. Plus, everybody knows how all the Florida teams like to talk during a game. I think that got to some of the younger guys.

It took a whole year for me to get over that [18–16] loss. It was one of the most disappointing times of my football career—probably the most disappointing loss. It was disappointing for coach Osborne, too, and the whole coaching staff. They had prepared us well for that game, and we just did not finish it up.

That was the battle cry for the 1994 season: "unfinished business." We worked out with "1:16" showing on our stadium clock, which is when Florida State began their final drive. It was a reminder for us to finish off games.

What can I say about 1994? It was a special year for us, but a frustrating year for me personally.

We were favored to win them all, and we did. When I got injured, some people in the media said, "The season's over with," but I knew it wasn't. I knew football was a team game, and we had a great team.

I just thought I had a bad bruise on my calf, because you get bumps and bruises all the time in football, but it just didn't go away. After the UCLA game—the third game of the season—it was very sore and tight. I played nine plays in the Pacific game, we scored two touchdowns [in a 70–21 win], and after that game they took me to the hospital for some tests. They did some blood tests and scans, and then they told me: "You've got blood clots."

I had questions. Coach Osborne had questions. Everybody had tons of questions. I thought, "I am too young to have blood clots."

I missed the next seven games, and it was very, very tough on me. Here I was, having the best time of my life—we were making a run at the national championship—and then this happened. I still have questions about why it happened to me. But it happened, so I had to deal with it and move on.

I spent the extra time studying, and I just got away from the team. I didn't really want to be around them because I couldn't play football. I had surgery behind my knee, and it took six weeks to heal properly, so I couldn't start practicing again until the week before the Oklahoma game. I was dressed and ready to play against Oklahoma, but the doctors said "only in an emergency" should I play.

Going into the Orange Bowl against Miami, we were 12–0, and I was going to play. As we got to Miami, there was some controversy over who would start—me or Brook Berringer. Some guys on the team felt one way, and I know other guys felt the other way. Coach Osborne just told everybody, "Both quarterbacks are going to play."

He made the final decision a week before the game—that I would start and play the first quarter, and Brook would play the second, and we would go from there.

To tell you the truth, I was out of shape and couldn't run that well because I had missed all that practice time. I had gained 10 to 15 pounds, but mentally I felt fine. After the first quarter we trailed [10–0], and Brook played the second quarter. When I came back early in the fourth quarter, we were behind 17–9. Brook had just thrown an interception in the back of the end zone, and we had lost a great scoring opportunity, so they put me in on the next series.

We were behind, but at that point, Miami's defense was tired. I think we just wore them out, and I felt fresh because I hadn't played the whole game. Their front four was tired, and that was the best part of Miami's defense. We trapped them, we cut them off, and we forced them to chase us outside to get them tired. Then we popped them up the middle with [fullback] Cory [Schlesinger] as we caught up and took the lead.

That was a great, great win [24–17]. I have to say it was my defining moment. I showed people that my goal was to win a national championship for Nebraska, and nothing—not even missing seven games with the blood clots—was going to stop me from doing that.

I remember getting on the bus after the game, I looked at coach Osborne, and he just smiled at me. I smiled back at him and went to my seat. We didn't say anything to each other.

It really didn't hit me what we had done until we went to spring practice a few months later as the defending national champions. We wanted to do it again and not settle for anything less. And we wanted to do it convincingly.

And we did that. The Washington State game [35–21] was the closest game we had in 1995. We fell behind for the only time in the season, 7–0, and then scored four straight touchdowns.

I never felt healthier, but I knew my medical problem wasn't exactly behind me. Mentally, I was fine because I knew I could play week in and week out.

When it came time for the Heisman Trophy presentation, I had no real hopes of winning it. I thought my chances were very slim because it was very rare for an option quarterback to win that award. I don't think you will see an option quarterback ever win it again. I was honored to be there, but my main focus was getting back to practice to focus on the bowl game. I have no problems with [Ohio State running back] Eddie George winning it—he was deserving of it. [Frazier finished second in the voting.]

When we got to the Fiesta Bowl to play Florida for another national championship, I knew they didn't have a chance. People said we couldn't play on grass, but I knew they wouldn't be able to stop our offense. I don't think the Dallas Cowboys could have stopped us that night. They were cocky—remember once again it was a Florida school—but I really didn't think the game would be close.

The defense figured out their offense early, and they never did stop us. In the end, I showed them that I was a much better quarterback than they thought I was coming out of high school. I showed them that I could go to another place and come back to beat them. [In the 62–24 Nebraska win, Frazier rushed for 199 yards and two touchdowns, passed for another touchdown, and was named the game's MVP.]

Lawrence Phillips had a big night, too, and he showed he was the best running back in the country. Lawrence is probably the best athlete I ever played with. He had the size and speed to do it all.

When it was all over, I can admit that I never thought I would have that type of career. I knew I was good coming out of high school, but not *that* good. But I worked hard. I worked really hard. I never took any shortcuts. I was always very competitive in practice, yelling at guys if they didn't do it the right way. And I yelled at myself when I made mistakes.

As far as my health goes, two years ago, I was diagnosed with Crohn's disease, and I am on medication.

Nebraska is very, very, very special to me. I believe there is no other tradition that rivals ours. To win as many games as we did over a 40-year period since 1962—and to have our bowl streak—I mean, no other school can say that.

There is a slogan here that says, "We have the greatest fans in America." That is true. Whether it is cold, snowing, or raining, they will always show up to see their team. They truly support the program, even on the road.

I can say I did what I set out to do coming out of high school—I proved wrong the people who doubted that I could play quarterback. I proved it to schools like Florida, Florida State, Miami, and Colorado. And with our two national championships, we beat two of those schools who doubted me. Playing at Nebraska made that all possible.

Tommie Frazier, the 1995 Johnny Unitas Golden Arm Award winner, finished his career with a 33–3 record as a starter. He holds the Nebraska school record with 43 touchdown passes, while ranking second in school history with 5,476 total yards. He completed 232 of 469 passes for 3,521 yards and rushed for 1,955 yards and 36 touchdowns in his career. He was named the quarterback of Nebraska's All-Century team. He currently works for the university as the assistant director for development.

AARON TAYLOR
GUARD/CENTER
1994–1997

GROWING UP IN THE HOUSEHOLD OF AN AIR FORCE master sergeant, I was taught that hard work, determination, and character could carry me through my life. I grew up moving all over the world and playing the game I thought I would play forever—soccer. Following my junior high school years in Bitburg, Germany, my father got transferred to Sheppard Air Force Base in Wichita Falls, Texas.

I had always wanted to play football from a young age, but was never able to since it wasn't available to me. After all, there wasn't much need for a 6', 240-pound soccer player.

My first day of football practice at S. H. Rider High School was one that I will remember forever. I never figured that putting thigh, knee, and hip pads into a pair of football pants could be so difficult. After all of the other players were already out of the locker room and on their way to practice, I had to have the trainer help me with my equipment problem. I finally made my way out to practice, but I had no idea what position I was going to play. I followed all of the other players that were my size, as the freshman offensive line coach told everybody to line up in the position they wanted to play. I made my way to left guard after seeing that I was the shortest player there among the five offensive line positions.

As it turned out, I went through my high school career playing several positions—guard, fullback, defensive tackle, punter, and even place-kicker. I even earned all-state honors at guard and punter. I figured that because I was able to accomplish these rewards in Texas, the high school football capital of the world, I would be able to write my ticket to a major university in Texas.

At that time, I was 6'1" and 300 pounds, and I was being recruited by Texas Tech, New Mexico State, and several small schools. Nebraska, too, was recruiting me, but I thought it was just because they were being courteous because they had landed a defensive lineman from my high school a year earlier.

However, Nebraska was steady during the whole recruiting process. I remember coach Osborne walking into my house and visiting with my parents in our living room, but little did I know that this man was about to change my life forever. He was courteous, polite, and never once pressured me to take a visit to Nebraska. He wouldn't have had to.

I received the invitation to go to Nebraska on the second weekend of January 1993. I left wearing the largest jacket I had in my closet and landed at Eppley Airport in Omaha, where coach [Milt] Tenopir picked me up, and we headed to Lincoln. As we approached the city, there wasn't much to see besides cornfields, a corn elevator, and then Memorial Stadium.

As we approached the stadium, it hit me that there was a huge history involved with the Nebraska program. I had never followed Nebraska during my adolescent years, but I was about to learn what it was to be a Cornhusker.

My recruiting trip was fast and exhausting. I was teamed with Scott Saltsman, the player who had attended my high school. Scott brought me up to speed on the tradition of Nebraska football. I can vividly remember seeing Christian Peter walking from the racquetball court, and he must have weighed around 340 pounds at the time. He was a monster, and I figured if I ever laced it up with him, I would be tossed around like a rag doll.

My fondest memory of that trip was sitting with coach Tenopir in his office and talking about my recruiting process. Milt asked me who else was recruiting me and I told him the truth, which was that no one was recruiting because of my height. He looked me in the eyes and spoke only the way Milt could speak, telling me, "I don't care how high you are, I care about the size of your heart." At that moment, I was sold on the program and on coach Tenopir.

My first year at Nebraska was tough because I was 10 hours from home and didn't know a soul besides Scott. The freshmen had to report a week earlier than the veterans, and I thought I picked up the complex Nebraska system

Aaron Taylor (No. 67), the only Cornhusker to be named an All-American at two positions, celebrates a Nebraska touchdown.

quickly. We had a great recruiting class that year: Jason Peter, Lawrence Phillips, Eric Anderson, Jon Zatechka, Fred Pollack, Tim Carpenter, and Jamel Williams.

When the veterans reported, we were all quickly put in our place by bigger, faster, and stronger players. I remember Brenden Stai coming down the offensive line on a pull and lifting me two feet off the ground and putting me on my back. I redshirted that year and was relegated to the scout team, which was a great learning experience for me. Every day, I went against Christian Peter, Terry Connealy, Kevin Ramaekers, Trev Alberts, and a bunch of other great athletes.

I called home to my parents several times and told them I didn't think I would be able to compete at this level. They told me I could not quit, to keep working hard, and everything would work out.

We went on to go undefeated in the regular season that year [1993], but lost the national championship on a last-second missed field goal against Florida State in the Orange Bowl.

I had worked my butt off as coach Tenopir had suggested, and it was starting to pay off by my second year. I backed up left guard Joel Wilks.

The offensive line is what many fans in Nebraska refer to as the "Pipeline."

In 1994, during my redshirt freshman season, the latest of the Pipeline were Rob Zatechka, Joel Wilks, Aaron Graham, Brenden Stai, and Zach Wiegert.

All of them were great to learn from because these weren't the type of guys to be outworked, outsmarted, or outplayed by any means. I played in every game that season behind Joel. One time in the first quarter at Missouri, I came in for him and Rob Zatechka looked at me and said, "Do not screw this up!"

I realized that he expected perfection not only from himself but from everybody next to him.

Coach Tenopir was right again—after the stars on the Pipeline moved on, I started during my sophomore year. Some people wondered how good the new line would play, but we ended up having a great line with Chris Dishman, Aaron Graham, Steve Ott, and Eric Anderson. We had so much unbelievable talent on that team, guys like Tommie Frazier, Ahman Green, Christian Peter, Jason Peter, Grant Wistrom, Mike Minter, Ralph Brown, and Mike Brown.

We ended up undefeated in the regular season, and all we had to do in order to win the national championship for a second consecutive season was beat the Florida Gators in the Fiesta Bowl. We got the impression from the media that we did not have the speed or the talent to play with them, but the final score was 62–24. I really have to say that game was the highlight of my career. We just dominated them in all phases of the game.

I think that team was in a class by itself. Our offensive line did not allow a single sack that year, and we averaged 399.8 yards rushing per game—second best in Nebraska history.

The next year, my junior year, I moved to center to replace All-American Aaron Graham. This move was something I knew I should make because Josh Heskew wasn't yet recovered from a knee injury. I had some doubts whether center would be the best fit for me, but Milt had asked me to help the team.

It was a tough season for us because we had a huge target on our back in the wake of the back-to-back national championships. We lost a night game at Arizona State 19–0 that will haunt me for the rest of my life. We don't play football at Nebraska to get beat this badly, especially to a program like Arizona State. But we rebounded and made the best of the year until we played Texas in the Big 12 Championship Game in St. Louis. We had to win it to have a shot at a third straight national championship game, but Texas played a great game to upset us. We ended the season by beating Virginia Tech soundly in the Orange Bowl.

I knew that the 1997 season, in which I moved back to guard, was my chance to become a leader and to expect perfection on every play just like Rob Zatechka did to me in 1994. Sure enough, we ran the table and were matched up with Peyton Manning and Tennessee in the Orange Bowl. I remember coach Osborne, who had announced his retirement a month earlier, giving his final halftime speech. We were leading Tennessee 14–3, but it could have been worse.

He told us that Tennessee was wearing down and the second half would be ours. He was never more correct—we rushed for over 220 yards in the third quarter alone—on the way to a 42–17 rout of the Volunteers.

We ended up splitting the national championship with Michigan that year, but our main goal was to send coach Osborne out a winner.

I have to say that the most rewarding experience of playing college football at Nebraska was being able to meet so many great people in the state. I loved it so much that I decided to stay in this great state, and that's a tough thing to do for a proud Texan, but that's what I think of the state of Nebraska.

As an offensive lineman, I was not a guy who wanted to be singled out because of my accomplishments. But winning the 1997 Outland Trophy was so special to me only because I was always the guy who was too short and not good enough to play major college football.

I made those years of hard work, determination, and perseverance pay off. The most memorable moment was at the Outland banquet when I could thank all of my fellow offensive linemen in helping me receive such a worthy honor. I would not have been able to accomplish any of it without them.

Aaron Taylor was named an All-American at center in 1996 and at guard in 1997, in which he became the seventh Nebraska player to win the Outland Trophy as the nation's best interior lineman. He was a captain of the 1997 national championship team, Tom Osborne's final team. He also was named to the Nebraska All-Century team. He was inducted into the Nebraska Football Hall of Fame in 1998.

AARON GRAHAM

CENTER

1992–1995

I WAS BORN IN LAS VEGAS, NEW MEXICO, but our family lived in Lubbock, Texas, for my first 13 years. My parents were educators—my father a high school principal and my mother an elementary school teacher. From there, we moved to Denton, Texas, where I attended junior high and high school.

My first taste of rejection came during junior high when one of the football coaches told me I wouldn't be good enough to play junior high football, let alone high school football. I was probably one of the weakest guys on our team and I struggled, but I made the varsity team during my sophomore year and became a starter at center as a junior. By the time I was a senior at Denton High, I was 6'4" and 260 pounds and was being recruited by pretty much every school in the country.

When the offers started coming in, I told my friends and family that it always had been my dream to play for the Texas A&M Aggies. When I would get all of those recruiting letters, I put them up as wallpaper in my room, and I took all of those envelopes from A&M and covered the entire back of my door. Then I visited College Station and the campus and was very excited about becoming an Aggie. Ironically, Tim Cassidy, who was the recruiting coordinator there at that time is now the recruiting coordinator at Nebraska.

But Texas A&M passed on me—for a center from Dallas Carter High School.

I had visited Texas Tech because that is where I spent my childhood, and I was a big [Texas Tech Head coach] Spike Dykes fan. I used to sit on the grass in the north end zone as a kid and watch Tech games, and I always had a spot in my heart for the Red Raiders.

I also visited Oklahoma, and it was top-notch. They really took care of their recruits. We walked into their locker room, and they had our names on the backs of jerseys hanging on the lockers. Then they had us run out onto the field as they played "Boomer Sooner."

But when I visited Nebraska, none of these schools compared to it. There were too many positives there for anybody else to compete with, even though Oklahoma had just beaten them 45–10 the previous season. That game didn't matter because I knew Nebraska was a better fit for me. After I saw Nebraska, there was just no turning back. The facilities, the program, the history, and the tradition—it was unparalleled in my eyes.

After I committed to Nebraska, [Texas A&M coach] R. C. Slocum called me up and said, "Listen, we made a mistake with you. We want you to have a scholarship—"

As he was talking, Mom snatched the phone out of hands and told him, "Look, my son wanted to go to A&M since he was a little boy, and you didn't want him, so now he is going to Nebraska and that is that."

When coach Osborne had visited my house, I verbally committed, and I'll never forget Dad asking him, "We are having a party for Aaron on signing day, can you come down to it?"

Coach Osborne said, "Well, under NCAA rules, I am not allowed to be there on signing day, but if you make it the following day, I will come."

So we did, and sure enough, he took a private plane from Lincoln to Denton to come to my house for a piece of cake. He met all of my buddies and family and then flew back, but that is the type of man he is.

Around Christmastime during my senior year in high school, my mom was diagnosed with leukemia, and she passed away the following May. Obviously, it was a terrible time for me, my dad, and my sister, but Dad wanted me to stay on track with our plans. We had planned for me to go to Lincoln early to enroll in summer school to get a jump on my freshman year. I went up there in June and took some classes and started working out at the facility, as we had planned.

Then two or three weeks into training camp, I came down with mononucleosis. I had always wanted to play right away as a freshman, but losing a parent and then getting sick—it all was too much for me. After practices, we would gather around coach Osborne for his talk, and at times, I would have tears in my eyes. It was a lonely feeling and a very terrible time for me.

I would call Dad and ask him, "What are you doing tonight?"

He would say something like, "Going to a movie."

I would ask, "With whom?"

"Nobody."

I hated that Dad was going through the same thing. I think we both were lonely.

People in the program were aware of what happened to me, and people were always checking up on me, but I knew it was one of those situations I really had to get through on my own. I leaned a lot on my faith at that time. I prayed and asked God to help me through the situation.

After I redshirted, the next spring I worked very hard, and I knew the offense really well. Jim Scott had been the starter at center the year before, and he was ahead of me, so I handled all the long-snapping duties for the season. Dad had helped teach me long-snapping when I was young because he figured it would come in handy some day, and it did. It got me on the field and allowed me to make the travel team for my redshirt freshman season.

285

I knew the way the Nebraska program operated, that very few freshmen and sophomores played, so that was my way of getting to play. I also knew if I was patient that my time would come.

You know, when Nebraska recruits you, they send a video that shows the team running into Memorial Stadium as the fight song plays. From that time, I imagined what it would be like to actually do that, and when I experienced it for the first time, there wasn't any comparison. What a great feeling.

Only two other freshmen traveled that year—Brook Berringer and Phil Ellis, and they were my roommates. Brook was from West Kansas, and, like me, he loved to hunt. He became my hunting buddy, and we would go out and hunt pheasant and quail a few times each week. When Brook died in a plane crash right before the [1996] NFL Draft, it was another terrible time for anyone that knew him. He was such a good friend. It was very sad.

Midway through the 1993 season, Kenny Mehlin was the starting center, but he moved to guard to replace Brenden Stai, who broke his ankle. That opened up a starting spot for me. It was a period of five or six games that I had to show them that they could rely on me as the future center of the program.

Aaron Graham, here snapping the football to Tommie Frazier, was a dominating run-blocker at center.

Being the long-snapper, we used to stay on the field after each practice with coach [Dan] Young to work with Byron Bennett, who would kick 15 or 20 field goals. We always ended with coach Young spotting the ball, and we would tell Byron, "This one is for the national championship."

So what happened? We won all of our games and got to play Florida State in the Orange Bowl for the national championship, and we got down to the end of the game, trailing 15–13. It was just like in practice. We all lined up for a field goal, and Byron got out to the huddle. I looked at him and said, "This is it. Just like practice."

He looked at me with all of this confidence and said, "I got it!"

I didn't think twice about it. The snap was good, the hold was good, and he drilled it [from 27 yards] to give us the lead with 1:16 left. Being a younger player, I thought the game was over, but I was guilty of celebrating too early.

And Byron was celebrating so much, he started to hyperventilate on the sidelines. When coach Young told him he had to kick off because our other kicker had been hurt, I don't think he was ready for it. I don't think he had kicked off at all that season, and he was still hyperventilating. Then he kicked it out of bounds, and here was Florida State starting from their own 40-yard line.

A few plays later, Scott Bentley was kicking a short field goal to put them ahead with 21 seconds left.

It was a mountain to climb for us even to have a shot at it, but we got a nice return and Tommie [Frazier] completed a pass across the middle to Trumane Bell. I remember looking up at the clock and seeing it tick down "4 . . . 3 . . . 2 . . ." and I grabbed this one official by the shirt and spun him around, screaming, "Time out! Time out!"

The clock had gone all the way to zero, and one official held the ball over his head, signaling that the game was over. They were dumping Gatorade on Bobby Bowden's head, and Florida State rushed the field.

Then the officials announced, "No, no, no . . . Nebraska has one more play."

As we huddled up a second time for another field goal with :01 showing on the clock, I looked at Byron and said, "You got it. You already did it once, so knock it through again."

287

But this time, there was no response from him. I don't know if he was still spent from what happened earlier or what, but I remember when I snapped it this time, I didn't have much confidence. And he missed it [45-yard attempt].

What an emotional game. Heading into that locker room, it was such a gut-wrenching feeling of being so close to winning a national championship. I mean, we were right there. I remember seeing Christian Peter at the back of the locker room. I just grabbed him and said, "We are coming back here next year and we are winning the damn thing!"

We all started working out right after that game because none of us could wait for the opportunity to get better and get back to the Orange Bowl the following year. You hear people talk about certain teams being focused. Well, let me tell you, that 1994 team exemplified being focused more than any other sports team I have ever seen.

Nothing knocked us off course that season. Tommie Frazier got blood clots and Brook came in and played well. Then Brook punctured a lung, and Matt Turman came in for the Kansas State game, and even though we had no passing game, we beat them. We couldn't lose. We *wouldn't* lose.

It culminated with another Orange Bowl, as we expected, but this time it was against Miami. Our goal going into that game was trying to wear them down. Our offensive line from left tackle to right tackle—Rob Zatechka, Joel Wilks, me, Brenden Stai, and Zach Wiegert—was so good and so focused that year. It had to be one of the best, if not the best, offensive lines Nebraska has ever had. And we knew that game hinged on us.

Miami's strength was their defensive front, and specifically Warren Sapp, but all we wanted to do that night was pound them, pound them, and pound them some more. Our game plan was that the fourth quarter would be ours.

Early in the game, on one of the first draw plays, the play called for Brenden, who was our strongest guy, to show pass protection and set, and then work the defensive lineman out of the hole. Brenden took his set and Sapp was on top of him. I turned and saw Brenden getting pushed backward and I'd never seen that before.

We got back to the huddle and Brenden asked me, "Did you see that?"

I said, "Yeah, he's pretty strong, isn't he?"

"Yeah," he told me, "but we are going to get them by the end of the game. All we have to do is keep pounding."

And that's what we did. By the fourth quarter, they were ours. We opened some holes and [fullback] Cory Schlesinger headed down the right sideline [15 yards] for one score and then down the middle [14 yards] for the touchdown to put us ahead. When Cory ran up the middle on that trap play, the one thing I remember is how loud the "boom . . . boom . . . boom" was in the stands. Nebraska fans were jumping up and down so much in the Orange Bowl that there was this thunderous thudding sound. I'll never forget that.

After the game [a 24–17 Nebraska win], it was euphoric. In the locker room, coach Osborne stood up and thanked everybody. The phone rang and they handed it to him, and it was the president [Clinton]. They talked for about a minute. Then he told us, "We owe it to our fans to go back out there and thank them for coming all this way."

So we took off all of our pads and went back out there to celebrate with our fans. It was awesome.

The next year, I was the lone returning offensive lineman, but I knew we had a lot of talent, too. Two years earlier, we knew what it took to get there, but now we knew what it took to get there and win it. But we also knew everybody would be gunning for us, too.

I think of the 11 starters on our defense in 1995, nine of them went on to start at least one game in the NFL. That's how much talent was over there, and on offense, we had Tommie and Lawrence Phillips, who was as good a running back as I ever saw in my life at any level.

We just rolled through the season to get to the Fiesta Bowl to play Florida for another national championship. We had been to three straight national championship games, and knew everything that went into it, all the press conferences and the preparation leading up to it. It was our little secret, because it was the first time for Florida.

In his pregame speech, coach Osborne told us, "We have been given the power and the strength, so let's go show 'em."

What I will never forget is when we came out of the tunnel, we headed straight to our sideline. When Florida came out, they ran to the center of the field and started jumping up and down with their fists in the air. We stood over there all calm and collected. I was thinking, "You are about to get your rear ends whipped, and you don't even know it's coming."

I remember looking over my shoulder to the left and then to the right, just looking at everybody on our sideline. We were so confident. It was like two armies prepared to do battle. One had the weapons and the other was thinking the battle was already over. By the third quarter, I think they were ready to throw in the towel. Lawrence Phillips was the best back they ever saw, and they couldn't tackle Tommie, either. It wasn't even close [Nebraska won 62–24].

Five years, three national championship games, and two national championships—I couldn't have dreamt of a better college experience. I wouldn't trade it for anything.

I left Texas to go to a foreign place, and now that place has become my home. The fans and people of Nebraska won me over. I don't think anyone could possibly say a negative thing about their experience playing football at the University of Nebraska. Like they say, there is no place like Nebraska, and if you play there, you know what it means to be a Husker.

Aaron Graham was named All–Big Eight in 1994–95 and an All-American in 1995. He also was an Academic All-American and team captain in 1995. He played seven seasons in the NFL, including four with the Arizona Cardinals.

The
NEW MILLENNIUM

ERIC CROUCH

QUARTERBACK

1998–2001

ONE OF MY FIRST FOOTBALL MEMORIES was when I was about nine years old and the coach of the Pop Warner League team was trying to find a quarterback. I had been a running back since I was seven, and then he asked me, "Can you throw the football?"

"I don't know," I said. "Let's find out."

So I threw a few passes, and he told me, "You are our new quarterback."

In the junior league, our team went to the national tournament in Daytona Beach and finished second. I can remember that I always had great coaches while growing up. I knew I wanted to play quarterback, and they worked on things like having quick feet, agility, and the discipline that comes with the position.

I was recruited by Lou Holtz at Notre Dame, John Cooper at Ohio State, and Gary Barnett at Northwestern. And Nebraska, of course. Those were the four schools I strongly considered.

Only at Nebraska did everything fit perfectly. Tom Osborne, Turner Gill, and Frank Solich all told me I would play quarterback. Plus, it was near home, and being born and raised in Omaha, naturally, I wanted to be a Cornhusker.

I knew the great history of Nebraska football, and I realized how deep it reached in the state, but I was never one to sit around the house and watch college football on Saturdays. I was just the type to be out doing things, rather than watching a game on TV, so I can't honestly say I sat around watching all of their games.

I will never forget the time coach Osborne visited my house. Before he got there, Mom told me, "Now when he gets here, offer him something to drink."

So he came in the door and I was in awe and my mom was in awe. We were sitting there talking, and Mom kept looking over at me with this grin on her face like I forgot something. Finally, I figured it out and offered him a glass of water. But he said, "No thanks, I am fine." After that, my nerves calmed down.

Right away, I accepted his offer. It was the best thing I ever did, announcing that I was headed to Nebraska before my senior season in high school. By doing that, I could focus on my senior year, have fun, and not have to worry about all the recruiting phone calls or decisions about college.

I ran track throughout high school, and I had a nerve injury in my knee that bothered me, so when I first got to Nebraska, I ground out two-a-days, but the pain was too much. It turned out that my right knee and left ankle each needed surgery, and I would need a medical redshirt year.

August 31, 1997, was an important day for me because that is the day I had both of my injuries operated on. Here I was, thinking I had the world on my shoulders and everything was going right, and I had just arrived at college and was being wheeled out of the hospital in a wheelchair. I went through all the doubts that I think are normal with that, wondering if I would ever be the same, if I would ever be as fast, or if I would run pain-free again.

I was on crutches, and both of my legs were out of commission for a while. I had to have homework shipped over to my dorm room. It turned out that I had a bone disease in my ankle, and they had to drill through the bone to make it bleed so it would heal properly. I had some soft tissue in there that was supposed to be hard, but it wasn't. That was extremely painful.

There is no question that year away from playing the game made me very hungry. I got back on the field in November with the scout team, but I never took that first hit again until the following spring. I remember that hit like it was yesterday. I got back up on my feet and felt great. My legs felt great and I was ready to go, and I felt a great sense of accomplishment for overcoming those injuries and coming through the rehab.

Still, I knew I had something to prove to everybody because I had not really been on the field yet.

At about this time, I really realized that I made the right decision because I felt we had such a stable coaching staff, and coach Holtz had just left Notre Dame. I thought, "This staff at Nebraska does stick around and will always be here for me."

Right about then, I started to hear the rumors about coach Osborne possibly retiring. I thought, "No way. No way. No way. It won't happen."

Then one day, coach Solich came into a meeting wearing a suit and tie, and we all wondered, "How often does he dress up for meetings?" That was the day of the announcement [of coach Osborne's retirement].

I thought, "Man, what am I going to do?"

But I felt good about coach Solich being named head coach because he was one of the guys who recruited me. It wasn't like somebody new was coming in from the outside, somebody who didn't know you. But a lot of guys didn't feel that way and went ahead and transferred.

In the spring of 1998, I thought the job at quarterback was wide open. Bobby Newcombe was moving from wingback to quarterback, Monte Christo would be a senior, and Frankie London would be a junior. I thought to myself, "It's wide open and I am going to be the starter."

When we went into the fall, I was No. 4 on the depth chart, but I started to work my way up slowly. I made fewer and fewer mistakes, and I really felt comfortable running our offense. I had been running the option since I was 14 years old, so I think I was a little bit ahead of the other guys in our offensive system. Not many of them had come from option offenses. Frankie London then moved to wingback, so that moved me up one more spot.

Bobby started the opener against Louisiana Tech, but he got hurt right away. They threw me in the game and then Monte played some. For the next three or four weeks, we never knew who was going to play between Bobby, Monte, and me. But then Bobby's injury required surgery, so it was up to Monte and myself.

They had a rule at Nebraska that an injured player could not lose his starting position, so when we went into the spring of 1999, the job was now Bobby's again. I felt that wasn't exactly right, but what could I do? I thought, "Let's duke it out in practice and see who the better quarterback is." But we went into fall camp and it was Bobby's job to lose.

Before the opener against Iowa, I was toying with playing receiver at that point, but they told me Bobby would start and I would get one series at quarterback in the second quarter.

Eric Crouch, here gaining yards against Iowa in 2000, set an NCAA record for rushing touchdowns (59) by a quarterback and became the school's third Heisman Trophy winner.

When we got down to Iowa 7–0, they put me in. I never left the field again, and we won 42–7. When we played Cal the next week, Bobby started again, but they told me I would get another series in the second quarter. They put me in, and in the second quarter, I threw for a touchdown, ran for a touchdown, and caught a touchdown [in a 45–0 Nebraska win]. The next day in the papers, they were calling me "the next Johnny Rodgers," and I couldn't believe what was happening.

Then they told us in a meeting that I would be starting in the next game against Southern Mississippi. Finally, I felt the job was mine for good. We had a great team that year, finishing 12–1 with only that screwball loss at Texas [24–20] in the middle of the season. I still feel the officials took that one from us. We had a third-and-15 at about midfield in the closing minutes when I was flushed out of the pocket and threw across the field to Matt

Davison. He cradled the football on his knees and clearly caught it, but they said it hit the ground.

Despite that, it was a good time for me because I had a newfound confidence in myself, and I had a sense that all of the tough times were behind me. I could focus on running the offense and not having to worry about who would be the starter.

We won the rest of the games and got back at Texas in the Big 12 Championship Game and then beat Tennessee, which was the defending national champion, in the Fiesta Bowl.

That following March, the build-up and hype for the Notre Dame game, which wouldn't be played until September, had already started. I have never seen so much publicity for a football game, even a national championship game. We were actually talking about that game during spring practice.

That led into the fall, when the build-up continued. Every day we were giving four interviews with all the networks. I mean, "Who had more tradition? Nebraska? Notre Dame?"

On the day of the game, our fans turned their stadium red. I thought we would come out and it would be all gold and navy blue, but the place looked like Memorial Stadium.

When we finally played, what a great game it turned into. We were ahead 21–7, and I thought we were going to run away with the game. Then they took a punt return and a kickoff return back for touchdowns and it was tied 21–21. I was thinking, "There is no way we are going to lose this game."

When it went to overtime, we converted that huge third-and-12 when Tracey Wistrom caught that little out route and we got the first down by about one half of a foot. We got down inside the 10, and Dan Alexander pounded it inside, then threw a good block to spring me on an option play. All I had to do was use my speed to beat the safety into the corner of the end zone, and that was it [a 27–24 Nebraska win].

That definitely was one of the most rewarding and satisfying wins of my career.

We later played at Oklahoma. We both were unbeaten, and we jumped up on them 14–0, and I thought it was going to be easy. That game was unbelievable because of how quickly it turned around. To their credit, they played a great game and came back on us [a 31–14 Nebraska loss].

Before my senior year, I thought we had a good enough team to win a national championship, but of course, at Nebraska, we felt that way every year.

The game I remember most is when Oklahoma came back to Lincoln. We were both undefeated again, and all week long before the game coach Solich would show us old tapes of the Nebraska–Oklahoma rivalry. He had put in this trick play and said we were going to do this in the game. It was called "41 flash, reverse right pass," which was a throwback pass to me. [On the play, I-back Thunder Collins took the handoff from Crouch, handed off to split end Mike Stuntz on the right side, who threw back to Crouch on the left sideline.] We worked on it every day in practice, and it never once worked. One time it would be knocked down. Another time it would be intercepted.

I thought, "This is the biggest joke in the world—this thing will never work." But I really figured he would never call the play anyway.

What is really weird is that Oklahoma tried to run the same play earlier in the game.

So we were clinging to a 13–10 lead late in the game and what did he do? He called the play.

I thought, "No way, I can't believe he is doing it now."

As I broke the line of scrimmage, I could tell that I would be wide open. The whole thing happened in slow motion. I was watching the ball in the air and it seemed like it was up there forever. I just thought, "If I drop this football, I will never live it down."

I can still see that perfect spiral coming over my shoulder into my hands. As I cradled it and headed down the end zone, I literally could feel the stadium shaking under my feet. It was the loudest I ever heard Memorial Stadium. It was just deafening. [The 63-yard touchdown capped Nebraska's 20–10 victory.] I'll never forget that play as long as I live.

We got to be 11–0 when we went to Colorado, and I have never played in a stranger game than that one. Nine times out of 10, we win that game. We missed every tackle that day and couldn't do anything right offensively as we fell behind 35–3 [in the second quarter]. Honest to God, we still thought we could come back and win that game, and it would have been the largest comeback in college football history. We got it to 42–30, and we were headed in again when Dahrran Diedrick fumbled at their 1-yard line.

They took that possession and drove 99 yards to put the game away [a 62–36 Nebraska loss].

The Heisman Trophy ceremony was coming up, and after that Colorado game, I thought there was no way I would win the Heisman. Earlier in the season, I actually told people privately that I didn't even want to win the Heisman Trophy, but I was just trying to talk myself out of it. It wasn't my main focus because I didn't want to come off as being an individual, instead of focusing on team goals. But really, who doesn't want to win the Heisman Trophy?

When they announced my name, it really was unbelievable. It is an emotional time to win an award like that, and so many feelings come to you all at once. To be on that list, I am very, very proud of it.

The ramifications of it will never go away, I don't think. You could be out of town, and just when you think nobody knows you, some sports guy will recognize you because of the Heisman Trophy and want your autograph. And because of it, I have become very close with Mike Rozier and Johnny Rodgers. It is a fraternity in which there is a lot of communication between previous winners.

By the time we got to Los Angeles for the Rose Bowl a few weeks later, I really thought we matched up well with Miami. But there was so much negative energy around us because the media kept saying we didn't deserve to be there. Our biggest mistake was that some guys never put that aside and focused on the game. We were run down mentally after the Colorado game, and I don't think our energy level ever rebounded.

Miami had so much talent and speed and quickness that after we committed four turnovers against a team like that, we were in big trouble. It wasn't a great way to go out [a 37–14 loss], losing our final two games, but I wouldn't ever let that dampen my career.

The only thing wrong with it all was not coming away with a national championship. I never thought in my mind I would ever be able to play at a school like Nebraska, or ever start at a school like Nebraska, but then to do it and win all of those awards and the Heisman Trophy was icing on my cake.

I became a better person and I learned so much, and Nebraska was my platform for that. The Nebraska tradition is as good as any in the country, and I strongly believe that the program is still the best in the country. Born and raised in Nebraska, I think it was my destiny to become a lifelong Cornhusker.

Eric Crouch, whose career record as a starting quarterback was 35–6, is one of the most decorated players in college football history, winning the Walter Camp Player of the Year Award, the Davey O'Brien Quarterback Award, the Heisman Trophy, and several more player of the year awards in 2001. He finished his career as the Nebraska record-holder in total yards [7,915] and season record-holder in total yards [2,625]. He also set an NCAA record for touchdowns [59] scored by a quarterback. He currently holds 21 school records and is one of three quarterbacks in NCAA history to rush for more than 3,000 yards and pass for more than 4,000 yards. He was named All–Big 12 in 1999 and All–Big 12 and All-America in 2001. He was inducted into the Nebraska Football Hall of Fame in 2002.

NN PRESNELL · FORREST BEHM · FRED MEIER · VIC SCHLEICH · JO

NNIS CLARIDGE · LYLE SITTLER · LARRY WACHHOLTZ · BOB CH

NEISS · JOE ORDUNA · JERRY MURTAUGH · BOB NEWTON · BILL K

A RUUD · JEFF KINNEY · VINCE FERRAGAMO · JIM ANDERSON ·

KROGER · DERRIE NELSON · JOHN MCCORMICK · TONY FELICI ·

H · TURNER GILL · WILL SHIELDS · MIKE MINTER · RUSS HOCHST

RON GRAHAM · ERIC CROUCH · GLENN PRESNELL · FORREST BEH

T FISCHER · LAVERNE TORCZON · DENNIS CLARIDGE · LYLE SITT

MER · LAVERNE ALLERS · DAN SCHNEISS · JOE ORDUNA · JERRY M

VE HUMM · JUNIOR MILLER · TOM RUUD · JEFF KINNEY · VINCE F

VE RIMINGTON · STEVE DAMKROGER · DERRIE NELSON · JOHN

HMAN · STEVE TAYLOR · NEIL SMITH · TURNER GILL · WILL SHIEL

MIE FRAZIER · AARON TAYLOR · AARON GRAHAM · ERIC CROUC

N BORDOGNA · MICK TINGELHOFF · PAT FISCHER · LAVERNE TO

RCHICH · KAYE CARSTENS · LARRY KRAMER · LAVERNE ALLERS · L

CH · JOE BLAHAK · LARRY JACOBSON · DAVE HUMM · JUNIOR MIL

NNY RODGERS · BRODERICK THOMAS · DAVE RIMINGTON · STEV

E ROZIER · MARC MUNFORD · TOM RATHMAN · STEVE TAYLOR

CHSTEIN · AHMAN GREEN · TREV ALBERTS · TOMMIE FRAZIER · A